Teaching Online
A Practical Guide

Teaching Online
A Practical Guide

Susan Ko

OnlineLearning.net

Steve Rossen

University of California at Los Angeles

HOUGHTON MIFFLIN COMPANY   Boston New York

Senior Sponsoring Editor: Loretta Wolozin
Development Editor: Lisa A. Mafrici
Senior Project Editor: Christina M. Horn
Senior Production/Design Coordinator: Jill Haber
Senior Manufacturing Coordinator: Priscilla Bailey
Marketing Manager: Jay Hu
Marketing Associate: Caroline Guy

Cover design: Diana Coe / ko Design Studio

Library of Congress Catalog Card Number: 00-133914

ISBN: 0-618-00042-9

3 4 5 6 7 8 9-EB-04 03 02

Brief Contents

Contents

Preface ||||||||||

In 1993, there was no World Wide Web. Today, it seems as if it is everywhere.

In 1993, if you had written a book about teaching, you would not have needed to describe the basic tools of the trade—the classroom, the rows of seats, the blackboard, the chalk. These were taken for granted; they never changed.

Today, you must describe how the virtual and real worlds intertwine in a process known as teaching online. You must talk about electronic bulletin boards, streaming video, asynchronous environments, and real-time chats.

Is it any wonder that so many instructors are both anxious and apprehensive as they try to make sense of this new phenomenon? There are so many questions to answer: What is the difference between teaching "on the ground" and teaching online? What are the fundamental techniques? Where can you learn them? What kind of equipment or software do you use? How do you assess how effective you are?

This book is written for the rapidly rising population of instructors who want to teach online, who have been told to teach online (sometimes in conjunction with on-the-ground classes), who are currently teaching online (but want to improve), or who are training or encouraging others to teach online. In other words, it is intended for lecturers, professors, teaching assistants, department chairs, academic deans, program planners, and information technology support personnel at both the administrative and departmental levels.

The book is as much for the tenured professor as for the graduate student or teaching assistant. It is for the college administrator who is trying to convince a skeptical and unwilling faculty to adopt this new mode of instruction, as well as for the part-time lecturer who drives seventy miles a day to teach four courses at four different institutions. It is for the trainer whose students range in abilities from those who do Java programming to those who barely know how to move a mouse.

The book is written from the unique perspective of two authors who have taught online themselves and have trained hundreds of other faculty to teach online. It is more concerned with the whys and hows of implementation than with theory, not because we do not value pedagogical theory but because it is discussed and critiqued more effectively elsewhere. Unlike other books we have read on the subject, this is not a collection of essays, not a general overview, nor is it—strictly speaking—a technical handbook. Rather, it is intended as a practical and concise guide both for instructors teaching completely online and for those supplementing a traditional classroom with online elements.

Our goal is to immerse instructors in this new environment as quickly as we can, using plain language and illustrating our points with case studies from colleagues or students that we have worked with or known, representing a wide variety of different disciplines and institutions. We hope to get you up and running as quickly as possible.

Organization of This Book

The book is divided into four parts.

In Part I, "Getting Started," we define and describe the new world of online learning and introduce the skills, training, and support you will need to become part of it.

Part II, "Putting the Course Together," covers the process of converting your course content to the online environment and discovering new possibilities for your course. We help you take inventory of your existing course and suggest areas for innovation, while guiding you through the conversion process and the creation of an online syllabus. We provide advice on using different types of software environments and offer a detailed look at opportunities for incorporating diverse activities and web resources. We shed light on the often-confusing issue of making effective use of multimedia, as well as on matters of copyright and intellectual property as they relate to the online classroom.

Although we strive to make the topics in Part II easy enough for beginners to grasp, there is much here to offer even experienced online instructors. Carefully chosen examples from real-life instructors help illustrate the approaches and solutions outlined.

In Part III, "Teaching in the Online Classroom," we focus on some of the techniques you will need to become an effective instructor, whether you teach totally online or are enriching in-class instruction with exercises on the Web. We discuss how to make sure your students are prepared for online classes, provide suggestions on the much-overlooked topic of online classroom management, and describe ways to integrate online activities into the face-to-face classroom.

Finally, in Part IV, "New Trends and Opportunities," we discuss how online teaching can affect your career and how to keep current with the pace of change. To help with this process, we have established a web site that will keep you updated with new trends and resources. Go to **http://college.hmco.com** and select "Education."

At the end of each chapter you'll find a list of resources mentioned in the text. As a handy reference, these resources are collected together and augmented in the Guide to Resources at the end of the book. Because web addresses change so frequently, we urge you to consult our web site for updates, corrections, and new references.

Because terminology is often a barrier for those unfamiliar with the Internet or computer software, there are numerous definitions and boxed sidebars throughout the text to help you understand the narrative. A Glossary at the back of the book offers additional assistance.

Acknowledgments

We would like to acknowledge the special assistance of our extraordinary editors, Loretta Wolozin, Doug Gordon, and Lisa Mafrici, without whom we would never have been able to complete this book. We also want to thank Esther Grassian, Dr. Sharon Packer, Lisa Weber, and Eva Gold, whose early review of our work proved so valuable. Finally, we would like to thank the many accomplished instructors—our colleagues in online education—who generously shared their experiences and whose many contributions have enriched this book.

SUSAN KO
STEVE ROSSEN

I

Getting Started

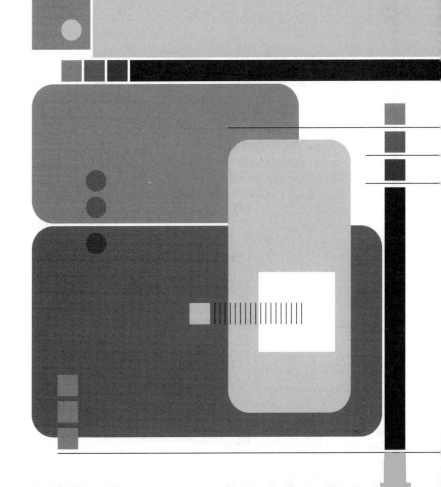

Teaching Online: An Overview

Because teaching online is relatively new, many people don't know what it is, or how it's done, or even what some of the terms used to describe it mean. Others may have a notion of what's involved, but they don't know how to get started, or they feel some trepidation about handling the issues they may encounter. Perhaps this is because the online environment is so different from anything most instructors have encountered before.

Teaching online means conducting a course partially or entirely through the Internet. It's a form of *distance education,* a process that includes courses taught through the mail, by video-tape, or via telephone hookups or satellite TV—any form of learning that doesn't involve the traditional classroom setting in which students and instructor must be at the same place at the same time.

What makes teaching online unique is that it uses the Internet, especially the World Wide Web, as the primary means of communication. Thus, when you teach online, you don't have to *be* someplace to teach. You don't have to lug your briefcase full of papers to a classroom, stand at a lectern, scribble on a chalkboard, or grade papers in a stuffy room while your students take a test. You don't even have to sit in your office waiting for students to show up for conferences. You can hold "office hours" on weekends or at night after dinner. You can do all this while living in a small town in Wyoming, even if you're working for a college whose administrative offices are located in Florida. You can attend an important conference in Hawaii on the same day that you teach your class in New Jersey, logging on from your hotel room's telephone.

Online learning offers more freedom for students as well. They can search for courses using the Web, scouring the world for programs, classes, and instructors that fit their needs. Having found an appropriate course, they can enroll and register, shop for their books, read articles, listen to lectures, submit their homework assignments, confer with their instructors, and receive their final grades—all online. They can assemble in **virtual classrooms**, joining other students from diverse geographic locales,

> **virtual classroom** Any online area in which instructors and students "meet," via their computer connections, for course activities.

forging bonds and friendships not possible in conventional classrooms, which are often limited to students from a specific geographical area.

The convenience of learning online applies equally well to adult learners, students from educationally underserved areas, those pursuing specialized or advanced degrees, those who want to advance in their degree work through credentialed courses, and any students who simply want to augment the curricular offerings from their local institutions. No longer must they drive to school, find a parking space, sit in a lecture hall at a specific time, wait outside their instructors' offices for conferences, and take their final exams in a stuffy room. They can hold a job, have a family, take care of parents or pets, and even travel. As long as they can get to a computer connected to the Internet, students can, in most cases, keep up with their work even if they're busy during the day. School is always in session because school is always there.

So dynamic is the Web that new technologies and techniques are emerging all the time. What's commonplace one year becomes old hat the next. The only thing that seems to remain constant is people's desire to send and receive information efficiently, no matter what the means. That's what drives people to shop, invest, and converse online, and it is this same force that is propelling them to learn online as well.

But all this freedom and innovation can sometimes be perplexing. If the conventional tools of teaching have been removed, how *do* you teach? If school's open twenty-four hours a day, seven days a week, when is school out? What is the role of the instructor if you don't see your students face to face? Do you become simply a lecturer, or are you more like a facilitator? moderator? or colleague?

And what if you're among the many instructors who teach face to face but maintain a web site as well? Does making your course notes available online mean that coming to class will become obsolete? How do you balance the real and virtual worlds so that they work together? And if information can be presented readily online, what should class time be devoted to: discussions? student presentations? structured debates?

There is no prototypical experience of teaching online. Some instructors use the Web as an adjunct to what they teach in class. Others teach entirely on the Web. Some institutions have sophisticated hardware and software that they make available; others offer little more than the bare bones.

You will get a sense of these differences in the chapters that follow. For the time being, take a look at two hypothetical instructors working online.

The Range of Online Experiences: Two Hypothetical Cases

The first of our hypothetical instructors, Jim Hegelmarks, teaches philosophy entirely online. The second, Miriam Sharpe, teaches a first-year physics course in a conventional classroom but uses a web site to help her students review material and get answers for their questions. If some of the terms we use seem unfamiliar to you, have a look at the box "Some Terms of the Trade."

Western Philosophy, a Course Taught Entirely Online

Jim Hegelmarks's course in Western philosophy is now in its third week, and the assignment for his class is to read a short commentary he has written on John Stuart Mill's *Principles of Political Economy*, portions of which the class has studied. He has asked the students to read his commentary and then

Some Terms of the Trade

web site   The "place" on the World Wide Web where online teaching and learning generally take place. A web site might consist of a page or pages of information you've put together yourself and made available on your local Internet service provider (ISP), such as EarthLink or America Online (AOL). Or it might take the form of an **electronic bulletin board** where you and your students can exchange comments and ideas. Or it might involve a full-scale **course management system (CMS)** containing a bundle of instructional tools such as a whiteboard, bulletin board, gradebook, and means to **chat** online.

In any case, the web site resides at a computer somewhere, usually at a college, but sometimes at a commercial hosting site. It typically includes a series of pages (a "page" is equal to a screenful of information) containing text, images, and **hyperlinks** to other web pages. These pages can be written in various programming languages, such as hypertext markup language (HTML), a coded language that defines the format of onscreen text or graphics through a series of descriptive tags, and JavaScript, a program that works with HTML to make web pages interactive. There are languages that create three-dimensional worlds, as well as languages that permit you to gather information and store it in a database.

Although knowing these languages is obviously useful, it isn't necessary to know any of them in order to be an effective online teacher, no more than it's necessary to understand the dynamics of an internal combustion engine in order to drive a car. Fortunately, a number of WYSIWYG ("what you see is what you get") editors, such as Netscape's Composer and Internet Explorer's FrontPage Express, permit you to create web pages without knowing a single tag or programming term. However, if you do want to learn more about the Web, its languages, and some of its terminology, we encourage you to visit the Learn the Net.com web site **(http://www.learnthenet.com/)** or look at some of the witty and enlightening guides and tutorials provided by Webmonkey **(http://hotwired.lycos.com/webmonkey/)**.

hyperlink or link   An element on a web page (typically an image, icon, or highlighted word or phrase) that makes something happen when you "click" on it with the mouse. Typically it takes you to another web page, but it can also cause a digital movie or audio file to play.

web browser   A software program that permits you to view and interact with web-based material. With a browser, you can read text, view

(cont.)

digitized videos, answer surveys, participate in discussions—the list of functions is long and continues to grow each year. The two most popular browsers are Netscape Communicator (Netscape is presently owned by America Online) and Internet Explorer (created and maintained by Microsoft Corporation). These browsers are available for free download from the companies' web sites, although either or both are often provided with the purchase of a new computer.

electronic bulletin board or discussion board (also known as a forum, conference area, or threaded discussion area) A software program that permits you to "post" messages online (much as you would post a message on a cork bulletin board with a tack) and allows others to reply to your posting with one of their own. With such software, structured conversations can take place. The instructor, for example, can post an initial commentary, and students can post their replies, with all of these entries appearing in an ordered row. (This hierarchical ordering of messages is what is meant by the term *threaded*.)

With an electronic bulletin board, communication is done **asynchronously**—that is, not at the same time. Thus one student might post a query on Monday, and another student in a different time zone might reply the next day. Conferencing software comes in all kinds of structures; it may be a standalone product, or it may be contained in a course management system. To gain some idea of the range of this type of software, visit David Woolley's site called Conferencing Software for the Web **(http://thinkofit.com/webconf/),** which provides annotated lists of asynchronous conferencing programs. This is also a great resource for finding free programs.

chat online communication that occurs **synchronously**—that is, in real time. Chat software is one of the most popular tools on the Web. Typically, two or more users chat with each other by typing notes in a common message space, although newer chat software permits audio and even video communication. Chat is especially useful to instructors holding virtual conference hours or small seminars. Chat programs are available as separate programs or as part of the suite of tools in a course management system.

course management system (also known as integrated application software, online delivery system, educational delivery application, or online tool suite) A software program that contains a number of integrated instructional functions. In a course management

(cont.)

system, course materials such as lectures or graphics can be posted, discussions moderated, chat sessions invoked, and quizzes given, all within the confines of the same software system. Not only can instructors and students "manage" the flow of information, but the instructor can both assess and keep track of the performance of the students, monitoring their progress and assigning grades.

Typical examples of such software systems are those produced by WebCT, Blackboard CourseInfo, eCollege, LearningSpace, IntraLearn, Web Course in a Box, and TopClass. There are many others, some in development and others undergoing radical reform. To keep track of these systems, and compare their various features, we urge you to visit Bruce Landon's comprehensive web site, Online Educational Delivery Applications: A Web Tool for Comparative Analysis **(http://www.ctt. bc.ca/landonline/)**. These systems are discussed in more detail in Chapter 5.

respond in some detail to a question he has posted on the online discussion board for his course (see Figure 1.1).

Connecting to the Web from his home, Hegelmarks types the **URL** of his class web site into the location bar of his Netscape browser and is

URL Short for Uniform Resource Locator, the address for a site on the Internet. An address such as **http://www.ucla.edu/** is a URL.

promptly greeted with a log-in screen. He types in his user name (jhegelmarks) and his password (hmarks420); this process admits him to the class.

The main page of Hegelmarks's course contains a number of navigational "buttons" he can use to manage the course. His commentary is posted in the course documents section, but the area he's interested in today is the discussion board, so that's where he goes first. With his mouse, he clicks on the navigational button that leads to the discussion board and reviews the messages that have been posted there. Several of the students have posted their responses to the assignment. He reads through the responses on screen thoughtfully, printing out the

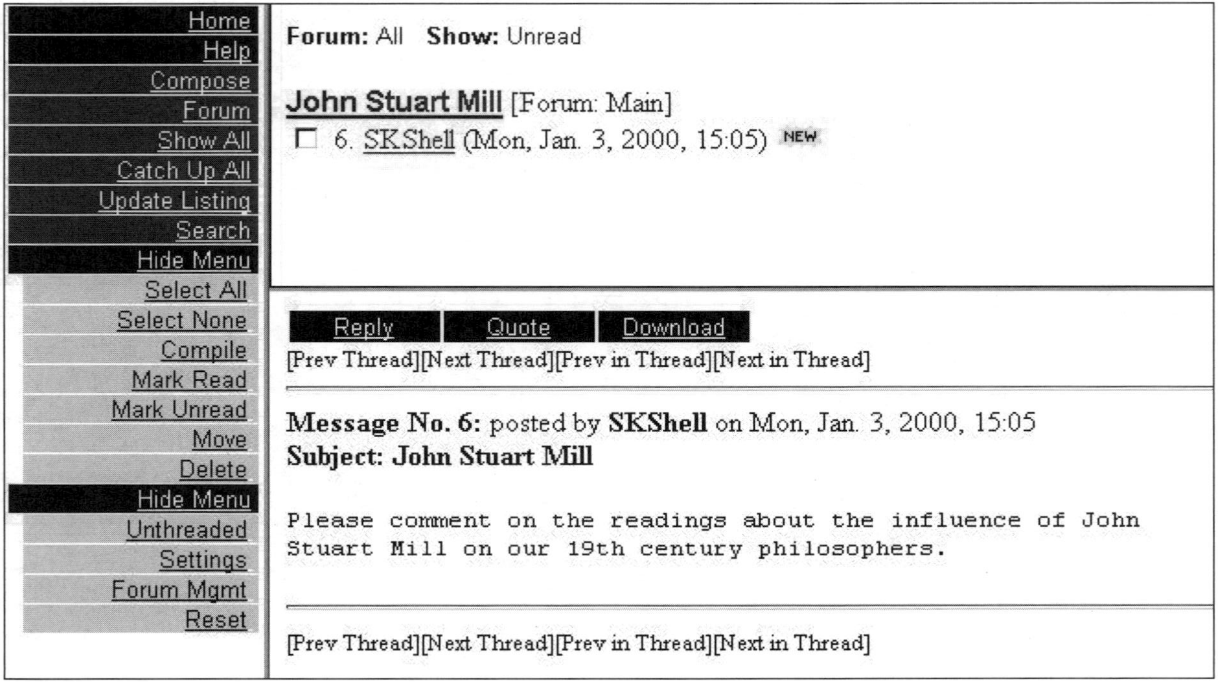

Home
Help
Compose
Forum
Show All
Catch Up All
Update Listing
Search
Hide Menu
Select All
Select None
Compile
Mark Read
Mark Unread
Move
Delete
Hide Menu
Unthreaded
Settings
Forum Mgmt
Reset

Forum: All **Show:** Unread

John Stuart Mill [Forum: Main]

☐ 6. SKShell (Mon, Jan. 3, 2000, 15:05) NEW

Reply   Quote   Download

[Prev Thread][Next Thread][Prev in Thread][Next in Thread]

Message No. 6: posted by **SKShell** on Mon, Jan. 3, 2000, 15:05
Subject: John Stuart Mill

```
Please comment on the readings about the influence of John
Stuart Mill on our 19th century philosophers.
```

[Prev Thread][Next Thread][Prev in Thread][Next in Thread]

Figure 1.1 Jim Hegelmarks's Online Discussion Question. Jim Hegelmarks posted this question in the online discussion board, which uses WebCT software, for his philosophy course.

longer ones so that he can consider them at his leisure. Each posting is about a page in length.

After evaluating the responses, Hegelmarks gives each student a grade for this assignment and enters the grade in the online gradebook, which can be reached by clicking another navigational button on the course's main page. He knows that, when students log on to the class web site to check their grades, each student will be able to see only his or her own grades—no one else's grade will be visible. Hegelmarks also knows that those who have failed to complete this assignment will be able to monitor their progress, or lack of it, by looking at the gradebook online.

What concerns Hegelmarks now is that only five of his fifteen students have responded so far. Because it's already Friday, and there's a new assignment they must do for the next week, he decides to take a look at some of the statistical information that the course management system offers for tracking student progress. What he finds is that, of the ten students who haven't responded to the question, eight have read his commentary, some for more than sixty minutes at a time. Two haven't yet looked at it at all.

Hegelmarks's first concern is with the two students who haven't even looked at the assigned reading. It isn't the first time they've failed to complete an assignment on time. Hegelmarks sends both of them a low-key but concerned e-mail asking whether they're having any special problems he should know about, gently reminding them that they've fallen behind.

The lengthy time the other students have been taking to read his commentary concerns him as well. From past experience he knows that students often struggle with some of the concepts in Mill's *Political Economy*. He had written the commentary and created the homework assignment in an attempt to clarify the subject, but taking a second look, he now realizes that the commentary was written far too densely. He makes a note to rewrite it the next time he teaches the class.

The last task Hegelmarks completes before logging off is to comment on the student responses that he has just read and graded. He doesn't comment on each one—that would take far too long—but he composes a summary message touching on the main points his students have made, and he posts this on the discussion board for all to see.

Introduction to Physics, a "Hybrid" Course

Our second instructor, Miriam Sharpe, teaches an introductory physics class at a large public university. Her course, a prerequisite for anyone majoring in physics, is what we call a "hybrid," combining both online and face-to-face activities.

The class is large, with eighty students enrolled, and Sharpe has two teaching assistants to help her. Three times a week, she lectures to her class, using PowerPoint slides projected onto a screen to elucidate her points. Because she relies on so many slides, she has decided to post them on the course web site for students to review. Figure 1.2 shows an example.

Although some of her colleagues disapprove of this practice, arguing that it will dissuade students from coming to class, Sharpe contends that relieving students of the tedium of taking copious notes during her lectures makes it easier for them to comprehend and remember the material. More importantly, by posting her slides online, she gives students the opportunity to review the material before coming to class. As a result, she has found that the questions raised in class, and the discussions they evoke, are far more relevant and lively.

Sharpe also uses the web site for discussion groups. Each TA leads a discussion group of thirty students, with Sharpe handling the remaining twenty herself. In these virtual discussion groups, students can post their queries and concerns and receive a response from Sharpe, from a TA, or from one or more other students. Sharpe and her TAs make a point of checking the discussion boards at least once a day.

Sharpe has one more major use for the web site: to post sample exams. When she first started using the site, she simply posted the exams as documents that her students could read. But after her university installed a new course management system, she was able to offer the sample exams in such a way that students could take an exam online and receive both feedback and a grade. This trial assessment, she has discovered, is quite popular with her students.

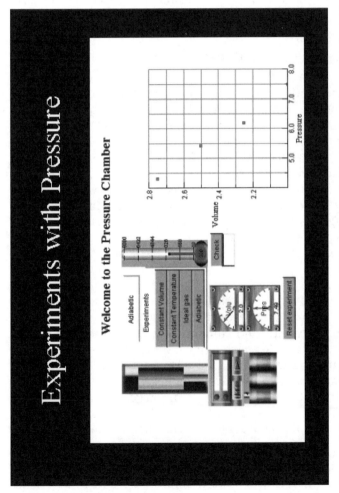

Figure 1.2 PowerPoint Slide Used by Miriam Sharpe in Her Physics Class. This type of graphic can readily be posted on a web page for students to review.

Teaching Online: The Basics

N ow that you have some idea of what it's like to teach online, and what some of the basic terms and concepts are, you may be thinking about how to teach your own class online. Later chapters will go into detail on many specific aspects of the task. Here we want to comment on some of the basic pedagogical considerations involved in teaching courses like those of our two fictional instructors, Jim Hegelmarks and Miriam Sharpe.

Teaching a Course Entirely Online

Perhaps the most daunting task is to plan a new course that will be taught entirely online, particularly if you've never taught online before. Composing the syllabus, assembling the exercises and quizzes, weighing the criteria for grades—all this presents a set of unfamiliar challenges.

Yet closer inspection reveals that the approach to solving such problems is similar to what you would use "on the ground." The same instructional strategy you've learned for a live classroom—setting the goals of the course, describing specific objectives, defining the required tasks, creating relevant assignments—applies online. Similarly, if you're converting an already-existing course into an online version, your basic approach need not change.

Where the online course differs is in technique. In a classroom, you have your physical presence—your voice, body language, intonation, expressions, gestures—to help you communicate with your students. Online, at least for the time being,* you don't. In a classroom, a smile can be a powerful signal of approval. Online, it's reduced to a ludicrous little emoticon **:)**—characters that look like a person grinning. In a classroom, the instructor is often the sage on the stage. Online, the instructor is more like the sage on the page. It is the written word, at least for now, that conveys the crux of what you want to say.

---

*As this book is being written, new tools are evolving that may radically alter the way instruction is delivered online. These are synchronous learning tools that permit instructors to "speak" to their students much as they always have. Such tools, and their implications, are dealt with in more detail in Chapter 14.

This fact puts an inordinate emphasis on style, attitude, and intonation as they are expressed in print. A sarcastic aside, a seemingly innocent joke, shorn of an apologetic smile or a moderating laugh, can seem cold and hostile to the student reading it on the screen. None of the conventional ways of modifying ambiguous or ironic statements—the wink, the raised eyebrow, the shrug, and the smile—are available online. Thus an instructor must pay particular attention to nuances.

In a physical classroom, moreover, you're always there to listen to your students or observe their interactions. Online, you're there only sporadically, at the times when you log on, whereas your students may post their comments at any time of day. These circumstances modify the instructional role you play, making you more a facilitator or moderator than the expert from whom all knowledge flows. Indeed, online courses depend heavily on the participation of students. As an instructor, you need to step back a bit from the spotlight in order to allow the students to take a more active part. Perhaps you will intervene only when the flow of conversation strays too far off the mark or when you need to summarize the conversation in order to move it along to another point.

Conversely, online participation is just as important to the student as it is to you. What makes the Web such an attractive medium—the ability to communicate instantly with anyone in the world—is what drives students to the Internet rather than to a conventional classroom. If, when they log onto the course, all they can do is read the voluminous course notes you have posted there, they will soon become frustrated and drift away.

It's your responsibility to bear all this in mind when devising your course. You will fashion tasks and exercises that emphasize student collaboration and deemphasize the traditional role of the instructor as the central figure in the pedagogical play.

This doesn't mean that an online syllabus should include only tasks that must be performed online: hunting for online material, for example, or linking to a host of other web sites. In fact, such tasks can often prove counterproductive, requiring as they do that students stay online an inordinate amount of time. Indeed, the sort of tasks you have your students perform need not, and perhaps should not, differ from what you would have them do on the ground. They may still need to go to libraries to perform the functions of sound research (unless their institution provides database and full-text resources online), and they still need to investigate, examine, and observe phenomena on their own. What's different is how they communicate what they have learned, how they talk to each other, and how you talk to them. A successful online course often includes challenging assignments that lead to publicly conducted discussions, moderated and guided by you.

Teaching a Hybrid Course

For instructors like Miriam Sharpe, who teach face to face but use the Web to augment the work in class, there's a somewhat different set of criteria. For these instructors, the Web may be a place to post information before class, in order to inspire a meaningful in-class discussion. Or the information on the Web may help give students the proper context for a lecture, so that the lecture falls on well-informed ears rather than becoming a mere oration accompanied by the sound of pencils furiously scribbling notes.

Conversely, the web site might be used to elucidate or elaborate a point that was brought up in class. It may become a place where students can comment, critique, or analyze material in a leisurely and thoughtful way, instead of having to contend with other students in impassioned face-to-face debates. Indeed, the Web provides a safe environment for those students who ordinarily might not chime in, too timid or shy to take part in discussions with those who are louder, more aggressive, or domineering. In this sense, using the Web as a means of communication can often provoke more thoughtful and reasoned discussions than might be possible in a classroom.

Later chapters will describe the options in more detail. Here, our point is straightforward:

Important! *There's no need to start from scratch to teach online. You can apply what you already know and add to it by using new tools and techniques adapted for the online environment.*

What About Support Personnel and Training?

It may have occurred to you that mastering new courseware and techniques is a task that ought to be handled by someone else—by computer support personnel, for example, or by graduate student assistants. On many campuses, however, neither the expertise nor the funds are available to provide the support each faculty member might like to have.

Most of the time, computer support personnel have to deal with problems concerning infrastructure, networks, and servers that shut down. When they respond to an individual faculty member, they're typically concerned with hardware or software problems: "I can't type the letter k on my keyboard"; "The cursor just dropped off my screen!" Teaching assistants, for their part, won't necessarily have more advanced skills than faculty members, and are more appropriately concerned with pursuing their degrees.

Some online programs do offer ongoing support to their teachers: the DIAL program at the New School and OnlineLearning.net, which handles online courses for UCLA Extension, are two examples. But even in these comparatively proactive programs, there's a limit to how much attention and help can be offered to each faculty member, particularly as the number of online courses continues to grow. Of course, instructors who aren't based on a campus have even fewer resources to help them troubleshoot problems.

Equally rare is the availability of reliable and effective training for online instructors. The vast majority must learn on the job. Often this means that the first course you teach is beset with errors, miscues, and miscalculations, much as may have happened when you taught your first class face to face.

Even for those who enroll in a formal training course, the results can be disappointing. Some schools of education, staffed as they are by professors who earned their degrees twenty years ago, aren't coping well with the exigencies of online instruction. Some tend to deal with the subject as if it were a phenomenon to be researched rather than a new set of skills to be mastered and employed. To make matters worse, training is often offered in a conventional classroom setting, depriving faculty members of the experience of learning online. The situation isn't entirely bleak, however. There are some reliable training programs, several of which are mentioned in Chapter 13. In addition, the amount of technical know-how you need before you begin is less than you may suppose. Newcomers to online teaching are apt to exaggerate the computer expertise required. Let's address that question directly.

Do You Have to Be a Computer Expert?

Instructors often wonder what qualifications—especially what level of technical computer skills—they need to consider teaching online. Do you have to be an expert or an advanced computer user?

In terms of technical computer skills, an instructor needs little to start with. A very basic familiarity with computers and the Internet will more than suffice. That means knowing how to do the following:

1. Set up folders and directories on a hard drive.

2. Use word processing software properly (for instance, cut, copy, and paste; minimize and maximize Windows; save files).

3. Handle e-mail communications, including attachments.

4. Use a browser to access the World Wide Web.

If you lack some of these skills, you can pick them up in on-campus or online workshops. Once you're comfortable with these basic skills, you should, with experience, be able to build on them and become more skilled.

Faculty of all ranks who are enthusiastic about the possibilities offered by online teaching—and who are willing to invest some time in learning new technology and methods for the sake of personal and professional growth—are good candidates for teaching online.

Important! *"Techies" don't necessarily make the best online instructors. An interest in pedagogy should come first, technology second.*

The Aim of This Book

In this book we will guide you through the world of online learning, introduce you to its tools and techniques, and help you evaluate whether teaching this way is the right choice for you. This book is a practical guide, not a pedagogical treatise. It will lead you through a fact-finding mission at the institution where you teach, show you how to convert your face-to-face course into one that you can teach online, and explore the different teaching environments available online. It will also help you reshape your syllabus and devise online exercises, manage both your class and your time, learn how to use some of the more popular software tools, and keep your career going by enabling you to stay on top of new developments.

In the next chapter, we will begin preparing you for online teaching by showing you how to explore your institution's resources and make practical sense of what you find.

Resources

Fundamentals of the Web and Distance Learning

Distance Education Clearinghouse. **http://www.uwex.edu/disted/definition.html**

Offers definitions of distance learning and links to other distance education resources.

Learn the Net.com. **http://www.learnthenet.com/**

A good site for learning the basics of web navigation, how to download files, and much more.

Webmonkey. **http://hotwired.lycos.com/webmonkey/**

Offers a "How-to Library" with sections on authoring of web

*material, design, multimedia, and more, as well as feature
articles and reference guides.*

Web Conferencing

Conferencing Software for the Web. **http://thinkofit.com/
webconf/**

*David Woolley's annotated lists of conferencing software,
including both free and commercial varieties.*

Online Educational Delivery Applications: A Web Tool for
Comparative Analysis. **http://www.ctt.bc.ca/landonline/**

*Bruce Landon's site designed "to help educators evaluate and
select online delivery software."*

Scouting the Territory: Exploring Your Institution's Resources

In Chapter 1, you learned a bit about how online learning functions. Now you're ready to begin planning the online environment of your course.

But where should you start?

A good first step is to scout the territory in which you plan to operate—that is, explore the technological and administrative environment in your institution to ascertain what is possible and desirable to do. The tools an institution uses and the support it offers very much influence the choices you'll need to make. Before you sit down to sketch out your course, you must be certain that what you're planning can actually take place.

Colleges and other institutions, after all, don't exist in a vacuum. They have administrators, department heads, and computer support personnel, all of whom have budgets, agendas, and rivalries. Investments have been made (or are on the planning board) in computer hardware, operating systems, software platforms, network cabling, computer labs, maintenance, support, and instructor training. All of these factors, in one way or another, may affect the shape of the course you plan to teach.

Of course, you can't be expected to know everything there is to know about these subjects. We aren't suggesting that you get on your hands and knees to follow the cabling from your building to the street outside. But we are suggesting that you arm yourself in advance with a bit of practical knowledge.

This isn't as formidable a task as it may seem. If you've been working at your institution for some time, you already know much of the information. What you don't know you can usually find out by visiting the institution's web site or by scheduling a few informal interviews with your department head, chief administrator, or head computer support person. If you know what questions to ask and what to look for in advance, you should be able to walk away with most of the information you need.

Imagine you're a manager visiting a plant for the first time. To familiarize yourself with its operations, you do a walk-through survey. You note which equipment is in use, heeding such factors as age, reliability, and maintenance records. You also notice which procedures are in force on the floor, as well as which have been most successful. You judge whether the foreperson and the floor workers seem friendly or enthusiastic, or whether that scowl on their faces denotes some deep-seated hostility you would do well to avoid.

The rest of this chapter will help you translate that metaphorical tour into specific questions to ask and ways to interpret the results.

Questions to Ask About Your Institution's Resources

The following sections describe some useful questions you can ask in your equivalent of a walk-through survey.

What's Already in Place?

This question is the most important of all. In practice, you'll break it down into a number of subordinate queries, such as these:

- Does your institution already provide courses online?
- If so, which courses?
- Who teaches them?
- What platform do they use?
- Who put them together?
- How long did it take to put them together?

Once you find out about online courses already being taught at your institution, make an effort to contact the instructors and talk to them at length. Tell them what you plan to do and solicit their reactions. Find out what their experiences have been. Ask about potential pitfalls you ought to avoid.

Information gained in this way is the most valuable you can collect. Not only will you learn first-hand what's going on, but you may, if you're lucky, forge a few strategic alliances with some of the technological pioneers.

What Kind of Hardware and Operating System Does Your Institution Support?

Does your college or department support PCs only? Macs? What kind of operating system is there?

If the hardware is of one type only, it will limit the kind of software available to you, and this in turn may influence the kind of course you design. This is true because the hardware can work only through the good graces of its **operating system,** which functions as a kind of United Nations interpreter for all the integrated communications of the Internet.

> **operating system** The software that controls a computer and allows it to perform its most basic functions.

The operating system is thus the key information broker or go-between that determines what you can and can't do when teaching online.

By "operating system," of course, we mean that wonderful collection of acronyms, abbreviations, and seemingly random names with which computer programmers have delighted us over the years: Mac OS X, Windows NT, UNIX, Linux, and so on. Windows is the most common operating system on PCs. Windows NT is a common information broker for PC networks. OS X (like its previous incarnations with lower numbers) deciphers what Macintosh chips will or won't do. UNIX is a venerable operating system for large networks.

Software is written expressly for a particular operating system. Thus the **web server** you use to run your course web site must be compatible with the operating system. Some of the more popular course management software programs, such as

Blackboard CourseInfo and WebCT, don't have a version that will run on Macintosh servers. Likewise, some operating systems will run only a few of the available bulletin board software packages. A program like WebBoard, a popular and relatively inexpensive bulletin board conferencing system, will run on almost any Pentium-based PC because the operating system is Windows based. But the same software won't run on a Sparc workstation, for which the operating system is usually UNIX based.

> **web server (server** for short) Software that "serves" out, or disseminates, web pages across the Internet; also may refer to the computer on which this software has been installed.

As these examples suggest, each operating system has advantages and disadvantages. Thus, if the operating system presents a major obstacle for your purposes, you'll need to alter your plans and your syllabus. You'll learn more about course management software systems, and the hardware and operating systems on which they run, in later chapters. For the time being, just take note of what's available at your institution.

What Kind of Network Has Your Institution Set Up?

It doesn't matter what kind of hardware or operating system your college may have if the information that's being "served" has nowhere to go. The "network"—about as vague a term as the "Syndicate"—consists of whatever hodgepodge of telephone, Ethernet, coaxial, and fiber optic cables your institution has cobbled together, complete with the hubs and routers that connect them to the campus "backbone," culminating in the "gateway" that opens to the great outside world in which you and your students live. This collection of stuff determines how quickly and effectively you and your students can communicate with each other. Collectively, it's often referred to as the "pipeline"—another vague term that conceals more than it reveals.

In investigating this pipeline through which you'll have to operate, pay attention to specific capabilities and hindrances. The kind of course you plan and the exercises you assign must take these conditions into consideration.

Imagine, for instance, that your university has an adequate network on campus, with a high-speed connection to the Internet that allows you to surf the Web and fetch useful software in a matter of seconds. Students living off campus, however, can connect with the university network only through a limited number of computer modems that allow **dial-up access** by telephone. Typical communication speeds for current telephone modems range from 28.8 to 56 kilobytes of data per second (kbps)—much slower than the speeds offered by cable modems, ISDN (integrated services digital network) lines, DSLs (digital subscriber lines), T1 lines, and other connections specifically designed for transferring large amounts of data. Thus, if your students are limited to dial-up access, you won't want to create a "treasure hunt" type of exercise in which they're required to go searching online for material or information. Staying online can often be both costly and frustrating for a student connecting from home via a relatively slow, 28.8 kbps modem. Nor will you want to schedule a lot of synchronous chat sessions when you know that the connectivity is tenuous. Text and graphics should become the elements of the courseware you provide.

> **dial-up access** Access to a network or to the Internet by modem through a regular telephone line.

If, on the other hand, the on-campus facilities include computer labs connected in a **local area network (LAN)** by **Ethernet,** you might plan for your students to accomplish their on-

> **local area network (LAN)** A network made up of interconnected computers in a relatively small geographic area, ranging from a single office or lab to a campus.
>
> **Ethernet** The most common technology for LANs, usually relying on coaxial cables or special "twisted-pair" wires.

line work in a scheduled way in one of these labs. In this situation, you might take advantage of the bigger pipeline by using more video, audio, or simulations in your courseware. It would also become more feasible to take advantage of resources available on the Web.

You also need to consider where you yourself will be working most of the time. If you'll work mainly at home and your institution doesn't provide dial-up service (or you live too far for a local call), you should consider obtaining unlimited access with a private Internet service provider (ISP). Also, if you anticipate spending part of the class time away from your normal environment, make sure that you find out about arrangements for network or ISP access when traveling. Can you obtain access without a long distance call? Check ahead with your hotel to find out if there are telephone data ports in the room for your laptop, or a business center that offers Internet access. Or consult an online travel guide to find out if there is an Internet café in the city you plan to visit.

What Kind of Computer Support Does Your Institution Provide?

Computer support comes in various sizes and shapes. Some colleges have computer support personnel who are strictly network maintenance types, with no time for wild-eyed academics. Still other institutions have well-meaning, but somewhat inexperienced, administrators in charge who aren't thoroughly familiar with what a web site can provide. The best have personnel who know their trade and are able to communicate what they know to faculty members.

So get to know your local computer support personnel and ask the appropriate questions. Will they assist you with such details as improving a scanned graphic in Photoshop? Will your students receive support and advice, such as through a troubleshooting telephone service? Or will you and your students be essentially on your own?

The answers to such questions will help you determine just how complex and demanding your online work can be, as well as which methods and software programs might best accomplish the task.

Different Resource Levels: Three Typical Scenarios

Now that you've made your walk-through survey of your institution, you should have a fair idea of what it can offer you. Of course, there are many shades of gray to consider, but in most cases your institution will fall into one of three broadly defined categories: low-tech, mid-tech, or high-tech.

The Low-Tech Scenario

A college or department in the low-tech category has little or no experience offering courses online. Its web site contains administrative information, but little else. Infrastructure is minimal; the majority of departments are connected to the Internet via an ordinary modem rather than a high-speed line. Students roll their eyes heavenward when you inquire whether there are enough computers on campus to meet their needs.

You may discover that a few intrepid faculty members have found a way to offer some of their courseware online, often using local Internet service providers to host their web pages, but these pathfinders have apparently accomplished this feat on their own. No one on campus, you're told, has sufficient skill, dedication, or patience to offer solid technological support. What's more, in order to produce their courseware, these instructors had to purchase their own computer equipment, scanners, and software.

The Mid-Tech Scenario

At a college or department in the mid-tech category, the web site probably does have pointers to individual courses offered online. Some of these courses even have their own web sites. The quality of these course web sites, however, varies widely. Some contain little more than a converted Microsoft Word outline of the course syllabus, whereas others are replete with animated icons, complex graphics, and links to other sites.

Speaking to some of the instructors and computer support people, you learn that the **webmasters** for the existing course sites are a mix of student interns, teaching assistants, and instructor volunteers, mostly self-taught. Hence they have different approaches and diverse sets of skills, accounting for the great variation you see in their web sites. Equally chaotic is the bulletin board software employed on campus—a mélange

> **webmaster** Person who administers and maintains the web server; usually a programmer.

of programs ranging from freeware obtained from the Internet to PC-based conferencing systems such as WebBoard.

There are several computer labs on campus, although the available seats in those labs only partially fill the needs of the student body. On-campus network cabling exists, with some of the major buildings and labs connected directly to the institution's backbone network. But communication with the world beyond the college gates is less reliable; students attempting to connect from home to a departmental web site often find the task frustrating. Many students, however, can connect readily from home to third-party web sites. Ultimately, all of your students have some Internet access, though it may not be high speed or very reliable.

The High-Tech Scenario

The high-tech institution has installed a full-scale course management system for its departments or colleges. It has purchased site licenses for course management software, such as Blackboard CourseInfo or WebCT, and has installed this software on its own web servers. Most of the online courses therefore have a uniform user interface.

The computer support service boasts a room full of humming computers connected to a bank of high-speed modems through which students living off campus can log onto the institution's LAN. Maintenance is handled by the institution's own staff.

The administration, apparently eager to promote the use of computer-mediated courses, has secured grants and alumni contributions to fund the construction of labs and cabling infrastructure on campus. Periodically, workshops are offered to both faculty and students to assist them in learning new computer skills. Or perhaps the institution has contracted with some **online delivery partners** to provide server access, technical support, instructional design, or training. An instructional technology or

> **online delivery partner** A private business set up to assist institutions or businesses in delivering courses online. Some maintain the courses on their own servers. Others provide training or course content conversion services, such as creating web pages from word-processed text. Some representative commercial providers are Embanet, OnlineLearning.net, and eCollege.

academic computing unit on campus has skilled personnel capable of assisting you in mounting your course.

Adapting to Your Institution's Resource Level

Even though it may appear that only the high-tech setting offers you a good chance to succeed as an online instructor, you can be successful in all three types of institutions if you're willing to tailor your demands to the available resources. In fact, a high-tech university doesn't always provide the most hospitable environment, or indeed the best results. You may find that a high-tech setting, with its integrated course management applications, amounts to a "one-size-fits-all" approach that doesn't suit your particular needs very well.

The following sections offer examples of solutions you might develop in each of the three environments.

Low-Tech Solutions

As an example of a low-tech setting, imagine you're teaching introductory biology at a small rural college with few technological resources. Because this course is required for biology majors and also fulfills the college's general education requirements, it's usually quite full, with upwards of ninety students crammed into a large, poorly air-conditioned classroom. The college has no graduate program to speak of and barely enough funds to provide TAs, so you rely on honors biology undergraduates for assistance.

You lecture, you assign homework (readings in a large, expensive, and somewhat daunting textbook), you give a midterm and a final, and you hold discussion sections three times a week, dividing up the class into groups of about thirty. On your office computer, you've created a series of overheads that you use as you lecture (as long as the bulb in the room's overhead projector hasn't burned out), and you make available to the students a set of your private course notes, complete with graphs and diagrams, for which they pay a nominal fee. Although your discussion sections help fill in the gaps, the atmosphere is often chaotic, with the students firing questions from all sides as if they were reporters at a presidential press conference.

Clearly, you're doing the best you can with the means available. Nevertheless, too many students seem to struggle with the material. Over the past several years, your students' grades have shown a downward trend, with fewer A's and more B's and C's. And in the student-prepared evaluation booklet circulated privately at the beginning of each year, your class is consistently deemed one of the hardest on campus.

You work hard to teach this class—so hard that you're exhausted much of the time—and you don't want to lower your standards merely to get more favorable student evaluations. What you'd like to do is improve student comprehension of this difficult and challenging subject while, paradoxically, lightening your own formidable teaching load. To do this, you know you must find a way to communicate more efficiently with your students. The obvious solution would be to increase your office hours. But, for a class of ninety-odd students, that might not be of much help. It also might prove overwhelming for you.

Given the limited means of your institution, what can you do?

Even in this difficult situation, there are ways to use online instruction effectively. Some of your students will have access to the Internet via dial-up modems. The question is, How many? Using whatever survey tools are available to you (personal letters to your students, information from the registrar's office, in-class polls, informal interviews), find out how many students either have a computer of their own or have access to a friend's or roommate's computer that is connected in some way to the Internet. To this figure add a reasonable estimate of the number of students who might gain access to the Internet via whatever on-campus resources are available to them.

Your goal is to set up an e-mail (and snail mail) mentoring system to supplement—and, in time, perhaps supplant—your regular office hours and some of your discussion sections. You want to have your students contact you when they need help.

These authors must be crazy, you may be thinking. Students who know how to use e-mail technology are capable of firing off fusillades of messages; within a week I'd have a thousand e-mails that I couldn't possibly answer, you're thinking. True, we respond, e-mail can be a dangerous thing; but, if used judiciously, it can lighten your workload and deepen student comprehension of course material. The keys to success are the rules you create and enforce.

Here, for example, are some rules for e-mail communication that you might set up in the situation we've outlined:

Rule 1 Students are encouraged to send you questions via e-mail (or snail mail). But you make it absolutely clear that you aren't going to respond to each and every message. Indeed, because your entire class doesn't have access to the Internet, you're going to collect the inquiries, group them according to subject, and provide a single answer on each subject once a week. Your answers will form, in effect, a page of "frequently asked questions," which computer folk often call "FAQs." You'll bring this page to class, post it on a bulletin board, distribute it to those who want a copy, or leave it in the library for students to peruse. You may even discuss the points in class.

Rule 2 Office hours are for personal problems only. Under no circumstances will you discuss content-related problems with students on a one-on-one basis in your office.

Rule 3 Don't break rules 1 and 2.

Even with such rules in place, the first time you begin the process, it will seem like an onerous task. You'll have to read each e-mail carefully and draft your replies. This may seem like even more work than you did before. But by the second term, your workload should decrease dramatically. You will have built an impressive database of written replies to standard queries, which you can supplement as new questions come in. When students raise questions in class, you can refer to your already-prepared answers, perhaps even read them aloud. Your posted FAQ page will become a resource students can rely on. Gradually they'll learn to look at the page first before sending you a note. And you'll have more time for more productive pursuits, as well as for your family and friends.

In time, you may be able to set up an electronic **mailing list**, often known as a **listserv**. A listserv requires special software that manages your e-mail communications, capturing all inquiries automatically and rerouting them to the entire class. This software does cost money and must be managed by someone. For references to information about listserv software and existing mailing lists, see the web page provided by Impulse Research Corporation at **http://www.webcom.com/impulse/list.html.**

> **mailing list (listserv)** An online discussion group, administered by a software program, in which each message is sent to a common e-mail address, which then forwards the message to all members on the list.

Mid-Tech Solutions

If you teach in an institution like the one described in our mid-tech scenario, you have many more options than in a low-tech setting.

For one thing, your students either have a computer at home, with limited modem access to the Internet, or can use one of the computers available in campus labs. Thus you can feel somewhat at ease in using the Web to help teach your class, circulate information, and cut down on your workload.

Unfortunately, you also know (or will soon find out) that, if you want to create a web site with lectures, quizzes, and bulletin boards, you're pretty much on your own. Your department computer support staff may help you a bit, but most of the work of designing, writing, and mounting the web pages will be yours, as will the worries and frustrations that arise when something goes wrong (as when the server goes down). The few software tools available to you are pretty rudimentary and difficult to use. Imagining the time it will take you to compose all the material for the Internet—not to mention all the software manuals you'll have to read in order to get it all right—you sigh heavily and set that plan aside.

Or maybe not. Although your college may not offer much help, others in the global village will. Now is the time for you to discover one of the great benefits of teaching on the Web—the incredible creativity and generosity of a vast percentage of its citizen proprietors. For the instructor like yourself, willing to take the technological plunge but wary of sinking too deep, there are numerous resources available to buoy you up. Some of them are free, and some of them cost so little that either you or your institution may decide they are affordable.

Using Free Online Resources   Many of the most advanced course management systems, such as WebCT and Blackboard or the lower-tech Nicenet's Internet Classroom Assistant, offer free access to course management software. For example, on Blackboard.com, you can conduct a course free of charge, using Blackboard's web server and software, as long as the amount of material posted doesn't exceed 5 megabytes. That's more or less the equivalent of fifteen chapters of a book, enough to post a considerable amount of information. (For information about contacting Blackboard and other such services, see the Guide to Resources at the end of this book.)

Using a free site like Blackboard's will make you feel as if you've made the leap from the Stone Age to the Information Age in one effortless bound. You'll find that you have these benefits, among others:

- You can control who accesses your course and who doesn't.

- You can create course syllabi and course notes simply by typing in your information online. (If you're a bit more skilled, you can create HTML files and send those to your web site as well.)

- You can create online quizzes that are automatically graded.

- You can divide your students into private study groups whose members can chat together online while they plan their projects.

These advantages are just the beginning. Every day there are more new resources available at free sites online.

Supplementing Your Institution's Resources If your college already has a web server, you'll probably use it for your course's web site. But you can also supplement the college's online environment by using some of the free tools available. Say you have a web site on which you've posted your syllabus, course notes, assignments, and course calendar, but you also want your students to take a self-grading quiz in order to test their mastery of the subject matter. How will you proceed?

To create such a tool from scratch—in other words, to write the program—would take a considerable amount of time, resources, and talent. Fortunately, there are a number of resources available online that will do the job for free. At the University of Victoria, for instance, researchers have developed a tool called Hot Potatoes that anyone can **download** free of charge (**http://web.uvic.ca/hrd/halfbaked/**). Running on either a Windows or a Macintosh server, this tool allows you to create a variety of quizzes and evaluations. For instance, you can construct "quiz and review" exercises, in which students have access to the answers, or fully graded quizzes (the software itself grades them). The University of Hawaii (**http://www.motted.hawaii.edu/**) provides an equally useful test generator that runs on a server housed on that university's campus. You create the questions and answers. Your students then connect to the university's server and take the quiz. Results are e-mailed to you and to them.

> **download** To retrieve a file from a remote computer and save it on your own computer.

High-Tech Solutions

In our high-tech scenario, the institution has set up a course management software system. This means that you won't have to go shopping around for a quiz tool here and some bulletin board software there. The shopping has already been done. Most likely, some training and support are also available to help you get up to speed using these tools. Thus, whether you want to teach entirely online or merely supplement regular classroom teaching with web-based tools, most, if not all, of the functions you require will be available.

You may think that, in such a technological heaven, your troubles are over. However, colleges are notoriously rigid. Having installed a course management system, they often begin to act like poker players nursing a good hand. They tend to stand pat, not drawing any cards and not discarding any either. When new software becomes available or new technologies come into being, they tend to dismiss these developments as too expensive, too difficult to implement, not practicable, or not necessary "at the present time."

A case in point: In 1998 and 1999, RealNetworks, the creator of RealAudio and a host of other products with "Real-" as their prefix, bolted to the front of the field with its **streaming media** products. Using free software, which Real-Networks made available to any interested user via the company web site **(http://www. real.com/),** an instructor could produce sound files—say, from a tape-recorded interview of a colleague—that her students could listen to with a RealNetworks player they had also downloaded free from the RealNetworks site. Or, as another example, an instructor could create a PowerPoint slide show, add narration, and (using one of RealNetworks' other tools) present it on the class web site as a streaming, narrated slide show that students could access with an ordinary modem.

> **streaming media** Audio or video files that are sent in a continuous stream from a source computer (usually via a web site) to a receiving computer. Using a "player" software program, the recipient can hear or view the content in real time.

As streaming media became widely available, many instructors, their faces glowing with enthusiasm, approached administrators with the request to put some of these multimedia creations on course web sites, only to hear that the software was out of reach of the department's budget at the present time. In most such cases, the administrator was thinking about the $600 fee for the basic server software (or the approximately $2,000 for the more advanced version). The administrator was often unaware of the fact that RealNetworks offered a *free* version of its software that would allow up to twenty users to request the use of an audio file at one time—more than adequate to accommodate the demands of most classes.

Often, when apprised of the existence of a free version, the administrators agreed to install it and make it available to faculty members. But this story has a clear moral.

Important! *No one knows everything, not even your computer support personnel. Even in a high-tech world, you have to do a little homework of your own to stay on top of new developments and be sure that those around you are on top of things as well.*

One other word about living in a high-tech environment: No institution will ever be able to provide the level of support to which you may think you're entitled. Even the most respected professors at Ivy League colleges sometimes complain that they can't get a decent web site designed when they want to. The fact that your university has purchased fancy equipment and software doesn't mean that you won't have to learn some skills. Sooner or later, you'll have to learn how to create a web page, download a graphic, or even create an audio file, just as once you had to learn how to use the overhead projector or the tape recorder.

In the following chapters you'll learn about these skills and how to master them. For the time being, pull your syllabus out of your desk drawer. We're about to convert it so that you can use it online.

Resources

E-mail Discussion Groups/Lists and Resources. **http://www. webcom.com/impulse/list.html**

A useful page designed to be a one-stop information resource about mailing lists (listservs).

Hot Potatoes Homepage. **http://web.uvic.ca/hrd/halfbaked/**

A useful, free suite of software for creating web-based quizzes and exercises.

Nicenet's Internet Classroom Assistant. **http://www.nicenet.org/**

A free course management tool.

RealNetworks. **http://www.real.com/**

Currently the leading supplier of streaming media software.

University of Hawaii QuizCenter. **http://www.motted. hawaii.edu/**

Free online quizzes that are hosted on the Hawaii site.

II

Putting the Course Together

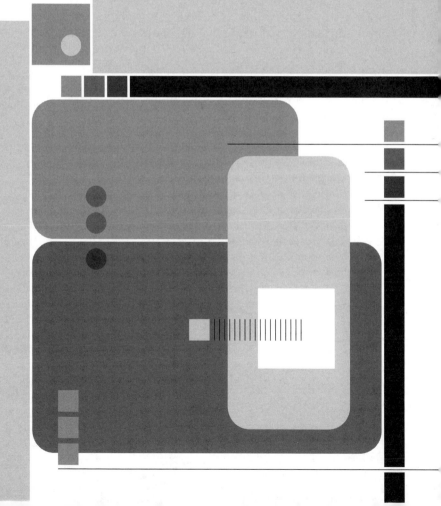

Course Conversion

All right. You've taken the grand tour of the campus and are now familiar with the lay of the land.

You're ready to get down to work, to convert your on-the-ground class to one online. You take your syllabus out of the drawer and stare at it. It reads just like it always did: It has your name, a description of the class goals and objectives, your grading policy, a schedule of your office hours, and a week-by-week listing of assignments and quizzes.

Nothing very exciting. Just the same old stuff. You take your syllabus, which you wrote using a word processing program, convert it into an HTML page (or ask instructional support staff to do so), and give it to your local computer support person, who displays it online. Or perhaps your institution has a handy web template (a premade form) that requires you to do little more than fill in the text fields with the appropriate information. You call several of your colleagues to tell them to have a look at your page. They congratulate you on your good work and tell you that it looks just fine. Your students, on the other hand, never look at it twice. Why should they, once they've printed it out?

Our point is this:

Important! *Putting your class online doesn't mean copying your lectures and syllabus word for word.*

Rather, converting your course to an online environment means adapting it to use some of the tools available in the new environment. If you teach a hybrid class (one that's both face to face and online), the conversion involves using the Web to complement what you do in class. If you're teaching exclusively online, it involves recasting your entire class in an online shape.

Two Examples of Course Conversion

Let's have a look at some actual instructors who have gone through this process. Here are two different situations: a pharmacology course delivered completely online and a psychology course that's a hybrid of face-to-face and online components.

Pharmacology Online

Anita Reach, a psychology instructor and coordinator of the Addiction Counselor Program at Kansas City (Kansas) Community College, decided to pioneer an online course in basic pharmacology. This basic course had been mandated by the state of Kansas for all those working with clients in substance abuse treatment facilities. The mandate, she said, "created a dilemma for individuals residing in remote areas of the state and unable to conveniently enroll in college courses." In addition, she noted that colleges in close proximity to potential students rarely offered the specific mandated course. Therefore, in the fall of 1997, she proposed to resolve this problem by making the course available completely online.

She knew that her students wouldn't all have their own personal computers and that many would be accessing the course through libraries or nearby colleges. So it was important that all classroom activity be made available online without requiring her students to download material from the Web. Because they'd be looking at the pages in a library, no audio or video tools could be used (the software or listening devices might not be available to everyone). Furthermore, because her college had limited resources to offer, it wasn't likely to purchase course management software to serve as the platform for her class. In fact, Reach joked, "I truly don't think the instructional technology staff even knew I was teaching a course online. But I did manage to get a laptop from them." Aside from the laptop, she had to go elsewhere to find her tools.

Because of the limited resources available to her in the beginning, Reach decided to use a free conferencing system, Nicenet's Internet Classroom Assistant **(http://www.nicenet.org/),** to support discussion forums in her class. She decided she'd use a mix of online materials, which she would create herself, along with assigned readings from a text. Class work would consist of weekly readings, both online and from the text. She posted specific questions in the discussion forum to which the students were required to respond. To ensure full participation in the course, each student was given individual questions to answer in the discussion forum, but her hope was that all students would benefit by reading the postings of their fellow students.

For each session, two web sites relevant to the topic were assigned for investigation. Students visited the sites and then submitted an individual e-mail to her, with a one-paragraph summary of the site. Students were given extra credit for finding and identifying additional sites of value to the course. These web site assignments were designed to give students experience in evaluating resources available on the Web. This training, Reach hoped, would prove valuable for students' future independent research.

Each week she assigned a discussion question that invited comment and reflection about socially related issues, such as legalization of drugs. By soliciting these subjective comments, Reach hoped to give students opportunities to "clarify their positions and share thoughts and values with others, for practice in the real world."

For assessment, Reach relied on short online quizzes about the reading assignments, participation in online discussions, and a final take-home exam submitted by e-mail or snail mail. For the online quizzes, she decided to use another free site, the QuizCenter at the University of Hawaii at Maui **(http://www. motted.hawaii.edu/).** The quizzes, a mix of multiple-choice and true/false questions, were graded automatically by the Quiz-Maker, which in turn e-mailed a report to the individual student with his or her grade. Cheating wasn't a dominant concern for Reach, because she knew that all of her students would be taking a proctored certification exam after this course, and most were aware that they needed the information and experience gleaned from the course to succeed with the exam.

Reach's course is a model of what we mean by converting a course to one that can be taken online. She took into consideration a number of key factors: software tools available to her, resources of her college and her students, and the goals and objectives of the course itself. She might have taken a different route. She might have assigned the readings from her text and sent her students videotapes of her lectures. Using Nicenet to deliver the course was "a little cumbersome . . . but it worked." Still, in her opinion, using the online tools produced a far richer learning experience for her students than a prerecorded lecture could ever have done. Requiring her students to discuss the assignments online engendered a sense of community that reduced the isolation many students would have felt working entirely on their own. Furthermore, having them use Internet tools not only afforded them the experience of using the Web to do research, but also taught them some of the skills they would need to be successful in their prospective careers.

Reach's first course had only six students, but in the spring of 1998 she was able to move the course to a more comprehensive software platform, FirstClass, which students accessed via a web-based version. Her college belongs to a consortium of seven institutions, through which a server and site license for FirstClass software became available for her course. Every term since then, the course has been filled to its enrollment cap of sixteen students.

Since her first course debuted, Anita Reach has gone on to steward an entirely online program at her community college. By the fall of 1999, over sixty online courses were being offered, and a move to the WebCT system was planned for 2000. With the use of WebCT, Reach is gratified that instructors will be able to make use of sophisticated online testing features and will also have the support of her new online unit in developing their courses. In her new position as Project Leader for Online Development at Kansas City Community College, she has gone from borrowing a laptop to having within her reach a fully equipped instructor lab that provides support for faculty members pioneering their own courses.

A Hybrid Psychology Course

For Lonnie Yandell of Belmont University in Nashville, Tennessee, there was no university mandate to create a totally online course. The problem he faced was how to use an online component to improve the quality of his course. As chair of the Psychology Department, Yandell taught a course in cognitive psychology, a course that required a great deal of problem solving and independent research projects, both of which tasks required a significant amount of one-on-one help.

Usually Yandell used the classroom period to lecture to his class. But he decided that standing up at a dais and lecturing wasn't a productive use of his time. In order to spend more time interacting with his students, he wanted to greatly reduce his time spent lecturing in the classroom and "free up face-to-face class time for one-on-one and small group discussion and problem solving."

Belmont University has a tradition of being very teacher oriented, encouraging innovative teaching techniques on the ground. In late 1998, although the university hadn't yet extended this support to online teaching, it had purchased a copy of the course management software suite TopClass, and Yandell was ready to try adding an online component to his course.

With these goals and resources in mind, Yandell determined to supplement his course by moving his lectures entirely online, while reserving his classroom time for "completing simulations, working on research projects, and getting individual help from the teacher." It turned out that putting all his lectures online was much more difficult and time consuming than he thought it would be. However, he reasoned that the students would get the best of both worlds: Besides receiving one-on-one guidance with their projects, they could read and reread the basic information they needed, including the material in his lectures.

When he taught this class completely face to face, Yandell routinely used graphics-enriched computer presentations for his lectures. These were graphs, charts, and problem sets generated by specific software programs, which he would demonstrate in class. Converting all these materials into an online format seemed to Yandell like an insurmountable task to do alone. So he decided to concentrate his energies on using the online environment to supplement the work on the many computer simulations his students were required to complete in the lab.

Previously, these simulations—over twelve in all—were presented only as lab components. Some could now be accessed online as well. These included simulations demonstrating aspects of memory and perception. Yandell posted a short commentary on each simulation online. He'd always asked students to answer a series of eight questions about each simulation, but now his students could post their responses online for everyone to read. Yandell's directions in his syllabus encouraged student-to-student interaction. After instructing the students to post their answers in the appropriate TopClass discussion folder, he added, "You can also read other students' posts and respond to them if you like. You can receive extra credit for the discussion grade by making appropriate responses to others' posts."

Yandell graded each student's responses separately, but he didn't offer his own feedback online to each and every one—that would have required far too much time and effort. Instead, he culled the best of the responses for each simulation question and compiled them into a page he called "comparison responses," which he posted online.

Belmont University still stipulated that actual exams be taken on campus, but to further assist his students in comprehending the great amount of challenging material (cognitive psychology is a formidable course), Yandell made use of TopClass's quiz-making features to create practice tests. Cutting and pasting from material he'd previously used in class, he created a host of multiple-choice questions with appropriate feedback for correct or incorrect answers. His students could take these practice tests or not, depending on their needs. Overall, Yandell "spent a long time posting multiple-choice practice tests on TopClass. I had to copy and paste each question *and* each of the four alternatives. Over the semester, I probably copied and pasted nearly 1,000 questions. Too much work! But the students commented very favorably about them, so I struggled through it."

Yandell also posted weekly questions on the lectures. He'd always fielded questions when he presented his lectures in class. Now he posted questions drawn from his long experience in teaching this class, and he required his students to discuss them, assigning a small portion of the students' final grade (5 percent) to their participation online. To his surprise, Yandell discovered that requiring his students to answer specific questions online increased the level of interaction with his class. "There is no way I could get every student to respond in discussions [in the face-to-face lecture class] the way they must online," he noted. "Many students who almost never talk in class expressed themselves very well in their online answers to questions. Regular classes tend to be dominated by a few articulate individuals, which is not so with online responses."

Lonnie Yandell is obviously an unusually dedicated instructor who was willing to devote a considerable amount of his own time to improving the way he taught his class by using online tools. It's a rare department chair who would do as much. What, then, are Yandell's rewards? For one thing, his class received high praise from the students. For another, the initial work he put into creating his web site would decrease significantly in the years to come, permitting him to spend more time with his students (not to mention with his duties as department chair). As it happened, Yandell ended up extending this online enhancement method to his honors course in Cognition, Research, and Analytics—with great success.

Initial Steps in Course Conversion

Now that you've had a look at these examples that introduce you to the process of converting a course, you're probably wondering where to begin.

Take a look at the resources you have available to you. In addition to your syllabus, you probably have some goals and objectives, a list of assignments, required readings, quizzes, papers, and grading policies. Do you also have lecture notes that you created using a word processor? overheads or slide transparencies that you regularly show to your class? audio- or videotapes? All of those elements comprise the raw material you'll use to convert your course to one that you can teach online.

It would seem at first glance that the essential task to be accomplished is to convert these elements into digital files to be posted on the Web. But the fact that someone has word-processed all of his or her lectures and transferred graphics to HTML pages doesn't mean that a course has been converted. In fact, this isn't even the first step! It's only the mechanical aspect of the job. We'll discuss the mechanics further in Chapter 7, but here we want to focus on more basic considerations.

As our two scenarios demonstrate, a strict translation of what you normally do on the ground into the online environment isn't always desirable. Like the art of translation, course conversion should not merely strive for a word-for-word equivalency, but should allow the new language of communication to be fully exploited. Just as there are some things one can say only in Chinese or Spanish, there are new and different forms of expression that can be attempted in the online medium. Although the communication of content and the achievement of course objectives will naturally be the aim of any course conversion process, there's a great deal more to be gained than a mere transfer from one medium into another.

Important! *If you simply post your lectures and syllabus on the Web, you haven't necessarily created a viable tool for your students. The missing element here is instructional design.*

Without necessarily becoming an expert in instructional design principles, you need to become aware of what you normally do to create a course for the face-to-face classroom and then think about applying these steps to the online course. The following sections provide a simplified view of this process, along with some additional elements that apply to the online environment.

Analysis

You'll need to have some idea of whom your course is for, what role it is to play in the curriculum, and what resources will be available to you and your students. Here are some questions you might want to ask:

1. What is your student audience? For example, is this course for 20 or 120 students? Is the course for beginners or advanced students? for majors or primarily nonmajors?
2. What types of materials should be made available to students online? For example, will any on-campus activities or labs be available, or must all class activities be delivered online?
3. What kind of Internet access will your students have?
   a. Will students access this online classroom from high-speed campus networks or from their homes?

   b. Do most students have unlimited Internet access through the university, or do they pay for their own ISPs?

4. What support will you have available to assist you in creating online course materials?

5. Is there an integrated suite of tools or course management software available, or will you have to create everything on your own web pages?

If you've done the survey of your institution's resources recommended in Chapter 2, you will already have most or all the answers to the more technical questions.

Design

"Design" really means the shape and direction you want your course to take. In thinking about the design of your course, you need to consider your course objectives, the preferred teaching strategies and approaches to the material that you want to preserve, and any new approaches you would like to try in the online environment.

   Here are some of the types of questions you need to ask yourself:

1. Is collaborative work among students or peer review appropriate or desirable?

2. What's the best way to assess your students?

   a. Portfolios?

   b. Multiple-choice quizzes? self-assessment exams or graded exams?

   c. Essays?

   d. Fieldwork reports?

   e. Individual projects?

3. What will be the balance of student-centered versus instructor-led activities? Will you mainly facilitate discussion and research, or does the course have a strong component of lecturing as well?

4. How central is discussion or student presentation to achieving the objectives of the course?

5. What are your preferred methods of presenting content?
    a. Do you have graphics or slides that you want to utilize in some way?
    b. Do you use lecture notes?
    c. Do you use overheads?
    d. Is it important for you to accommodate as many different learning styles as possible?
6. How might your available resources affect the implementation of your design?
    a. Will you have online testing forms?
    b. Do you have a bulletin board or conferencing discussion forum, or will you have to rely on e-mail and mailing lists?
    c. Do you have easy access to a scanner for your preexisting slides?
    d. Will you be able to use streaming audio?

Perhaps this is the time to consider whether a direct "translation" is either possible or desirable. Say that you have PowerPoint slides with lots of text on them. These probably won't translate very well to an online setting, although simple figures and images may be directly convertible. But look at the other side of the question as well: Do you really *want* to replicate the combination of lecture and slides that you've always used, or would it be possible to consider some new combination of presentation methods?

Important! *The move to an online format offers you opportunities to try out new methods and approaches. Preserving the quality of your course need not mean finding an exact translation of what you've always done in the past.*

Course Development

The development stage involves the actual creation of a syllabus, class schedule, content, and exams, as well as activities the class will follow. Having assembled your materials and analyzed the needs of your class, and with your basic design considerations in mind, it's now time to make a few decisions about what you're going to do.

The activities in most college classes can probably be divided into a few large categories:

- *Instructor presentation:* Typically this includes lectures, simulations, charts, and graphs, as well as computer-assisted presentations using tools like PowerPoint. Guest lecturers are also included in this category.

- *Discussion:* Small group, guided discussion sections run by teaching assistants are a common format for discussion. So are question-and-answer sessions as adjuncts to lectures, labs, and exams. In seminars, instructor presentation and discussion are often combined.

- *Group-oriented work and student presentation:* Collaborative, cooperative, and other peer activities are included here. These might include a group project, peer-reviewed compositions, and an independent project presented to the entire class.

- *Research:* Research may be conducted either by individuals or in groups. A separate category may be carved from research to encompass practical applications, experiments, fieldwork, interviews, and apprenticeships.

- *Assessment:* Assessment activities typically involve exams, essays, and projects; portfolios that combine different types of work; and evaluation and credit for participation.

Let's look at some of the factors you need to consider in converting these various types of course activities to an online format.

Instructor Presentation: Lectures

Lectures are probably the most common method of presenting content in a college classroom. Often they're accompanied by transparencies, slides, blackboard writings, or computer-assisted PowerPoint presentations.

To translate this type of activity into an online environment, you can use several different online formats alone or in combination. Here are some notes on these possibilities, along with their advantages and disadvantages.

Text   Text in the form of web pages is a logical choice for converting lecture materials. (See Chapter 7 for discussion of ways to create and format web page text.) Compared to a conventional lecture, text on a web page has the advantage that students can copy the materials and make their own notes; in addition, they have more time to reflect on what you've said.

The main pitfall here is trying to transcribe your speech without taking into consideration that the lecture will be read, not listened to. You don't want to create documents that are tediously formal or that appear as overly long blocks of text when viewed on a web page.

Tips for Writing Online Text

- Strive for a style midway between casual speech and formal writing.
- Chunk your writing into short paragraphs with space between them.
- Use headings, italics, colors, and other indicators to allow the eye to quickly take in the gist of the presentation.
- Graphics can be interspersed as well, or presented via links (see Chapter 7).

PowerPoint Slide Shows   As we mentioned in earlier chapters, you can incorporate PowerPoint slide shows into a web page. In fact, PowerPoint itself allows you to save a slide as an HTML file for a web page. Remember, though, that in the face-to-face classroom, the students have you to observe, but online the slides themselves must carry the entire presentation. Therefore, design, images, and graphics are essential to the success of such presentations.

Keep in mind, too, that slides are accessed rather slowly online, and this can make such presentations very tedious. If you wish to use slide show presentations, divide up your slides and test them so that each segment takes no more than ten minutes.

Don't try to directly replicate long PowerPoint presentations that are mainly bulleted text. If your slides are primarily of this type, consider converting them into short text paragraphs with bulleted items. This web page format can replace your slides.

Narrated Slides and Audio- or Videotaped Lectures   Narrated slides can be an effective way to present materials online. However, you should avoid simply narrating bulleted text. Here are some tips for using narrated slides effectively online:

- Make sure each narration extends over a series of slides rather than stopping for five or more minutes on one slide.
- Use a casual narration with lots of color in the voice.
- Use graphics, arrows, or other visual means to enliven the presentation.

A narrated slide presentation is particularly good for taking students through a series of steps—say, the steps for learning a computer software program. Audio alone or in narrated slides can also be a very effective instructional method in foreign languages, art, and music. Audio might be used to replace a short lecture or a guest lecture. Audio can also serve as a personalized introduction to the course or to the instructor. In the latter case, a short audio welcoming message might be combined with a still photo.

Some online programs feature videotaped lectures that have been converted into streaming video files on the web site. Although this is indeed an option, it isn't a particularly good choice, given the present state of modem access. Students who don't have high-speed connections will find this a frustrating way to access lectures. In addition, there's the familiar problem of "net congestion": when the Internet gets busy, the student will find that the video being streamed will become garbled, or the picture will blur or drop out altogether. For these reasons, even though many students do enjoy the videotaped presence of an instructor, a little video may go a long way.

Effective uses of streaming video might include a demonstration of an experiment and a presentation of vignettes for a language course. For longer or numerous videos, consider distributing the material on a CD-ROM or even on videotape.

When offering audio and video, you should also take into consideration students' disabilities. Prepare a text transcript or summary of audio or video presentations for the benefit of those who have sight or hearing disabilities. This will also serve to give all students other options for accessing the material—

including those who have technical problems and those for whom the text option is a learning preference. You can best prepare your transcript or summary *before* making your video or slide narration. Preparing transcripts afterward is quite labor intensive. By creating the textual materials ahead of time, you also generate, in effect, a script or storyboard from which you can more efficiently produce your audio or video.

Instructor Presentation: Simulations and Experiments

If you use computer simulations and experiments, you'll often find it possible, as Lonnie Yandell did, to have students access them via a web page. But you should test any simulations under the real conditions in which students will access them. If they involve long download times or could be interrupted by net congestion, they may prove less effective than you wish. In that case, you may want to continue using a computer lab.

But what if no actual lab is available, and you have a large number of computerized simulations to demonstrate? In such cases, you might consider distributing your simulations on a CD-ROM. This will require extra preparation on your part and perhaps the enlistment of instructional media services as well.

Discussion

Earlier, we mentioned the following types of discussions that are normally held on an on-the-ground campus: TA-run, small group, guided discussions; question-and-answer sessions as adjuncts to lectures, labs, and exams; and seminar models in which instructor presentation and discussion are often combined. All of these may be successfully transported to the online environment.

In planning these activities, however, you'll need to decide which can best be carried out in an asynchronous (not-in-real-time) forum and which in a real-time, synchronous mode. Here your audience and course analysis comes into play. If you're conducting a primarily face-to-face class, for example, you may want to have all real-time discussion carried out in the live classroom and utilize an asynchronous forum for follow-up discussions that allow for more reflection. Or you may want to utilize an asynchronous forum for preparatory exploration of topics before the face-to-face discussion takes place.

If your course is entirely online, a synchronous mode of discussion might seem to offer the best parallel to face-to-face interaction. Yet, if students are logging in from multiple time zones or are primarily working adults, the synchronous mode will allow too little flexibility in scheduling.

Later chapters will discuss specific strategies and techniques for getting the most out of both asynchronous and synchronous discussions. The following sections look at factors you need to consider when planning your course discussions.

Asynchronous Discussion   To prepare for your use of asynchronous discussion opportunities, you should first decide on how you want to use discussion in relation to your presentation and assignment elements in the course. In other words, decide whether discussion topics will closely follow the questions you raise in your lectures and other presentations, or whether the topics will provide opportunities to introduce additional materials and further applications of ideas you've presented.

For example, one instructor we know ends each short lecture with two or three questions. The discussion scheduled in coordination with this lecture starts out by repeating these questions and having students respond to them. After the discussion based on the questions, the TA may then open up the forum to additional questions.

What about a seminar type of discussion? Even though a face-to-face seminar is synchronous, you will find it possible to organize the same type of activity in an asynchronous mode. To do so, you need to create a *segmented* lecture or dialogue. First, you create some initial or topic questions to pose, or short minilectures followed by a series of questions. After allowing an interval of time (say, two or three days) to permit students to respond to the initial minilecture or question, you proceed to ask some open-ended questions, such as, What other ramifications might there be to this set of circumstances? or simply, Are there any other aspects of the lecture that you want to comment on? Questions may be prepared in advance and used or not used as you deem appropriate.

Discussions that are coordinated with assignments must be scheduled to allow enough time for reflection and response. If assignments are presented in the online classroom and students are asked to comment on them, guidelines and procedures must be set up in advance to make sure that the discussion is structured and focused. Even though this activity may be asynchronous, you will probably not want to allow unlimited time for participation, especially if one of your goals is giving students feedback that they can apply to their subsequent assignments.

You'll also have to decide who will lead discussions—you, the instructor; the TA; or a student appointed for this purpose each week? What guidelines will you use for TA- and student-facilitated discussions?

Asynchronous Discussion in the Sciences

Some instructors we know in various sciences—including some of the social sciences, computer science, and math—have told us that discussion isn't an appropriate activity for their students. Their idea of discussion is that it's connected to the realm of the soft, fuzzy, inexact, and ambiguous fields of the humanities. We believe, however, that all instructors can utilize discussion forums in online environments.

A good example of a "hard" use of online discussion is a question-and-answer forum. From such a forum, a "frequently asked questions" (FAQ) page can be created to serve as review material. In fact, posting an FAQ page can eliminate some of the chit-chat and elementary questions that, however essential, are time consuming for the instructor to answer; thus it can permit the instructor to broach new or more in-depth topics.

Another use of the discussion forum is to ask students to offer possible solutions to problems. Discussion then consists of analysis of these solutions, with the instructor contributing comments as well. Some instructors have a slightly different approach to this process: First, they receive and evaluate the solutions, then they choose the best ones to post and discuss with students online.

The discussion area may also be used to post student homework or to allow students to present projects. Questions may then be posed by other students, and the instructor may offer his or her input for the benefit of the entire class. Students in the sciences can benefit from seeing how others approach the material. Drew Bianco, who teaches a course on Microsoft Access for UCLA Extension, frames this approach in simple terms: "Post problems and assist your classmates in solving challenges related to this week's assignments."

Synchronous Discussion   Most synchronous discussion is text-based chat. In chat, everyone participating must log onto a particular site at the same time. The entire conversation then takes place in real time, although some chat software does permit saving the chat transcript so that it can be read after the actual event. Figure 3.1 illustrates the appearance of a typical "chat room."

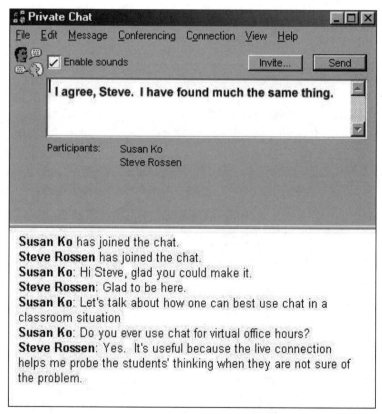

Figure 3.1 The Structure of a Simple Text-based Chat Room. Words are typed in the upper box; the participants' names and the transcript of the conversation are recorded below. Each typed-in phrase is automatically prefaced by the name of the participant. The chat pictured here is on an Embanet-hosted FirstClass 5.5 platform.

While chat is more spontaneous than asynchronous communication, adequate preparation and forethought are still essential to its success. The timing of chats, for example, is an important factor in planning. If your students are in different time zones, you'll need to make multiple times available for the same discussion topic: Say, topic A will be discussed on Tuesday at noon Pacific time and the same subject repeated on Thursday at 7:00 P.M. Pacific time. You might indicate to students that you'll be surveying them to find the most convenient times for all. Or you may set up two or more chat times and require that each student sign up for a particular time so that you can control the number participating in each session. You need to decide all of this ahead of time.

Chat is a fast-paced and often confusing forum. Topic and response often may be separated by other questions and comments.

Important! *To get the most out of chat, we recommend that students be given adequate preparation by announcing the topic ahead of time and publicizing the rules for the conduct of the chat.*

For example, you may have a series of questions that you want students to think about before the chat. Or you may have students view a web resource or read a particular passage before the chat. See Chapter 10 for an extensive discussion of how to use chat in an effective manner.

Some synchronous chat tools also provide a **whiteboard** and a "follow me" function. The former allows an instructor or student to draw or write on the whiteboard screen in real time (and, in some cases, to use math and science symbols as well) while students can type in their questions. The questions appear, chat style, in the space below the whiteboard. "Follow me" functions permit an instructor to guide students to view an external web site by typing in a URL. The instructor can then write on the displayed web page, initiate chat

> **whiteboard** The online equivalent of a chalkboard, on which one or more users can write or draw.

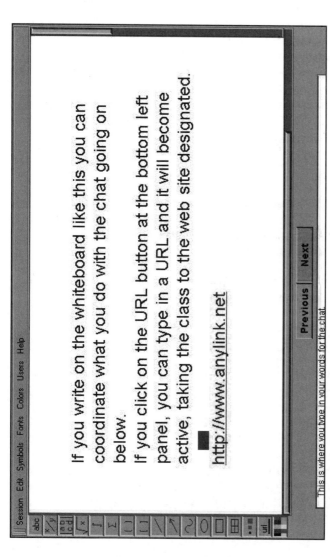

Figure 3.2 Sample Whiteboard on Which the Instructor Has Typed a Message, with Chat Entry Line Below. Math symbols and writing and drawing tools are available on the left-hand side of the whiteboard. A URL may be typed on the whiteboard; when clicked on, it will take participants to the web site indicated. This whiteboard chat is bundled with Web Course in a Box, version 4.

discussion, and encourage student questions about the site being viewed by all. Figure 3.2 illustrates a chat environment that includes both whiteboard and "follow me" options.

If you plan to use such a tool, you must plan ahead carefully to coordinate this activity with your topics and assignments. Students will need to know the protocol to follow for such an activity. For example, you might want students to first visit on their own the URL of a site to be discussed, or you might ask students to work on some preliminary problems before using the whiteboard to show them the correct solution.

Group-Oriented Work and Student Presentation

All types of group activities, from peer review to true cooperative learning exercises, are possible in the online environment. To be effective, however, group activities must be well organized and well timed. In Chapter 6, we'll discuss how to conduct specific types of group activities and presentations. Here we'll outline the considerations related to planning and implementation.

In terms of your planning, consider how many group activities will be included in your course. Also, if you decide to reconstitute groups during the course (that is, not have students remain with the same group throughout), make sure that you allow enough time for students to get to know each other and develop working relationships.

Important! Group organization and working procedures take longer to develop in the online environment.

Always consider in your planning how, where, and when groups will be able to meet and work together online. Also consider how you will monitor and evaluate individual contributions if this is an element you're concerned about.

Groups will need guidelines for working together. It's a poor idea to allow groups to evolve naturally. This isn't likely to happen online in a way that will be satisfying to the entire group of students. You may want to specify a method of group organization or particular roles to be filled; for instance, a rotating chair plus a recorder and a spokesperson.

Allow student groups as many avenues for communication as possible, with an emphasis on asynchronous discussion forums, synchronous chat, whiteboards, and document-sharing areas. If an asynchronous discussion board is available to you, that's preferable to relying only on e-mail and listservs. E-mail and listservs aren't the most efficient forums for group work, because documents and comments can't be viewed in sequential order without creating unwieldy e-mail messages.

For each group, try to plan an ice-breaking, getting-to-know-you activity as early as possible. This can include an initial casual get-together opportunity—in a face-to-face class, for example, or in a totally online setting. Online ice-breaking activities may involve paired chats, exchanges of private e-mail, or participation in an online student "lounge" area (a discussion area specifically set aside for casual talk among students).

Decide how you'll determine the composition of groups. For example, will groups be chosen by random assignment? Will they mix male and female students? Special practical considerations may apply. For instance, if students will rely heavily on real-time communication, it would be wise to factor in time zone residence when constituting the groups.

How will students be graded on group work? Some instructors give a grade for the entire group, and others for each individual. This is easier to arrange online because you may specify that all group work be done in an asynchronous area visible to you or that the transcript of all chat sessions be saved and sent to you. You may want to prepare a grading rubric for students to see, in order to clarify your criteria for grading.

What role will student presentations by groups or individual students play in your course? To which assignments, activities, or topics will the presentations be connected? What will be the structure of each presentation? Will it involve a simple presentation of text, such as posting a paper or a group summary of the week's lessons? Or will the presentation involve the display of multimedia projects? There are more examples of these types of activities in Chapter 6, but here we want to emphasize that such activities must be carefully planned, and areas for their implementation must be chosen or organized.

Research

Research activities, including fieldwork, may be carried out in a number of ways in an online class.

Web Research   Web research is an obvious option. There are open-ended activities, and there are guided activities. In the former, instructors typically propose web searches in which students are told to go find information on a particular topic. But in these open-ended research opportunities, it's vitally important that you give students some guidelines for both evaluating and searching out web resources. Because of the enormous growth of the Internet, open-ended research is becoming increasingly frustrating and difficult. Web search engines typically discover only a small percentage of the sites actually available.

We suggest that you not only give students some training in web search and evaluation, but also consider providing them with initial home-base sites from which they can fan out to find others. You could offer this guidance in the form of edited or reviewed collections of hyperlinks. For example, there may be an economics department at a university that maintains a site of the best links related to economics. Or a reputable and well-established association or journal might provide a selective list of relevant sites in its field. These provide reliable starting points for students to begin their searches.

Another way to approach this problem is to give students your own list of preevaluated sites to use for their research. This is similar to distributing a bibliography for research papers in an on-the-ground class. You might want to enlist the help of your campus librarian in assembling a list of web sites for your students. Or you might encourage students to consult with their local librarians. Librarians are increasingly engaged in the review and evaluation of web sites and electronic reference materials, and they can be a great resource for students who are doing research on the Web.

Library Research   Library research will depend on the facilities that your library or those in your consortium make available online. If your school subscribes to an electronic full-text service, that will make library research much easier for your students.

There are a few databases available online free of charge, as well as many others that charge for their services.

If full-text documents aren't available to your students, you may still be able to direct students to databases that will help them expedite their in-person research at nearby libraries. Here's another case in which it's vitally important to consult with your librarian and survey the resources that will be available to your students, as well as the costs of accessing them.

Fieldwork   Fieldwork isn't as obvious an option for an online class, because it implies experimentation or apprenticeship in a live, on-the-ground environment. However, although the fieldwork itself may be accomplished outside the online classroom, its results may be presented online, and a discussion and evaluation may also be accomplished online.

If you're using field studies or internship periods as part of your class work, it's essential that you carefully schedule the before-and-after activities that will take place online. Any prerequisites, such as a secured internship position or a prearranged fieldwork site, should be stated in your course description at registration time and in any catalogs that list your course.

If a proctor or supervisor's report is required for fieldwork, this should also be clearly indicated. You will need to create the necessary forms and make any arrangements required to allow this aspect of the course to be implemented.

Assessment

After you've surveyed the resources available, you can make some choices about the types of assessment you'll use. If online testing is available to you, you'll have to decide which types of questions to create and whether a specific test will be used for self-assessment and review, or for a grade.

Some online testing programs allow for relative security: They may be set so that students can access them only at a specific time, after obtaining a password, and they may be timed or made to record any pause in execution. Even so, if students aren't taking such tests in a proctored environment, there's naturally some possibility of fraud and cheating. However, this is also true for many testing situations on the ground. (How many large lecture classes check student IDs before exams?) To cut down on fraud and cheating in graded online testing, in cases in which a campus-based or proctored test is not an option, you should consider the following techniques in your planning:

1. The test should be lengthy enough that it isn't easy for students to look up information and still complete the test on time.

2. A good proportion of questions should relate directly to in-class discussions. Even if students can access the transcripts of such discussions, these aren't easy to locate in time to respond to timed tests. In addition, this type of question isn't easily answered by "stand-ins" who haven't actually participated in the class.

3. Don't rely only on online testing for grading individuals. Make sure you have at least two other methods of evaluation, such as essays and discussion participation. You can even include one real-time online "debriefing" that can serve as a basis of comparison with the student's other work.

4. Find out if other security measures are available and use them. You may have the option to issue a password to enter a test, or you may be able to arrange that a student contact you before gaining access to the test.

Portfolio methods of assessment have become quite popular in recent years, and it isn't difficult to assemble a portfolio of work in the online environment. The key is planning an adequate variety of activities from which students can assemble portfolios of their work. You can even create a special online area, equivalent to a folder, where student work and evaluations of student work can be stored.

Choosing Textbooks, Coursepacks, and Software for Your Course

Even though your course may be totally online, there's no reason to discount the idea of ordering a textbook for your students. A textbook may provide the most effective and most easily procured source material for your course. (It can even be ordered and purchased online.) Few students want to read book-length materials completely online, and it can be expensive and time consuming for students to print out copious amounts of text.

Some publishers provide companion web sites to support their textbooks, and the best of these can furnish your students with valuable resources. You can also create your own online resources that will help students get the most out of the text, for instance, self-assessment quizzes, guideline questions for use in discussion, and web site reference lists for further exploration of the textbook topics.

A coursepack anthology of writings from different sources can also be ordered. This may be essential when you wish to make use of copyrighted materials. A coursepack also makes sense when the instructor's own authored materials aren't easily transferred to the online format or when students are best served by having a hard-copy reference. Raymond Urgo, an instructor in technical communications for UCLA Extension, had long used hard-copy examples of technical writing that he wanted students to use as models. Although these could have been scanned and posted on the Web, the examples were quite numerous, and putting them online would have necessitated more technical support and labor than was available to him. In this particular set of circumstances, the low-tech solution was the best one.

In ordering software applications for use in a particular class, the pricing and compatibility of programs are important issues, as well as your analysis of your student audience. These factors can make the difference between a successful and an unsuccessful online course. For example, Chris Moggia, a continuing education instructor who was designing "Advanced Microcomputers," a California credential-clearing course for K–12 teachers that would meet the state requirement for basic computer knowledge, was faced with some hard choices in stipulating the software to be used. As he framed the problem, "knowing that the creation of electronic files to be shared would be an important and integral part of this course, I needed to have some sort of common platform with which to share files. So I decided to give teachers the option of using either Microsoft Office or ClarisWorks in my class, but not to allow other programs." This choice reduced the chance of students' producing "unreadable" files, and it meant that Moggia didn't have to spend valuable time helping students decipher their classmates' documents.

Some Final Tips on Course Conversion

Before you begin to convert your course, here are some final tips:

1. Even though you may ultimately create web pages written in HTML (a topic we discuss in Chapter 7), make sure you save all content that you create, whether it be lecture notes, quizzes, or announcements, in some word-processed format, so that you'll be able to reuse or revise it for a future course. In other words, don't simply post your materials online without saving them in clearly marked files on your own hard drive, on floppies, or on a Zip disk. Include the date of the latest revision of your documents.

2. When you do create your course materials, you may place them in one of the integrated course management systems (such as WebCT, eCollege, Blackboard CourseInfo, or First-Class) or in some combination of web pages and conferencing tools (such as WebBoard or HyperNews). We discuss many of these systems in more detail in Chapter 5, but be aware that each system is different. Therefore, be sure to give yourself enough time to experiment with different ways of organizing the material. Try out all major features of the system; knowing the limitations of your software will save you time in the long run. Also be sure to try out a sample unit in your course from the students' perspective, or ask your teaching assistants or others to play this role and give you feedback. Then go back and make changes in your syllabus.

3. Be sure to develop a schedule for preparation and delivery of any materials that need processing by teaching assistants, technical support staff, or instructional designers. Make sure you ascertain the turnaround time necessary for anything you'll be doing that requires some mediation by

others. Draw up a time line and then work backward from your due dates to plan your own work.

Resources

Instructional Design for Online Course Development

http://illinois.online.uillinois.edu/IONresources/
   instructdesign.html

From the Illinois Online Network, this page explores topics related to instructional design and development of online courses. The information is presented in clear and easy-to-read fashion for nonspecialists.

Instructional Design Models

http://www.cudenver.edu/~mryder/itc/idmodels.html

Martin Ryder at the School of Education of the University of Colorado at Denver offers this collection of links organized according to different models or theories of instructional design.

4

Creating an Effective Online Syllabus

The syllabus is an important part of any course, whether delivered online or face to face. Defining *syllabus* broadly here, we assume the traditional syllabus should include not only a schedule of topics, readings, activities, and assignments, but also such elements as goals, objectives, or expected outcomes for the course, grading policies, procedures, and any other information necessary for students to succeed.

Some instructors separate these various elements and call them "Course Information," "Course Requirements," "Grading," "Schedule," and so on. For the purposes of this chapter, however, we'll cover all these essentials with the term *syllabus*.

Although the details of course requirements, expected outcomes, schedule, grading, and procedures are staple elements of any course syllabus, they are perhaps even more important for an online class. Students tend to feel somewhat disoriented without the familiar first-day speeches from the instructor, and they may wonder if any of the same old rules will apply in this new online territory.

It's typical for first-time online instructors to include too little detail in their syllabi. One instructor we know changed nothing in his regular on-the-ground course syllabus except to add the words "This course is delivered completely online." Unfortunately, students had a hard time even finding his syllabus, as he posted no welcome at the "entrance" to his online course, and then they were puzzled by his schedule, which still listed "class sessions" as once a week. Some students reasonably thought this phrase referred to online, real-time chat. Others wondered if the phrase meant that their asynchronous communications should be posted only once a week, on the particular day named in the schedule. As a result of this lack of clarity, the first week's discussion forum was dominated entirely by questions about where, when, and how to do the assignments, and the main topics for that week were nearly forgotten in the confusion.

Even after the instructor's hurried explanations, students continued to experience confusion about dates and times, procedures and grading. They could refer back to the first week's forum and search through the various discussion threads in which these questions had been raised, but they had no clear reference document to which they could turn. One student even had a grade dispute with the instructor that arose from an ambiguity in the syllabus. In the syllabus, the instructor had declared that all late assignments would be penalized at the rate of one-quarter grade point each day, but hadn't clearly specified that the due dates for assignments were based on the instructor's time zone, not the student's. Thus the student claimed that, when he posted an assignment at 11:00 P.M., Pacific time, on the due date, he was unfairly penalized because the server on which the course was housed, located (like the instructor) on the East Coast of the United States, had recorded the time as 2:00 A.M. the following day. These examples, both serious and trivial, illustrate some of the problems that can ensue if online syllabi (and, naturally, subsequent directions) aren't thorough and detailed.

Even in hybrid courses—those that are taught face to face with an online component—clear directions are vital. It's important, for instance, to explain to students how the mixture of different venues will be integrated. Which course activities will take place in the on-campus classroom, which in the online classroom, and what's the sequence of procedures students should follow each week? Imagine that, before the live class meeting on Wednesday, you want students to read the online lecture and post a preliminary report, but you want them to wait until after the class meeting to take part in that week's online discussion. In many cases, they won't understand that sequence unless it's carefully explained to them.

There are three aspects of an online syllabus we want to emphasize in particular: the contract, the map, and the schedule.

The Contract

▪▪▪

Increasingly, the syllabus has come to be the contract between students and instructor, laying out the terms of the class interaction—the expected responsibilities and duties, the grading criteria, the musts and don'ts of behavior. Let's look at some features of the contract that are especially important for an online course.

Class Participation and Grading Criteria

What's meant by "participation" in the online setting won't be obvious to students. Participation should be defined. For example, is it posting, that is, sending messages to the classroom discussion board? Or is it just logging on and reading (an activity revealed to an instructor only when course management software has the capacity to track students' movements online)? Perhaps participation includes taking part in an online group presentation or showing up for a real-time chat?

Important! *Whatever kind of participation you expect in your course, you should make that explicit in the syllabus.*

If you're going to count participation toward the final grade, you should define how that will be calculated. We recommend, in fact, that you always give a grade for active participation in the class, that is, for contributing to discussions and asking or answering questions. The plain fact is that, if students aren't graded, the great majority won't actively participate. Besides judging the quality of students' contributions, you may want to set a minimum level for quantity of participation. (We'll return to this subject in Chapter 10.)

Another consideration in asynchronous discussion is the degree of self-pacing allowed. Must students follow a chronological order of topics in their participation, or can they go back and respond to previous weeks' topics? Can they do assignments at different times during the course? The answers really depend on the nature of your course. For example, if your course has a set number of tasks, which can be completed at any time within the ten weeks of the session, then you may not be concerned about students' skipping about or restarting conversations about previous weeks' topics.

If you're going to allow some measure of self-paced activity, then you must make this clear to students in your syllabus. The danger in this sort of arrangement is that students may get confused about the progress of the course, and they may feel that they must continually look back at earlier weeks to see if some new discussion has been posted. However, there are course management platforms and standalone forms of discussion software that alert students entering the classroom to the fact that they have new, unread messages in a particular discussion forum. In this case, students will easily discover that there are discussions going on in any of the various units of the course. If students don't have this sort of alert, you should remind them via announcements or in your syllabus instructions to check the previous weeks' discussions.

Defining Participation and Grading Criteria: Examples from Online Syllabi

Here's an excerpt from the syllabus for Chris Moggia's Advanced Microcomputers class for UCLA Extension's teacher education program. Note that Moggia discusses both quality and quantity of participation and the application to grades:

I have created a grading policy which basically rewards two things: the **quality** and **timeliness** of your responses and assignments.

In terms of quality my expectations are simple. Responses should be well written (please spell-check!) and clearly address the issues being discussed. When responding to a question about gender equity in technology access, please don't talk about baseball, for example. Though it is the national pastime and one of my favorite subjects it is off topic and not relevant (especially when the Dodgers are in last place . . .). Also please submit assignments within the week assigned. I will accept discussion responses and written assignments up to FOUR DAYS after the week ends, however. . . .

A note on attendance and class participation: Regular and active participation is an essential, unmistakably important aspect of this online

(cont.)

course. The expectation of the instructor is that students will log on a minimum of three times every seven days. It is critical that you read all of the lecture and assignment materials as well as all of the public discussion materials. Your full participation ON A WEEKLY BASIS is not only a requirement, it is an essential aspect of the online course process. All students are expected to do the work assigned, notify the instructor when emergencies arise, and make up missing assignments no later than four days after they are due.

Nancy Shepherdson, who teaches Nonfiction Writing for UCLA Extension's online writing program, addresses these needs for definition equally well but in a manner appropriate for the different nature of her course.

Since it is difficult to mandate writing improvement, your grade in this class will depend heavily on your participation. Seventy-five percent of your grade will be based on completing assignments and participating in discussion. That is, you could receive a B simply for turning in all of the assignments and participating regularly, as long as your contributions demonstrate that you tried your best. (Last-minute schlock will be recognized and penalized.) The other twenty-five percent of the grade will depend on the quality of your work and your participation. How well have you understood the elements of a particular nonfiction form, and how well have you executed them? Does your writing show publishable flair? Has your writing improved since you began the course?

Managing Student Expectations

The task of managing student expectations is very important in the online classroom. Some students enroll in an online course expecting it to be much easier than a regular course. Others imagine that the course will be something like independent study. Still others think the instructor should be available for twenty-four real-time hours a day. Your syllabus as well as your introductory comments can help manage such expectations, correct false impressions, and set the stage for the smooth unfolding of your course.

It's also helpful if your institution has a general student orientation (or at least a student handbook) that explains how the online course will work, how much student-instructor interaction can be expected, and so forth. If your institution doesn't have such an orientation, you may need to supply some of this information in your own syllabus.

A continuing education instructor we know, who has a busy professional practice, complained after a few weeks of her online class that students had "unrealistic expectations." When pressed to explain this remark, she commented that, if she didn't reply to each and every student comment in the discussion forum or if she appeared not to be in the online classroom every day, she would receive plaintive e-mail queries or even classroom postings inquiring about whether she had read a particular message. She further explained that she had expected students to work on their own during the first part of each week and only then to post their thoughts in the discussion forum. Unfortunately, neither her syllabus nor her introductory comments ever mentioned these teacher expectations.

This case shows that managing student expectations can also require an instructor to communicate his or her expectations of the students. This type of problem can be handled by a simple statement in the syllabus to the effect that the instructor will look in frequently during the week but may not be in the classroom every day, or that students should work on the week's assignments during the first part of the week (say, Monday through Wednesday) and then post their responses later in the week (Thursday through Sunday).

Other information of a "contractual" nature that you might want to incorporate in your syllabus includes the following:

- Your policy on late assignments
- Whether due dates are calculated by your time zone or the student's (or the server's, as that might actually be in a third time zone)
- Your availability for real-time chat appointments (which some call "virtual office hours")
- Specifications for writing assignments (formal essay? informal journal? of how many total words?)
- Your institution's policy on plagiarism and cheating

The Map

■ ■ ■ ▬▬▬▬▬▬▬▬▬▬▬▬▬▬▬▬▬▬▬▬▬▬▬▬▬▬▬▬▬▬▬▬

In this new territory of the online classroom, students will seize upon your syllabus as if it were a map. Students will want to know how to proceed and where everything is located. So, one of the first things you must do, whether through the syllabus or in an introductory message, is to explain the geography of the course.

In fact, if the syllabus isn't visible on the first level of the course, but instead can be arrived at only by one or two clicks of the mouse, then this introductory set of directions must be given in an announcement area or even delivered prior to the course, by e-mail. Figure 4.1 shows an example of an announcement area with explicit directions to the syllabus.

What else does "explaining the geography" mean? If your course consists of various web pages plus a discussion forum, you'll need to let the students know where to find the component parts of the course and under what headings: "Lectures will be on the page whose link says 'Lectures,' and these are arranged by weeks." If the discussion forum is hosted on an outside site, students need to be told that this link will take them off the university server, that they must use a password given to them, and so on. If you've created a discussion forum dedicated to casual communications and socializing for students, let them know that the area you have imaginatively labeled "Café Luna" is intended to be the online equivalent of a student lounge.

This is particularly important when using course management software that has its own unique and not customizable category headings. Students will need to know what you have stored behind each of these generic headings. For example, to students taking courses within the course management system Web Course in a Box, it may not be obvious that the main page heading "Learning Links" is where they will find the threaded discussion forum. Similarly, the "Water-Cooler" forum created by the instructor in Blackboard CourseInfo, to which students are guided in Figure 4.1, might remain a mystery without explicit directions.

In a hybrid course that combines face-to-face and online components, it's essential that you specify where to do each

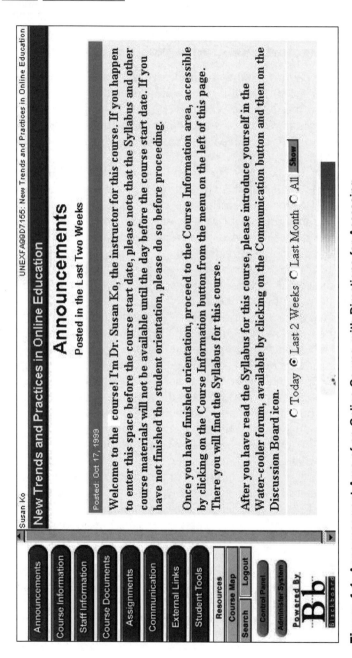

Figure 4.1 Announcement Area of an Online Course, with Directions for Accessing the Course Syllabus. In this instance, the course management software was Blackboard CourseInfo 3.0.

activity. For example, in Lonnie Yandell's Cognitive Psychology class for Belmont University, his syllabus gave clear instructions for combining face-to-face and online procedures. Here's an excerpt from the "Course Requirements" section of his syllabus:

> This course will include a major computer Internet component. Assignments, lectures, practice tests, simulations, and discussion will be held online. Time spent in class will be on computer lab simulations, in-class discussion, group work, and textbook chapter tests.

And this excerpt from his assignment schedule explains the procedures:

> The course is divided into 24 modules. Each chapter has from 2 to 4 modules. Each module has a related textbook reading, online lecture, online discussion question, and online self-test.
>
> You should read the textbook section first, then review the online lecture. The lectures will be summaries, elaborations of the textbook material, and links to related information on the Web. To get to a lecture, click on it in the schedule on this page.
>
> After you have completed reviewing the lecture, you should then log into "TopClass" and post answers to the lecture discussion question. You can also read other students' posts and respond to them if you like. You can receive extra credit for the discussion grade by making appropriate responses to others' posts. Discussion posts must be made by the date on the schedule to receive full credit.
>
> You should also complete the short self-test. The self-tests are designed to help you make sure you understand the material.

Other procedural and geographical issues you might want to cover in the syllabus include these:

- The URL for your home page
- How e-mailed assignments are to be labeled in the subject line
- Which file formats you'll accept for attached documents (for instance, Microsoft Word, Rich Text Format, PowerPoint, Excel)
- Any contact information for technical and administrative support

- The proper sequence for accomplishing weekly activities and assignments (for example, do the exercises before taking the quiz, post a message in discussion before e-mailing the assignment)

The Schedule

The course should be laid out by weeks for students, because this is commonly the unit by which students gauge their own participation and work. If your class starts on a Wednesday, then Tuesday will become the last day of your week unless you state otherwise.

We recommend that you think in terms of subdivisions of two- or three-day spreads. For example, if you post your lecture on Monday, allow students through Wednesday to read and comment on it, rather than asking them to do so by Tuesday. Students can be told to log on every single day, but it is perhaps wiser to take advantage of the asynchronous flexibility of the online environment. Assume that some students will log on and read on Monday night, some on Tuesday morning, and others at midnight. The Monday reader may return on Tuesday night to reread and post. The Tuesday reader may respond with comments at once. This scheduling flexibility is even more important for those who have students in different time zones or in foreign countries.

It's also good to gauge your students' access to computers and their probable work schedules. This goes back to what we discussed in Chapters 2 and 3. If your students are accessing the course web site from a campus lab, the dorms, or branch campus libraries, then they'll follow a different pattern than will continuing education students, who may want to use the weekends to do most of the time-intensive assignments. A Monday or Tuesday due date for assignments will allow working adults to make the most of their study time out of the office.

Using Specific Dates

Instead of simply listing the course schedule for "Week One" and "Week Two," your schedule should include the specific

A Checklist for Your Online Syllabus

Here, in summary form, is a checklist for creating your online syllabus. You needn't include all of these items (some may be more appropriate for your class than others), nor do you have to include them all in one document called a "syllabus." You can distribute this information among several documents if desired.

- ❏ Course title, authors' and instructor's names, registration number, and term information; syllabus web pages should bear creation or "last revised" dates if the term date isn't included at the top
- ❏ Course instructor's contact information, plus contact information for technical support
- ❏ Course description, perhaps the same as the description used for a course catalog listing, but probably more detailed; should list any prerequisites or special technical requirements for the course
- ❏ Course objectives or expected outcomes; what students can expect to learn by completion of the course
- ❏ Required texts or materials: any books or other materials, such as software, not made available in the course but required for the course
- ❏ Explanation of grading criteria and components of total grade: a list of all quizzes, exams, graded assignments, and forms of class participation, with grade percentages or points; criteria for a passing grade; policies on late assignments
- ❏ Participation standard: minimum number of postings per week in discussion and any standards for quality of participation
- ❏ Explanation of course geography and procedures: how the online classroom is organized; how students should proceed each week for class activities; how to label assignments sent by e-mail; where to post materials in the classroom; any special instructions
- ❏ Week-by-week schedule: topics, assignments, readings, quizzes, activities, and web resources for each week, with specific dates
- ❏ Any relevant institutional policies, procedures, or resources not mentioned above

Sometimes it's difficult to anticipate every issue that may arise during the class and to include that in your syllabus. There's obviously a bal-

(cont.)

ance between readable brevity and a syllabus so voluminous as to be intimidating. Whatever you don't include in your initial documents may still be introduced by means of announcement areas, weekly e-mail sent to all students, or postings in an appropriate forum. You will also want to use these means to reinforce important elements of your syllabus as the course progresses.

dates for each unit, week, or topic area covered. This is particularly important for asynchronous courses in which students may be logging on at diverse times and days during the week. It's quite common for students to lose track of the weeks in the term when following an asynchronous online schedule.

If you don't want to include dates on the main syllabus web page because you want to reuse it for subsequent terms, then send students an e-mail version of the syllabus or post a downloadable document version with the relevant dates inserted. Some course management software includes a calendar feature that you may use to reinforce the dates for each segment of the course.

Supplying Information More Than Once

It's easy to lose track of where and when something was said in threaded discussions or via e-mail. When you give directions, it may not be possible for students to simply link back to them at a later date. For that reason, you should provide important instructions in more than one location.

Important! *In an online environment, redundancy is often better than elegant succinctness.*

Although students in some course management platforms may be able to use a search function to find your instructions, in most cases students will have to waste energy and time to sift through materials before they can locate that one crucial sentence of direction. Therefore, even if you intend to explain assignments and procedures later in the course, it's best to state them up front in the syllabus as well. Then, if your course is laid out entirely in web pages, make sure that each page permits students to link back easily to essential information in the syllabus.

Resources

Faculty Orientation Online Syllabus Checklist. **http://online. valencia.cc.fl.us/Faculty/VOfacultysyllabuscheck.htm**

Valencia Community College's guidelines for online course syllabi; the site is maintained by the college's Internet Development Center.

The Online Course Syllabus. **http://ollie.dcccd.edu/Faculty/ InfoForFaculty/DistrictResources/secure/olsyll2.htm**

A syllabus template offered by Dallas TeleCollege of the Dallas County Community College District for the district's distance learning "telecourses."

Syllabus. **http://oit.idbsu.edu/fp/syllabus.htm**

Skip Knox at Boise State University Computing Services offers guidelines on the basic elements of an online syllabus and tips on how to use an online syllabus for a face-to-face class.

Appendix: A Sample Syllabus

The following is an excerpt from a syllabus used in a real course taught by Susan Ko. It was made available to students as a Rich Text Format document that could be easily downloaded and printed out. Key points of information contained within this syllabus were repeated during the course in other areas of the classroom. For example, an introductory message gave a general overview of the course and directed students to the main geographical areas of the classroom. Frequent announcements reminded students of upcoming deadlines or reemphasized the requirements for assignments. Any e-mailed questions about the syllabus were redirected to the shared classroom space, so that all students could have the benefit of instructor responses.

Please note that web sites mentioned here are from a version of the course taught in 1999 and may no longer be active.

NEW TRENDS AND PRACTICES IN ONLINE EDUCATION

F1675, May 25–June 22

SYLLABUS

Instructor: Dr. Susan Ko
Class e-mail: Through internal e-mail, type in Susan Ko. Available for real-time chat by appointment through e-mail.

Course Description and Goals

As one of the advanced enrichment electives in the UCLA Extension Online Teaching Program, this course is designed for busy professional educators, administrators, distance learning coordinators, online instructors, and others who have already begun to involve themselves in the delivery, design, management, or teaching of online courses.

Although there are many ways that those of us involved in online education keep ourselves posted about recent developments—through word-of-mouth, conference, or listserv-derived information; web reports; and references—these seldom provide us with a coherent view of how we might apply these new developments to our own areas of interest. This course will provide a brief but focused exploration of trends and possibilities. Due to the nature of the subject matter, both topics and readings will change each term this course is offered.

In a short but intensive four-week period, we will focus on new developments in online technologies, teaching and learning approaches, online course management, and miscellaneous issues related to online education, such as faculty training, property and copyright questions, accreditation, testing security, etc.

This course will emphasize real-life examples rather than theories. Visits to web sites, demonstrations, and guest speakers will offer concrete and varied perspectives. Participants will also benefit from sharing the experiences of others enrolled in the class in our seminarlike discussion forums.

Grading

100 points total:

- Participation, 40 points: reading, posting at least twice a week in class discussions. Note: Quality of contributions counts. You will not get extra points for simply posting beyond the number required. You can continue to contribute to previous weeks' discussions up until June 21 of the last week and still get credit.
- Journal 1 and 2 assignments, 30 points total. Journal assignment #1 due June 7 and #2 due June 14 in my e-mail box.
- Final assignment, 30 points, due June 21, in the classroom's final commentary area within the discussion forum. Participants may continue to read and comment on these final papers until June 25. Participation credit is given based on the quality of your comments on classmates' contributions.

The journal and final assignments are due by midnight PST of the date indicated; $\frac{1}{2}$ point per day will be deducted for late assignments.

How to Send and Name Assignments

All assignments should bear the subject line as follows: First initial+last name+J1 or J2 or Fin (Example, SkoJ2). Also, if you are sending the first two assignments as attachments to e-mail, your name and the assignment number must be included in the text of the document attached. The final commentary should be pasted into the discussion forum, not attached.

Procedures

Each week, follow the instructions contained in the syllabus for activities and readings, read the materials I've posted in the "Topics" presentation area, then discuss the issues raised there and in your readings and activities by replying to the discussion topics established in the discussion forum for that week. . . .

WEEK THREE: Messages and Media, June 8–June 14

Topics:

New uses of technologies; networks and applications, standards, and their impact; Steve Rossen, guest, to discuss integrating RealPresenter.

Week Three Readings:

1. Kenneth Klingenstein's "The Technical Realities of Virtual Learning: An Overview for the Non-Technologist" at **http://www.educause. edu/ir/library/html/cem9815.html.** This article might be more technical than you might like, despite the title! However, it is worth reading for the perspective it gives us on issues that have an impact on the directions online education might take.

2. Read Steve Rossen's sample web page, "Web Resources," and then view his RealPresenter, both offered in the topics folder.

3. (Optional) Take part in *one* of the two real-time chats scheduled for this week on June 9 at 5:30 P.M. or June 12 at 9:30 A.M., U.S. Pacific Time. Each chat will be 45 minutes long, and transcripts will be logged in this week's presentation area for the benefit of those who cannot attend. The topic for each chat will be the promise of Internet2, and there will be 5–10 minutes reserved for open forum–style questions and comments about any aspect of the class.

Activities:

1. Internet2 Activities:

   a. Read a very brief introduction to Internet2 by visiting the Internet2 site at **http://www.internet2.edu/html/about-i2.html.**

   b. Visit the Internet2 applications page at **http://apps.internet2. edu/sept98/applications.htm.** Explore these pages on applications to get an idea of the range of activities that would be enabled by the greater power of the networks envisioned by Internet2.

   c. Listen to the audio or read the transcript of an interview "What's New with Internet2?" with Ted Hanss, at **http://seminars.cren. net/events/internet2.html** as well as the update from April 1999, "Update on Internet2," with Doug Van Houweling, at **http://seminars.cren.net/events/net2net.html.**

d. Optional: If you already have the G2 RealPlayer, you might want to watch the excellent seminar presentation on Internet2 by Judith Boettcher, entitled "Why Does Higher Education Need Internet2?" It's available at **http://seminars.cren.net/internet2.html.**

2. Visit the IMS standards site at **http://www.imsproject.org/** and read the links to Background **(http://www.imsproject.org/backround. html),** Scenarios **(http://www.imsproject.org/scenarios.html),** and FAQs for Providers **(http://www.ims.org/faqProviders.html).**

3. *Journal assignment #2:* Due in my e-mail box by June 14. Please write 150–200 words on *one* of the following questions:

   a. What are the most challenging technological developments or issues related to online education in your own professional life?

   b. Please comment on your own interest in any technological issues referred to in this week's reading and activities and what impact this (these) might have on you or your institution's work in online education.

5

Building an Online Classroom

Now that you've done the necessary design, planning, and development work on your course and fleshed out your syllabus, it's time to actually build your course.

This means that it's time to put your work online—compose web pages, set up discussions, post assignments, create quizzes—in short, start learning about and working with the software you will be using to run the class.

As you move from the planning to the implementation stage, you may find that some of the features you planned to incorporate don't work as well as you thought they would. You may also find a few functions in your software that you didn't know existed. The fact is that this stage of preparation involves a bit of trial and error. As you experiment with sample units to create a prototype for your course, you will soon learn how to get the most out of whatever course management software structure you are working in—whether it be a fully developed course management system or some combination of web pages, discussion forum, and online testing. In fact, as you become more familiar with the particular software environment you will be using, you may find that you will want to go back and revise your course plan to reflect the opportunities or limitations that you have discovered.

In this chapter we will be discussing the various types of functions and features available in today's software and how best to exploit them. In doing this, we will use examples from a variety of different existing software platforms. As you examine these features, be aware that this is a rapidly changing, highly competitive field. Our descriptions of particular features correspond to the versions existing at the time of this writing. Our purpose is not to tout one software platform over another, but to show (1) the opportunities presented by certain types of features and (2) how you can adapt and implement your favored teaching strategies.

This is not to say that a particular software or course management system may not be better suited to your pedagogical needs than another. However, we do recognize that many instructors will not have the final say about which system is chosen, so our intention is to help you make the most of whatever you have. If you would like to compare and track the changes and innovations in software platforms, we refer you to the web site mentioned in Chapter 1, Online Educational Delivery Applications: A Web Tool for Comparative Analysis, created by Bruce Landon of Douglas College, New Westminster, British Columbia. This site is continually being updated as new versions of software debut; in addition to comparison and review charts, it provides links to the web sites of the different software platforms. The URL is **http://www.ctt.bc.ca/landonline/.**

So, by all means take advantage of any special features afforded by your software system, but don't feel that your system must dictate your choice of teaching methods and approaches. Generally, if you have the desire to include a particular kind of activity, you can find a way to implement it in almost any system.

If you were fortunate enough to receive special training on the system you are going to use, you probably received some tips and techniques for exploiting that system. If you haven't received this type of training, we recommend that you join a user's group or mailing list devoted to users of that software, or share information and strategies informally with colleagues at your institution who may already have had some experience with the system. You may discover that a colleague at your own institution—or at one half a world away—has found a new approach to solving the same problems that you face.

Now let's look at some of the structures, features, and built-in functions that are available in course management systems and components.

Presentation Areas

Presentation areas are where you present your basic course content, lectures, and so forth. Web pages are the most obvious presentation format.

If you are using course management software, you will find that, in some systems, presentation is clearly defined and set apart from other functions. This is the case, for example, in eCollege, WebCT, Blackboard CourseInfo, and TopClass. The presentation areas allow one to type or paste in text and to **upload** text and HTML files, PowerPoint slide shows, and so on, into what is, in effect, a document storage area (see Figure 5.1). This storage area, which can be filled only by instructors, is entirely separate from the discussion forum and other areas where students can post or upload documents.

> **upload** To transfer a file from your computer to a remote computer; the reverse of *download*.

If, however, you are using a discussion-board-only format (such as FirstClass, Allaire Forums, HyperNews, or WebBoard), in which the underlying structure for posting messages remains the same for all areas, then you will have to designate areas by name to serve as your presentation spaces. You might set these off by using special titles, bold text, or some other distinguishing marks, depending on what your software system permits. Figure 5.2 offers an example.

Announcement Areas

Some systems have an announcement area, that is, a special form of presentation area that is seen by students as they enter the online classroom. The announcement may appear on the main entrance page (as in eCollege and Blackboard CourseInfo), or it may simply be an icon available to click on (as in Web Course in a Box and TopClass).

For the instructor, the announcement area offers a quick method of typing in announcements and updates for the course. Even if it is set up as a separate document storage area, students will know to consult it each time they enter the class-

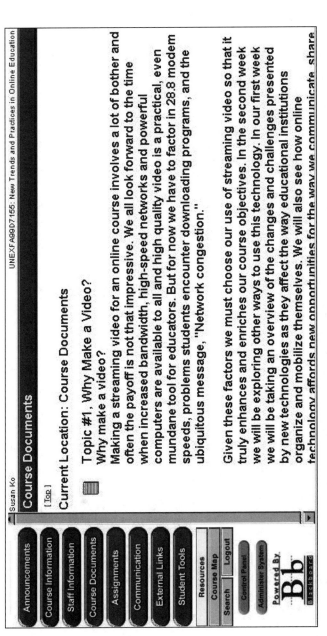

Figure 5.1 Presentation Area in Blackboard CourseInfo, Version 3.0. The Course Documents area on the right displays an open document presenting a topic. Students access this area by clicking on the appropriate navigation button on the left.

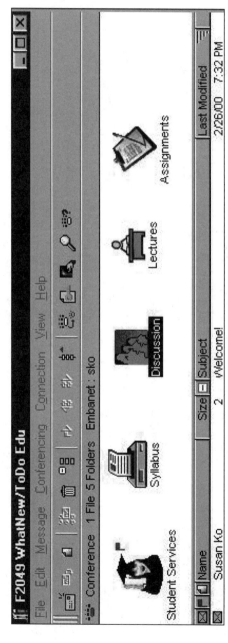

Figure 5.2 An Instructor's Designation of Presentation and Discussion Areas in Embanet-hosted FirstClass 5.5. Each of the icons represents a conference folder, and inside each is an identical messaging structure. The instructor has labeled some of these folders as presentation areas (such as "Syllabus" and "Lectures"), while others are for student participation ("Assignments" and "Discussion"). The welcome message posted in the main window explains the organization and instructs students in how to proceed.

room. For an illustration of an announcement area, look back at Figure 4.1 on page 72.

Syllabus and Schedule Areas

Depending on your software, you can post a syllabus and schedule in a document storage area, or you can create separate web pages for this purpose.

Important! *Make your syllabus available in a download-able or easily printable document, because this is the "map" students will follow in your course.*

This means that, if you use graphics in your syllabus or if the syllabus is divided up into a group of hyperlinked web pages, you should also make it available in a text-only, scrollable document. This will permit students to print it out readily.

In some course management software, the syllabus area also serves as the chief organizing tool, the "home page" or outline for the course content. For example, in IntraLearn and in Learning-Space's "Schedule" section, each item on the syllabus becomes a clickable link to respective sections of course material. In eCollege, the syllabus is housed as a complete document in an area designated for the syllabus, while on the main home page it appears as an outline hyperlinked to individual sections of the course.

Discussion Forums

We will cover the management of asynchronous and synchronous discussions in Chapter 10. Here, we will note that the asynchronous discussion areas in various software programs are structured in different ways, have different options for student use, and allow messages to be viewed or sorted in different ways.

Structure of Discussion Areas

Many systems are comprised of a hierarchical architecture. Forums or message groups form the highest level, with each containing a number of subordinate threads that together make up the discussion. In this case, it is important to decide how you want to divide up your forums—by week, by topic, by unit, or by some combination of categories. For example, you may decide not only to have weekly forums but also to create a forum that can serve as an open discussion area, a sort of "student lounge" (see Figure 5.3).

Take note of the arrangement of threads and responses within the system you are using. As mentioned earlier, in a messaging system such as FirstClass (Figure 5.2), the basic discussion unit, the "conferences," must be designated clearly as discussion areas to differentiate them from those used for presentation. The messaging system remains the same whether the "conference" is used for presentation by the instructor or discussion by instructor and students.

The way you structure your discussion forums will probably affect your decisions about the number of topics you wish to introduce each week, whether to break down larger topics, and the instructions you need to give students about procedures.

User Options

In FirstClass, both students and instructors may initiate new topics; in other systems, such as eCollege and WebCT, only instructors may start new topic threads. Still other platforms, including Blackboard CourseInfo, may allow the instructor to set the options, using a switch that enables or prevents students from starting new topics.

Other user options in some systems include being able to add HTML files, use attachments, and change the subject line without having to create a new thread.

Viewing and Sorting of Messages

How are conversations viewed in your software? Do the messages have to be opened and shut one at a time in order to be read? Is it possible to open and read all messages in a linear fashion, one following the other in a scrollable page? Many systems are moving to a dual capability, allowing conversations to be viewed both as individual messages in threads and as continuous conversations. Blackboard CourseInfo, Virtual-U, First-Class, and eCollege all have introduced these double views.

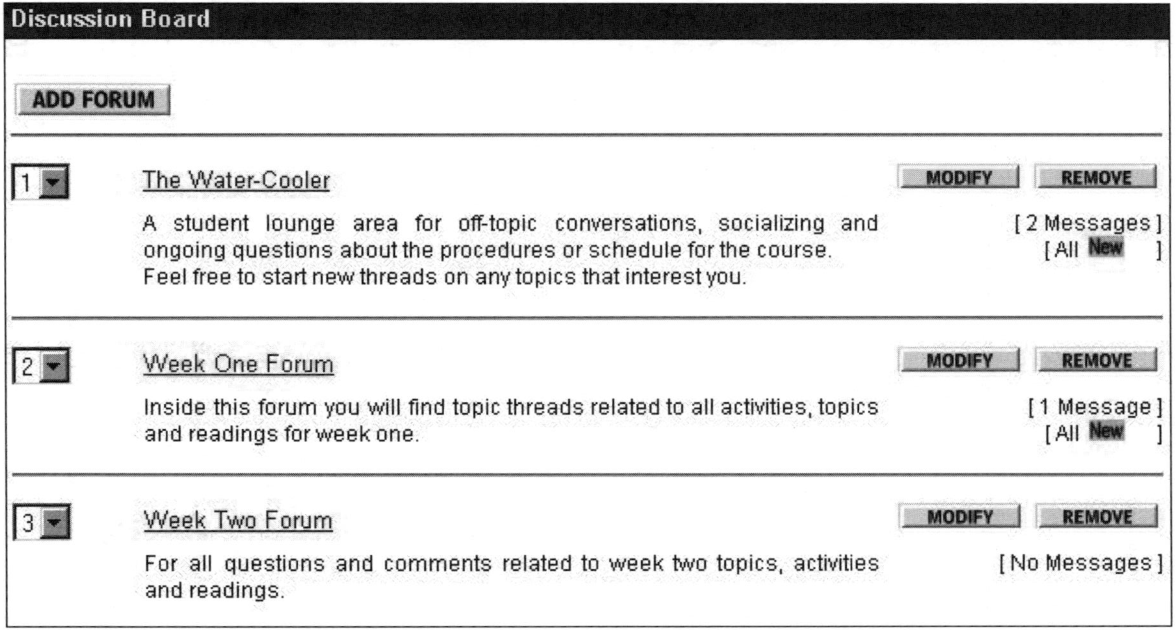

Discussion Board

ADD FORUM

1 ▶ The Water-Cooler   MODIFY   REMOVE

A student lounge area for off-topic conversations, socializing and   [2 Messages]
ongoing questions about the procedures or schedule for the course.   [All New]
Feel free to start new threads on any topics that interest you.

2 ▶ Week One Forum   MODIFY   REMOVE

Inside this forum you will find topic threads related to all activities, topics   [1 Message]
and readings for week one.   [All New]

3 ▶ Week Two Forum   MODIFY   REMOVE

For all questions and comments related to week two topics, activities   [No Messages]
and readings.

**Figure 5.3 The Creation of Discussion Forums in Blackboard Course-
Info, Version 3.0.** The "Water-Cooler" forum has been designated as a student lounge area. Each forum contains threads on different topics.

Many systems also allow multiple ways for users to sort messages for their own viewing. For example, messages may be sorted by date, by topic, or according to the people who posted them. (This has some utility for classroom management, as explained in Chapter 10.)

E-Mail

Some systems, such as TopClass, WebCT, IntraKal, and First-Class, contain their own internal course e-mail, which does not need to go to an outside e-mail address. Students and instructors can use this mailbox exclusively for all correspondence within the course, sometimes by just typing in or selecting the name of the student.

Other systems, such as Blackboard CourseInfo versions 3 and 4 and eCollege, have a convenient e-mail roster, which allows students to send mail to all or part of the class from a central area that lists the addresses of all class members. These rosters also allow the sender to receive a carbon copy of sent mail at the sender's home e-mail address.

Chat and Whiteboard

Chat is a synchronous (real-time) communication tool. There may be one or more chat rooms available for a particular class, depending on the software. As mentioned in Chapter 3, chat is sometimes combined with a whiteboard. Whiteboards are also a synchronous tool, running the gamut from those offering the ability to write on the screen (using text or simple drawing functions) to those that can display specialized math and science symbols. Some, like those bundled with Web Course in a Box, Blackboard CourseInfo, and WebCT 2.0, combine several functions, including a "follow me" function that allows an instructor to bring web pages or uploaded images onto the screen and annotate them for all to see.

Synchronous tools like chat rooms and whiteboards are particularly appropriate for your class if you have students living in the same time zone or logging on from campus locations. If your students live in separate time zones, careful schedule accommodation is required to make this a worthwhile and attainable learning experience.

If your software allows you to save whiteboard and chat sessions, and make them available to view later, this can be a major asset. This feature enables students to refer to and reflect on chat and whiteboard activities, thus considerably increasing their value to your class.

Check, too, to see what options your software affords for student direction of whiteboard activities. If you can hand over the reins to students, this will allow you to arrange for individual student or group presentations in real time.

Group Activity Areas

Groups may be formed online when an instructor wishes to divide up the class for the purpose of certain tasks. Group activities may range from discussion to peer review to collaborative projects and cooperative learning activities, as explained in Chapter 6.

If you are using Blackboard CourseInfo, you may want to take advantage of its built-in group areas, each of which contains its own asynchronous discussion, real-time chat, and document-sharing capabilities (see Figure 5.4). This means that the members assigned to a particular group can engage in discussion and document sharing within their own small, private group environment, apart from other members of the class. Similarly, in LearningSpace, you can designate "team" areas within the main discussion area. A comparable capability exists in Web Course in a Box and WebCT, in which you can create a separate discussion forum and limit the participants to a designated group of students.

If you are using a system that does not have built-in group functions, you can still find ways to carve out group areas. For example, in FirstClass, you can simply designate and label particular conferences as group areas for asynchronous communication. To accomplish the document-sharing function, group members will attach or paste in documents in the appropriate conference area. If you are using a system that consists mainly of

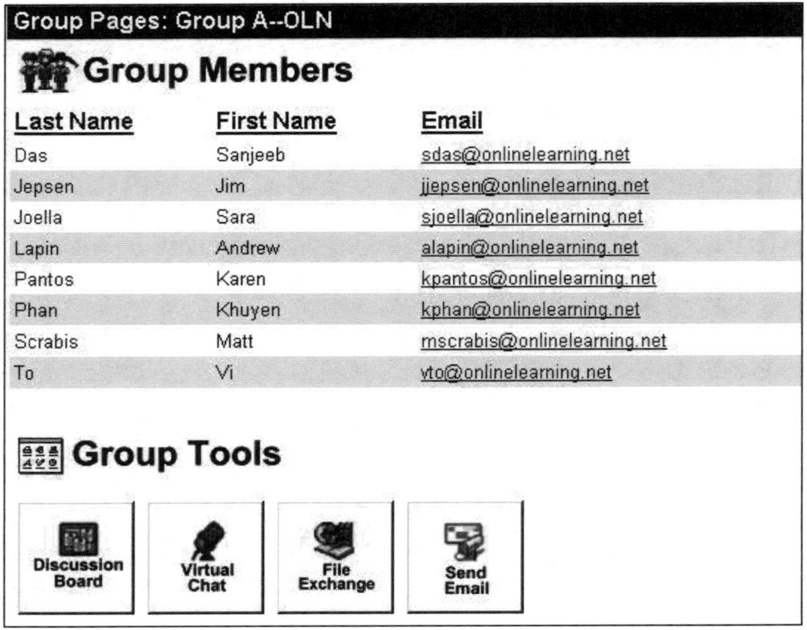

Group Pages: Group A--OLN

Group Members

Last Name	First Name	Email
Das	Sanjeeb	sdas@onlinelearning.net
Jepsen	Jim	jjepsen@onlinelearning.net
Joella	Sara	sjoella@onlinelearning.net
Lapin	Andrew	alapin@onlinelearning.net
Pantos	Karen	kpantos@onlinelearning.net
Phan	Khuyen	kphan@onlinelearning.net
Scrabis	Matt	mscrabis@onlinelearning.net
To	Vi	vto@onlinelearning.net

Group Tools

Discussion Board   Virtual Chat   File Exchange   Send Email

Figure 5.4 The "Group Pages" Area in Blackboard CourseInfo, Version 3.0. Each icon of the Group Tools opens to permit communications, whether on a discussion board, using real-time chat, by e-mail, or via file sharing among members of the group. Every group in a class can have its own area of this type.

web pages plus a discussion messaging system, such as Caucus (used by the New School's DIAL program) or WebBoard, you can assign topic threads within the system for use by particular groups. For example, you might name one threaded topic (or perhaps a whole forum) "Group A Discussion" and indicate to the class that this is only for a particular group of students to use. Students in that group can then post, read, and respond in that area.

Some software has additional special features that may be of value to you in setting up groups. In WebCT, for example, the instructor can request that students be randomly divided into groups of a certain size—a function that has obvious utility for very large classes.

Web Resource and Linking Areas

Some systems allow both instructors and students to insert activated hyperlinks (URLs on which one merely has to click to be taken directly to a web site) into discussion messages. Often these can be inserted into real-time chat as well.

If a separate web resource area is available, you may want to create a reference list for all the links that will appear in the course. WebCT, for instance, offers a "Resource" section, eCollege has a "Webliography" area, and Blackboard CourseInfo includes an "External Links" area. Such areas provide places where you can organize a reference list of relevant web sites, making it easier for students to find and retrieve them as the course progresses.

Depending on the software's options, you may want to organize your links according to each week of the class or in a topical fashion. Some systems, such as eCollege, allow both instructors and students to add Internet links in the resource area, while others, such as IntraLearn, limit this capability to instructors.

Searching Capabilities

Some software platforms provide search capabilities. These can be very selective—for example, allowing users to search only in the discussion section. Or they can be comprehensive, as in IntraLearn, which allows you to choose whether to search all sections of the course or to limit your search to a single area.

Search functions can be useful not only for your students but for you as well. They permit you to find that one passage or comment you only dimly recall.

Resume and Bookmark Features

The bookmark feature in a web browser allows you to record the URL of a web site and return to it later, by clicking on the name of the site in your list of bookmarks. Unfortunately, it is not usually possible to set your browser bookmarks to mark a specific URL within a course management environment.

Some systems, however, have their own "resume" or "bookmark" feature that allows students or instructors to stop working and later return to exactly that portion of the course they were working on. WebCT and IntraLearn are two systems that include such an option. Although this feature may not affect your own course planning, you should make your students aware of it, because it will be particularly helpful to them when they are working through long or complicated documents.

Assessment

Some systems make available multiple-choice, short-answer, and true/false exams. Even if you don't normally use this type of test, you may want to consider creating some assessment instruments that make use of the feature. For example, you might create self-assessment quizzes to help students review the material at the end of each unit, or you might ask students to take a diagnostic quiz at the start of your course.

Important! *It is recommended that you rely on more than one form of graded assignment.*

From a security standpoint, it is better to be able to compare several different types of samples of a student's work than to base all the grades on a single type of assignment. Also, from the standpoint of multiple learning strategies, it is best to give students the opportunity to display their achievement and comprehension in a number of ways.

To increase security, find out the capabilities of your quiz-making system. As noted in Chapter 3, various features can help increase the security of an exam—for instance, timed, one-time access; password-protected access; and the ability to create pools of questions that permit individual randomization. There are many different approaches to quiz security issues. WebCT's version 2.0, for example, can limit access to a quiz to a certain IP address, thus allowing the instructor to control the student's point of access. IntraKal offers a posttest analysis that looks for similarity among student answers.

Another option available in some systems is the ability to give students automatic feedback. For example, in many quiz-making programs, students who answer a question incorrectly can receive automatic instructions for remediation: They can be told to review pages 10–15 in the textbook or to reread the instructor's Unit I lecture. Another handy feature of some software is the ability to postpone access to a quiz (for example, by withholding a password or blocking access) until the student has finished a particular section of the course.

Finally, there are options that permit an instructor to insert images or sounds into an exam. With these features, the instructor can pose questions based on graphs, charts, or bits of music and language. Depending on your subject field and teaching methods, these may be important features for you.

Student Progress Reports and Tracking

Progress reports that can be accessed by the students themselves allow them to keep track of their own accomplishments. This is particularly helpful in courses in which the assignments may be accomplished in any order. If this feature exists, you won't have to be as vigilant in reminding students of their progress in the course.

Student tracking by instructors—that is, obtaining statistics about when students log on, how long they remain in a specific area of the course, which specific documents or messages they have read, and so on—is increasingly recognized as an important feature for any course management software suite. Some systems allow tracking by the number of browser "hits" in a specific area of the course. Some give the duration of time spent in each area or reveal whether or not an area or item has been opened. These tracking abilities are invaluable in helping you assess participation.

Bear in mind that these indicators are not always accurate, because they can be manipulated by students. For instance, a student can open an area of the course and simply let the clock run. This will give the appearance of the student's having spent a great deal of time studying that section of the course.

However, if statistics reveal that the student hasn't even entered a certain area of the course, that will tell you that he or she hasn't read the material contained within it. Or, if the student has spent only five minutes in an area of relative complexity, this is a sure sign that he or she hasn't dealt adequately with that portion of the course.

Thus the best way to use tracking functions is as a contribution to a more comprehensive evaluation, including student assignments, student postings in discussion, student presentations, objective quizzes and essays, and so forth. The online course does permit you to know a great deal more about a student's attendance and participation than is possible in an on-the-ground course.

Most tracking systems permit the instructor or administrator to track student statistics, but not the student to track the instructor. One interesting feature of FirstClass, though, is that students can see, through the "History" of each message, whether or not their instructor has actually opened (and presumably read) any posting they made. This can be reassuring to students, because they will realize that the instructor has read their messages, even if the instructor has not replied.

Adapting to Your Software's Tracking Functions

If tracking is available in your software system, it's important to find out exactly how it functions. For example, if you can track the responses a student makes in discussion but can't tell whether the student is reading the topic messages you post, you might want to require a specific number of postings in specific threads each week. As another example, assume you can track students' access to your presentation documents, but only on a unit basis; that is, you can't tell whether students have read individual documents within a unit. In this case, you might want to place the most important documents in their own individual units.

If you have little or no tracking capability, then student work submitted to you directly by e-mail or posted in the classroom will assume greater importance, as will quiz questions that test comprehension and familiarity with material.

Online Gradebooks

An online gradebook is a tool that allows you to record and compute grades for students and permits students to access their own grades (see Figure 5.5). Some of the course management systems that offer such gradebooks are IntraKal, Blackboard CourseInfo, and eCollege.

Whether or not you have an online gradebook as part of your course management software, you can create your own electronic gradebook in spreadsheet form. Even though you may feel that you can always refer back to the online classroom for a record of activity, it is easy to lose track of individual students in a busy class. Thus it is no less important to keep detailed records of student activity in an online setting than it is for the traditional on-the-ground class. See Chapter 10 for more information on record-keeping strategies.

Other Course Areas and Features

If your course is conducted completely online, think about creating the sort of asynchronous "student lounge" area men-

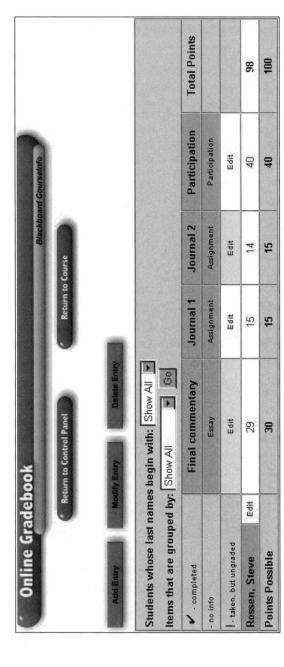

Figure 5.5 The Online Gradebook in Blackboard CourseInfo.

tioned earlier—an area where students can socialize. Another useful area is one in which students can address questions to you throughout the course, questions that either are "off topic" or concern ongoing procedural matters. These two types of messages can be combined into one area or separated, depending on your wishes. Having such areas available benefits the students, many of whom need the added interaction and feeling of camaraderie with classmates, as well as one central place where they know they can address urgent questions about the course.

Other helpful devices for personalizing a class include a discussion forum where students introduce themselves during the first week of class and student web pages where students provide some brief biographical information about themselves. Besides helping to break the ice, these areas provide an important service by allowing students to refer back to identifying details about their classmates as the course progresses. Always inform students whether web pages are open only to the class or can potentially be accessed by the public on the Web.

Some course management systems make it easy for students (or you) to upload a photo to the classroom. This should always be voluntary. There are many reasons not to push this option. Although it does help give each student an identifiable face in the classroom, it undercuts the egalitarian advantages inherent in an online classroom. Not knowing the race, ethnicity, attractiveness, or even gender of a student—except by that individual's own choice in self-identifying—often allows students (and you) to pay more attention to the ideas and words of class members without all the assumptions and subtle biases that we all harbor.

Another desirable area to carve out is a technical support area or help link. For instance, you may set up an area of the classroom or web pages that contain downloadable programs and **plug-ins** (or hyperlinks by which one can access software), plus either a simple FAQ for the course management software or a full instruction manual. If support

> **plug-in** An application that supplements a web browser, automatically activating itself when it is needed.

staff are available, they may monitor this area. In the absence of a full student orientation, the area plays a vital function in providing self-help to students or a connection to support materials or staff. As a backup to these technical support areas, provide, via an initial e-mail or letter, some instructions for getting started and any other relevant information, such as phone numbers for support in the event that students have trouble logging onto the class.

Dividing Up Your Material and Activities

In building your course, no matter which system you use, you will have to make decisions about organizing and dividing your materials.

For example, in terms of your overall organization, do you want to divide the course into units according to week or topic or some combination of both? As mentioned above, your ability to receive tracking reports might be one consideration. Other, more obvious factors include how many topics you will cover each week, how large your documents are, and whether the portions you create will be easy to digest (and, if necessary, download) for your students.

Another basic question must be whether you want presentation materials to be housed in areas apart from discussion and conferencing areas and, if so, what coordination you wish to have between these areas. For example, if you present a "lecture" in Unit 1, do you want to create a discussion forum that will match it and provide direct reference to it? Or do you want to post minilectures directly in the discussion forum thread, culminating in questions to which students must respond?

Similarly, do you want web resource links to be woven in among your assignments, discussions, and lecture materials, or do you want to house these in a separate area (when available)? How many assignments are to be delivered to you alone, and how many are to be shared with the class as a whole? Do you want students to work in groups? If so, you need to give them a space to work as a team and a place to present their work as well.

Important! *The overall guideline here is to create or make use of a space for every activity you devise.*

Timing of Access

Before you actually begin to build your course, find out exactly when students will first be able to access your classroom and whether they will have access to the entire course at that time. For example, will they be able to enter the course management software environment two days before the class officially starts? At that point, will they have access to an outer web page but not to the discussion area?

Also, find out if your software allows you to work on a section of the course without making it available for students to see. Some systems allow you to set specific dates for the release of a section or document or simply to toggle an on/off switch to determine the availability of a specific area. If you have no way to control the timing of your students' access, you should consider laying out and arranging your course on paper or in a practice course shell, and making all changes in your word-processed and HTML documents prior to posting the final form. This will prevent students from becoming confused if you need to revise your materials at the last minute. However, do post at least an announcement or syllabus for students to access on the first possible day, and remember to give detailed guidance about how and where to proceed. There's nothing more discouraging to students than entering an empty, unattended online classroom!

How much of your course materials should you actually make available to students at one time? This is a tough question to answer, because there is no one response that will suit all teaching situations and approaches. If you post all the lectures for all the weeks of your course so that students can see ahead, this does offer two advantages:

1. Students can gain a more detailed understanding of what the course involves.
2. If they choose, students can work ahead.

The disadvantages are that, in an asynchronous class, even one with defined start and stop dates, you may be detracting from the sense that the class as a whole moves and learns together. If you also allow students to post in discussion forums as many as two or three weeks ahead, you further lose the sense of class cohesiveness. You may also prevent yourself from adapting to the class's needs by revising materials. You may find, too, that simultaneously keeping an eye on two, three, or four discussion forums adds significantly to your workload.

Often, a good compromise is to restrict the advance posting of materials and the opening of new discussion forums to no more than one or two weeks ahead of the time when you expect the class as a whole to be ready for them.

Pacing Considerations

A final important consideration is the method of pacing your students in your course. Everything takes longer online. Even if your students don't have to endure Internet congestion or slow modem speed, you will still find that you must factor in the "click time"—the time it takes to open and close documents, to download and access documents and web pages, and to perform special tasks such as accessing large graphics, slow Java-operated functions, or streaming media and animations.

Even though you want your course to be as rigorous as its on-the-ground equivalent, you don't want to overload students with materials and tasks for which the payoff isn't worth the time expended. Leave students enough time to delve deeply into the material. Presumably, you will already have factored in these considerations when composing your online syllabus. However, these matters often become more apparent once you begin to lay out the course within your course management software or web pages. In that case, don't be afraid to go back and make adjustments to your syllabus.

Resources

Online Educational Delivery Applications: A Web Tool for Comparative Analysis. **http://www.ctt.bc.ca/landonline/**

A site with reviews, comparisons, and links for the major course management software providers. Maintained by Bruce

Landon, Douglas College, British Columbia, and regularly updated.

Web Based Learning Resources Library. **http://www.outreach. utk.edu/weblearning/**

Maintained by Robert Jackson, University of Tennessee, Knoxville, this site contains information on many types of web educational resources. See especially the sections on "Asynchronous Web Based Software Suites" and "Synchronous (Real-Time) Web Based Training Solutions."

6

Student Activities in the Online Environment

In this chapter we suggest a few rules and guidelines to help you make use of the Web for student activities. We also present some concrete examples of activities that instructors have found to be effective, and we suggest how these might be organized.

You may well be familiar with theories of "learning styles," and perhaps you have applied these ideas in your on-the-ground classroom. An example of the learning style concept would be the idea that a visual/verbal learner prefers to read information, while a visual/nonverbal learner might learn best when there are graphics and pictures to supplement the text. There's nothing to prevent you from designing your online course with such learning styles in mind.

We know of at least one online instructor who gave students a learning style assessment within the first week of class and then followed through with this approach in devising weekly assignments. Students were allowed to choose one question from an array of exercise assignments, each question choice having been designed according to a different learning style.

Here, however, we won't attempt to define online activities in terms of any of the complex learning style matrixes that have been developed. (See the "Resources" section at the end of this chapter for some guidance on this subject.) Rather, we will approach the subject from the standpoint of the desirability of incorporating different types of learning opportunities. Variety is as important online as on the ground, and using multiple approaches will both reinforce student learning and allow students to view the subject matter from different perspectives.

Using the Web as a Resource

One often-overlooked aspect of planning and building a course is the use of the Web itself as a basis for assigned work. The frequent neglect of this option arises, in part, from the sheer vastness of the Web. To most of us it is like an immense sea of information. There are so many documents, databases, archives, and collections to be examined that looking out at it is somewhat like standing at the edge of the ocean. It seems safer to stay within the confines of our own web sites, with their more familiar course materials and tools.

But when you do limit student activities to your own course site, you and your students are totally dependent on information that you provide, and this inevitably restricts the course's breadth and scope. We hope, therefore, that you will make use of the Web's rich potential for student activities. In this section we will suggest how you can do so without allowing yourself or your students to become inundated in a sea of minutiae.

Preparing the Way

Whenever you use the Web as part of an assignment or activity, you should take care to examine the material yourself before assigning it to your class.

This point may seem obvious, but it is all too often ignored. Instructors often prefer to employ something that might be called the "treasure hunt" approach. They tell their students that somewhere out there on the Web sits a valuable nugget of information yearning to be found. They arm the students with either a list of possible sites where this precious nugget might be found or instructions for using a search engine to hunt it down. The students then spend more time than they can afford clicking through links that lead nowhere or scrolling through pages of irrelevant text until the desired information is found, copied, and bookmarked, and the requisite posting is made on the course discussion board.

It's fun to explore and rewarding to make discoveries, but the treasure hunt approach is often both impractical and unsound. To do all that hunting and tracking requires a reliable connection to the Web that, as we have noted before, is often unavailable to students working at home. Spending an inordinate amount of time waiting for web page after web page to appear on their monitor can become a frustrating experience for students—one that is even more bothersome if it seems irrelevant. If the task is to examine a given piece of data, why not simply direct the students to it rather than require them to ferret it out?

There is a place for such web exploration, of course. If a student is trying to refute a given piece of information—or to affirm it—he or she may very well want to search out applicable material to make the case. Similarly, when researching an essay or a project, students often will scour the Web on their own, because they feel it is effective to do so and because they feel confident they can assess the material they find.

For most situations, however—such as a homework assignment or a question on a quiz—you should probably do the hunting yourself and let the students spend their time learning instead of searching.

Evaluating Web Sites

What criteria should you use in choosing web sites for your course? You should evaluate each site for quality, just as you would any other resource.

First, you can apply the same guidelines you would use in choosing a book or article for a reference list supplied to your students. For example,

- Check the site's sponsorship.
- Check the authorship of any articles or sections on the site.
- Assess the relevance of the material to your topics. Does it bear only a tangential relevance to what you intend to examine or discuss, or is it closely connected?

Second, you can apply some additional scrutiny to the web material that you probably would not need to apply to books and articles. You can ask questions like these:

- How well is the site designed?
- How difficult is the site to navigate? Will students be able to find the most relevant material without wading through extraneous details or unnecessary links?

Varieties of Useful Web Sites

Once you begin exploring web resources, you'll find that articles are not the only web materials that will prove useful for your course. Equally valuable choices are sites that provide graphic examples, documentation, or illustrations of your main topics and principles. Works of German expressionist art from the 1920s might provide a good starting point for a discussion of the impact of World War I on Germany. Photographs found online might provide the basis for an essay. You may also base a research project on students' exploration of a web site. In that case, you would want to provide some questions or pose specific problems for the students to tackle during their visits to the site.

Here are some of the different types of potentially useful sites you can expect to find on the Web:

- Some sites on the Web offer photo essays, documents, articles, and recordings. These provide raw materials with which you can fashion a focused and relevant assignment or discussion. Some examples are:

  - The National Archives Online Exhibit Hall, which offers an array of different topics on historical themes: **http://www. nara.gov/exhall/exhibits.html**

  - The National Geographic Map Machine: **http://www. nationalgeographic.com/resources/ngo/maps/**

  - The ImageBase of the Fine Arts Museums of San Francisco, which offers a searchable collection of art: **http://www. thinker.org/fam/thinker.html**

  - The World Radio Network, which carries "on demand" audio programs from radio stations all over the world: **http://www.wrn.org/ondemand/**

- Online magazines and news sources include the *New York Times, The Economist, Salon,* and CNN (see the end-of-chapter "Resources" for the URLs), as well as news sources published online in languages other than English. There are also specialized sites for those interested in finance, literature, art, photography, and science. These can provide the basis of a single assignment or research project, or a continuing series of such assignments. However, not all of these offer open access to all sections of the site, and some charge if you want to access anything but the most recent issue. Others require registration even though they may be accessed free of charge. So, always research the access policies of online magazines and news sources if you intend to ask students to use them.

One of our favorite specialized sites is ZoneZero, a bilingual (Spanish and English) site dedicated to contemporary photography. Offering articles, exhibits, and photo essays, ZoneZero makes good use of multimedia and encourages viewer feedback: **http://www.zonezero.com/**

- Commercial sites, maintained by major corporations for the purpose of promoting their products and services, often contain valuable information but should be carefully identified and used in conjunction with targeted objectives. The same is true for sites maintained by nonprofit organizations.

- Sites maintained by individuals with a particular passion—for Mozart, bamboo, or World War II weapons, for example—are often quirky (and sometimes verge on the crackpot), but they can provide valuable collection points for hyperlinks, photos, and documents. These sites do not always provide the necessary citations and references to evaluate their material, so their inclusion in a course should probably be supplemented with warnings or commentary from the instructor to put the material into proper perspective.

- Online classroom materials, posted on the Web by educational institutions, may prove worthwhile for your own class, especially if they cover topics similar to the ones you teach. But beware! These materials are notoriously ephemeral and may not last beyond next semester. If you want to use such materials, take note of the dates they were posted and contact the instructor listed to determine how long the site will remain available.

- Finally, some sites provide annotated collections of links to other sites in a particular field. These are often hosted by universities. For example, EcEdWeb, the Economic Education Website, offers links to resources and lesson plans for incorporating web resources on economics and related topics: **http://ecedweb.unomaha.edu/home.htm**

There are some other excellent methods for finding resources in your field. You might consider joining a mailing list (listserv) or discussion forum in your discipline that shares information about web resources. This is a great way to quickly accumulate some solid leads. Second, you might look for professional association or academic web sites in your area of study that provide annotated links to web resources. Finally, there's no substitute for visiting and evaluating sites on your own. Try to budget short periods of time a few times a year that you can use just to search the Web for resources in your field.

However you decide to use the Web, whether as a resource or as part of a group activity or exercise, think twice before making a specific site optional rather than required. Often instructors post a list of links (or resources) and encourage students to use these for valuable supplementary information. But when students learn that they aren't required to visit a site, they usually won't. This doesn't indicate a lack of intellectual curiosity on their part. Rather, it indicates that students have other priorities: jobs, families, lovers, friends, finding an apartment, fixing the plumbing, walking pets, not to mention handling a full load of coursework from other classes. So, when they see the word *optional* attached to a given item on their syllabus, their natural instinct is to pass it by.

Using the Web as a Resource: Two Examples

Richard Rains teaches an online course in astronomy for Mission College in California. As he implemented his course in the fall of 1999, he was progressively refining his approach to using web site resources, and he told us about his experiences.

Each week in his course, students were required to submit a report "on two web sites assigned by the instructor." In addition, Rains asked each student "to find a new, different web site relating to the chapter of the textbook for the week." But Rains did not stop there; he provided additional guidance for the students. His instructions stipulated that every report on a web site should include "a description and evaluation of the site. (Did you like it? Was it easy to understand? Could it be improved? etc.)." Further, he listed the following criteria for each report:

1. It must be between 200 and 500 words in length.
2. Please do not take, verbatim, your description from the Internet site you are describing and evaluating.

3. The Internet site you choose must be related to the textbook chapter being studied that week.

4. Use standard forms of English, and check spelling and grammar.

5. This is an independent, noncollaborative assignment.

Rains offers an example of how the web site visits complemented his learning objectives. One of the shortcomings of college astronomy textbooks, he points out, "is that when it comes to the planets, most textbooks talk about the science of Mars, Venus, and the Moon, but they don't emphasize them as actual places with named features. So I assigned some sites with labeled maps, so that the students could familiarize themselves with the geography of the terrain." In reporting on their visits to these sites, students mentioned the ease of attaining different views of the geographic features; they could use site-provided tools such as "zoom" and "recentering" to enlarge or modify the area of inspection.

Rains would like to use the Internet much more in his course, because there are so many astronomy-related animations and graphics available on the Web. He would eventually like his students' web site visits not only to supplement the textbook, but even to replace it. However, he concedes that "it would be a huge job to develop an inventory of sites comprehensive enough to be the primary source of information . . . a concern is to ensure that there are no gaps in the resources." There is also the problem of web sites' becoming obsolete or disappearing over time. Nonetheless, he is actively compiling a list of sites that he and his students have evaluated, and he hopes to rely more on these and less on the textbook in subsequent iterations of his course.

Another example is provided by Pam Taylor, a nursing instructor at the University of Tennessee at Chattanooga. She built a series of seven online exercises that employed guided web search for specific information related to disease processes. Explaining the design of these exercises, she says they "provided for the increasing sophistication of the student's understanding of the pathophysiologic processes and web search skills."

In several cases, Taylor combined a case study method with the guided web research, asking students to apply the information learned to answer questions about a hypothetical patient. For example, she directed students to a series of web resource sites on hematology and cardiovascular topics. She then posted a case study of "John Smith" and asked students to answer a series of questions about Mr. Smith's health, based on the knowledge gleaned from the web sites. This was an individual assignment, in which students input their responses into an online form. The case study included graphic elements, such as a diagram of Mr. Smith's heart, as well as questions related to the graphics: "Mr. Smith is diagnosed with an inferior myocardial infarction. Use the following diagram to locate where the infarction occurred in Mr. Smith's heart." The student then had to check one of three boxes showing the location of the infarction.

What were Taylor's goals in using this approach to teaching? She hoped to "present students with increasingly complex technology-related skill-building situations related to their course of study," as well as to "provide students with increasingly complex opportunities to apply their growing knowledge base of pathophysiology to situations which also require critical thinking skills."

Group Activities

Group activities constitute an obvious strategy for large online classes, but they can be equally effective in classes of fifteen to twenty students. A mixture of individual and group-oriented activities can help provide a variety of contexts within which students may learn skills and concepts and demonstrate their mastery.

Group activities can range from the most informal small group discussion to a highly structured and scripted arrangement. A group may include several students, or it may be just a pair of students who work out their own consensus about how to approach a mutual assignment. Some of this range of possibilities is illustrated in the following discussion.

Icebreaking Activities

As we mentioned in earlier chapters, online students need opportunities to get to know each other. By an *icebreaking activity,* we mean any activity that allows students to begin to form some sense of community online.

We recommend that every online class—and every online component that features a discussion forum—begin with an exercise in which each student introduces himself or herself to the class. This can be accomplished via a discussion thread or through the creation of student web pages. If you carve out a separate area for this activity or create a page of links to students' own web pages, your students will be able to refer back to the biographical information throughout the course.

It is best to keep the requirements for introductions simple: "Please say a few words about yourself and your reason for taking this class" or "Let us know from what part of the world you are logging on, and tell us a little bit about your background in this subject." Begin the process by introducing yourself. Generally, you should include both the formal details of your career and academic interests and some informal information. How much of the latter you offer is up to you. You can also include information about how you prefer to be addressed, either explicitly ("call me Dr. Ko") or implicitly (for instance, signing off your introduction with just your first name).

In addition to these initial icebreaking activities, many instructors find it helpful to have the members of small groups engage in some sort of icebreaking team-building activity. This may involve asking each person for initial comments about how he or she visualizes the common project. It may include questions about people's typical online schedules and times when they might be available for a real-time chat. The more concrete and specific the icebreaking questions, the better, because specificity allows students to respond without worrying about whether they have stayed within the expected boundaries of the activity.

Some instructors encourage students to add photos, either by uploading them to web pages or by attaching an image file to a discussion thread or e-mail sent to the entire class. This is also an option for the instructor. Photos personalize the biographical information and help classmates form a clearer image of their fellow students. As mentioned in Chapter 5, however, photos also have disadvantages. Our only recommendation is that, if you encourage the use of photos, you always make it a voluntary matter.

Dividing Students into Groups

Generally speaking, it's best for the instructor to play a role in dividing students into groups. It's difficult, confusing, and irritating for students when they are simply left to their own devices to form groups. Many online instructors don't realize how clumsy it can be for all but the most outgoing and determined students to join or form groups on their own. In addition, if the task will involve synchronous activities, the time zone in which each student resides becomes a major factor, and the instructor is in the best position to take this into account.

Nonetheless, you may want to include some measure of student volition in the process of setting up groups. Student choice may be desirable under two circumstances in particular:

1. The group activity involves a diversity of choices, and you would like as many students as possible to choose the area that truly interests them.

2. There are already "natural" groupings of students in the course that you would like to incorporate in your assignments in order to promote group camaraderie.

An example of the latter situation would be a course in which three students enroll from the same corporation, and all of them have an interest in working together. Other examples might include mothers and adult children in the same course, or a husband and wife studying together. However, in some cases you might want to break up these groupings to make it easier to distinguish the individual contributions.

When you would like to give students some measure of choice in forming their groups, we recommend that you ask students to e-mail you their preferences. Tell them simply, "I'll try to take into consideration your preferences in forming the groups, but please be aware that it isn't always possible to satisfy everyone."

Size and Duration of Groups   Don't make the groups too large. A group formed only for the purposes of discussion can easily accommodate ten or more, but when the group members must collaborate on an assignment, a group of four is probably the optimum number. For online collaboration, any number larger than four risks creating problems of organization and communication that will consume valuable time.

Try to maintain the composition of the group for the duration of the course. It takes time for groups to develop a working dynamic. Changing the groups just as members are getting familiar with one another leads to needless waste of time as students adjust to their new circle of collaborators.

Group Roles Assigning and rotating roles within each group is an effective method of ensuring true sharing and cooperation in the work. For example, assign one member of the group to summarize, another to record the group's conclusions, and another to lead the discussion or allocate portions of the work. Then request that these roles be rotated during the duration of the course. Make the rotation frequent enough to give each member a chance at several roles, but not so frequent as to interfere with group continuity.

To some extent, the frequency of the rotation will depend on the length of the course. In a course of eight weeks or less, more than three rotations would be an unnecessary bother.

Supervision of Groups

Although some instructors like to give groups complete privacy—from the instructor as well as from other class members—we don't advocate excluding yourself from the groups.

Important! *You need not participate in group activities, but your supervision will encourage participation by all group members and ensure that an individual's contributions to the group are recognized.*

Students are often concerned either that they will expend effort not matched by others in the group or that they will be unduly hurt by uncooperative or inactive group members. An instructor who directly supervises groups can assign grades based on both the whole group's output and the work of the individual members. Combined assessment of this sort is reassuring and encouraging to well-intentioned students.

If you perceive that a student isn't holding up his or her end of the group assignments, you may want to e-mail that student privately. Some instructors also ask group members to privately evaluate each member of the group, using a well-defined set of criteria. This provides additional input that can aid the instructor in discerning what each student has contributed to the group effort.

The question of whether groups can observe the activities of other groups raises a different issue. We tend to feel that groups need a sense that they are coming up with solutions as a result of their own efforts and will be given credit accordingly. If you provide a forum for presentation of group work to the entire class, there is no need for the class as a whole to examine earlier, preliminary stages of a group's efforts.

Collaborative and Cooperative Group Activities

To organize group activities, you need to provide guidelines for each group's collaboration, set reasonable goals and objectives, and provide both a place for the group to work and a place or method to present its work. These matters often depend to some extent on the course management system you're using, a subject we discussed in Chapters 3 and 5. Here, rather than going into the mechanical details of setting up a communal online working space, we'll focus on general principles and on examples from actual courses.

You may have already learned a hard fact about collaborative activities in your on-the-ground classes: collaboration doesn't just happen. Many students have no idea how to collaborate on a task in a course. Thus it is vital to provide detailed guidelines on the responsibilities of each member of a group, as well as explanations of how groups are to proceed with their task. As mentioned earlier, you may want to define such roles as group recorder of the activities, group manager or leader, and group spokesperson.

It's also necessary to define clearly what the end product of each group's project should be, what it should include, and where in the online environment it should be presented. Timing may be critical here, if you want the entire class to have the chance to read and critique what a group has produced. Make sure you clarify the deadlines for each stage of the process.

A Collaborative Exercise in Education   In Tamara Jackson's course for UCLA Extension, "Principles and Practices of Teaching Exceptional Learners in the Regular Classroom," she used three major classifications—definitions, characteristics, and modifications—to organize her lectures. She applied this same format to a collaborative group exercise. The point of the exercise, originated by the creator of the course, Stephanny Freeman, was to compile and analyze information on types of exceptionality.

Students were allowed to state an interest in one of four types of exceptionality, such as communication disorders or disabilities of vision and hearing, as well as in one of the three major classifications noted above. Taking these preferences into consideration as much as was practical, Jackson organized students into four groups, one for each of the types of exceptionality. Then, in each group, she assigned one member to focus on each of the three classifications.

Jackson provided each group with a series of web resource sites pertinent to the type of exceptionality the group was to research. She asked the group members to cull information from both the web sites and their assigned text readings. Each student was responsible for one aspect of the final group report, which was to be posted in a group folder online.

As you can see, the exercise was greatly simplified by applying the overall organization of the subject matter to the structuring of group tasks. Jackson's provision of screened and evaluated web resources was also important: Students could spend time on the objectives of compiling and analyzing information rather than on web searching.

A Team Marketing Plan   In Nancy Levenburg's "Marketing Principles and Practices" course, which she teaches for UCLA Extension, she bases 40 percent of each student's grade on the development of a marketing plan through team effort. As she notes in her syllabus, "The marketing plan is a team project, which will provide you with an opportunity to actually apply many of the 'textbook' principles which you will learn throughout the course. . . . Your team will be expected to develop and present a basic marketing plan for a product or service that your company has decided to manufacture and market."

Levenburg points out that a major reason for doing this project collaboratively is that "students can cross-check each other's understanding of concepts and how they can be applied." Students can test their ideas on their fellow group members and receive feedback. This is particularly important in marketing, Levenburg adds, a field in which, "with few exceptions, there are no truly right or wrong answers." Another advantage of this collaboration in the online environment is that students gain experience in working as a geographically dispersed team—an increasingly common occurrence not only in marketing, but in many other fields as well.

Levenburg limits groups to no more than four students. In larger groups, she has found, "somebody is always left out" because "it becomes more of a challenge logistically for them to coordinate the input and work of more than four people."

Levenburg provides students with a list of eight potential products, such as Asian frozen dinners and a home cholesterol test. At first, she allowed students to choose their own products, but she discovered that a predetermined list reduced the opportunities for plagiarism of marketing plans from the real world. In fact, because Levenburg has students from all over the world, she has found it necessary to provide an explicit definition of "original work" and to state her institution's policy on plagiarism.

She also includes guidelines for the content and format of each team's marketing plan. For example, she stipulates that the plan include an "Executive Summary," "Situation Analysis," "Marketing Strategies and Tactics"—in all, a total of eight components. The plan should "demonstrate knowledge and correct application of marketing terminology and concepts" as well as "evidence of critical thought" and "scholarly research," including the proper citations and references. Levenburg further requires that the plan be prepared as a Rich Text Format or plain text file that can be shared with all in the class.

Levenburg provides online group areas for all to work on their projects, with subareas available for the various tasks or modes that each group might choose. For example, one asynchronous area is set aside for groups to post the transcripts of any real-time chat sessions they have conducted. Another area is devoted to a record or schedule of group tasks.

Levenburg has further instituted a team assessment process, in which each student is asked to evaluate his or her own contributions, as well as those of teammates. Students are made aware of the assessment plan early on. They know that they will be asked to evaluate each member by assigning him or her a certain number of points, as well as to justify each score with a brief explanation. Students who score below a certain level, according to their teammates' evaluations, do not receive the full value of the overall group's score. Students who score exceptionally well receive bonus points. Levenburg also asks students to comment on what has made their group effective or ineffective and to provide feedback on their experience in working with a team.

This team evaluation, says Levenburg, "lets learners know up front what the game plan is." Students understand "that there are rewards for true teamwork and also costs associated with less than true teamwork." Judging from the reaction she has received, her students seem to feel that this is a good and fair system for evaluating team members' contributions.

Role Playing and Simulations

Role-playing activities have been used to great advantage in such subject areas as human resources, business, counseling, international relations, and economics, as well as in history and foreign languages. The same kinds of role playing can take place in an online instructional environment.

Online, role-playing exercises can be carried out in small groups, with each member taking a different role. For example, in a human resources class that is studying hiring interviews, one person becomes the interviewer and the other the interviewee. Alternatively, an exercise can be designed for teams: for example, one team playing the role of Germany in World War I and others representing Britain, the United States, and France. A third alternative might involve an individual student's making a presentation in which he or she assumes a particular role.

Online Debates

In an online debate, students may be asked to defend their views in a public venue or to argue a point of view different from their own. Online debates can involve some of the same activities as role playing, such as preparatory research of the position the student is assigned and postactivity reflection and discussion. Yet debates can also be more pointed and more focused on a specific issue: For example, students might be asked to debate the question of whether the states should be able to tax Internet commerce or whether intervention in Kosovo was justified.

You can arrange students in pairs, with each student taking one side of an issue. Or you can divide students into groups, with each group doing the research and consultation necessary to represent a particular point of view. Each group would then appoint a spokesperson to debate another group's spokesperson on the issue.

In order to make this process work online, students need to be given the information or scripts necessary to play their roles, or they need to be directed to research the material. In the first case, you need to make sure the preparatory materials are posted online or sent in course packets to students. In the second case, you need to provide adequate time and proper guidelines for students to research their parts.

To provide an exciting learning activity online, role playing can be combined with a simulation of a changing situation. Mark Freeman from the University of Technology in Sydney, Australia, devised an award-winning role-playing online activity for his graduate school course in business finance, "Securities Markets Regulation." Students were anonymously assigned the roles of real Australian figures who were involved in the deregulation of Australian securities markets (such as the prime minister, the treasurer, and tycoon Rupert Murdoch). Students then had to respond to "events" announced to them online in a "public forum" (set up with TopClass software) over a period of ten days. The responses could be posted in the public forum (read by the whole class), or the students could approach each other privately via TopClass's internal e-mail.

The anonymous role players were unmasked only at the end of the simulation, when students were asked to reflect on their experience. The anonymity and asynchronicity provided by using the Web, rather than face-to-face meetings, meant that attributes such as ethnicity and gender (and even language proficiency) were less likely to interfere with the role playing. You can read a description of this activity on the Web at **http://www. bus.uts.edu.au/fin&econ/staff/markf/roleplay/rp_outline.html**; a link there provides access to a full paper on this experience by Mark Freeman and his colleague John Capper.

One key to the success of this type of role-playing project is adequate preparation by students. They need to understand the concepts and issues of the subject matter, the roles they are playing, and the instructions and guidelines for carrying out the exercise. In Mark Freeman's class, students had to thoroughly research the roles they were assigned before they began to act "in character." They were also given explicit instructions and rules for "play." The instructor must not only create these guidelines, but also give a great deal of forethought to the simulated events so that they will evoke relevant and worthwhile student responses.

Equally important is the time spent afterward in reflecting on the role-playing experience and integrating what one has learned into an assignment. Reflection can be prompted by individual papers or by whole-class discussion. Integration can be accomplished by having students contribute their newfound understanding to a work in progress or a final project.

Scenarios and Case Studies

Scenarios present concrete situations that can be used to stimulate analysis, requiring students to imagine how they might respond to a particular set of circumstances. In an on-the-ground classroom, scenarios typically involve hands-on activities. Online, scenarios can be used to provoke responses related to matters such as procedures and planning. Either in individual assignments or in group activities, scenarios are a particularly good vehicle for stimulating students' thoughts about step-by-step planning.

Elizabeth Stokes teaches a nursing course, "Role Development for Clinical Nurse Specialists," for Arkansas State University. She uses scenarios to get students thinking about the changing roles and procedures for clinical nurse specialists. Students read the scenarios and then respond in asynchronous discussion threads. They also comment on their classmates' responses. A typical scenario goes like this:

> You are a clinical nurse specialist (along with three other CNSs) in a 300-bed comprehensive health/medical center. The clinical nurse specialist group has been assigned a leadership role in changing to computerized nursing documentation. Because you have worked with the Informatics/Systems personnel in developing the computerized ordering function, your colleagues have elected you to be in charge of this project.

More details follow, and then Stokes poses some questions based on this scenario.

> What will be your plan of action? Who should be involved? What are the major parts of this project (example, training of personnel)? Develop ideas to accomplish the work parts/sections needed in order to complete the project. What strategies will be useful in making this a positive experience? What resources will you need? What strategies will you use for acquiring necessary resources?

Similarly, in her "Principles and Practices" class described earlier, Tamara Jackson provides two scenarios that serve as the basis of an assignment posted in the classroom. Each scenario describes the situation of a child with a disability whose parents want the child to be mainstreamed in the general education population. Here's an excerpt from the assignment description:

> Please read the two scenarios (below) and provide at least four questions you may have about each situation (you'll probably have a lot more!). . . . You might be able to do this by taking on the role of either the parent, the parents of the other children, the teacher, or an administrator. Please do look at other people's questions. You can elaborate by asking questions that relate to other people's questions, or you can ask new questions.

The point of this activity is to get you thinking before you hear about the current laws and the rights of students with disabilities. Then you'll read lectures 5 & 6 with some reference points, and many of your questions will be answered.

These types of scenario questions can transform an abstract or theoretical discussion into one in which students demonstrate concrete problem-solving skills in a particular context. Scenarios may also stimulate debate on a variety of approaches, thus acting as a valuable tool for bringing multiple perspectives to a problem.

Case studies, similar to scenarios, but typically less open ended, are easy to transfer to the online environment. They are basically stories that present a specific situation or a set of facts, so there's little difficulty in posting them online. Case studies call for analysis or for the application of principles learned in the class. For example, a case study in an accounting class for CPAs might describe the financial profile and statistics of a business and ask questions about its tax status.

Case studies can easily form the basis of a written assignment, questions for a quiz, or a series of questions that you pose for a discussion forum. Like scenarios, case studies may be used for both individual assignments and group assignments.

Computer-Based Simulations

Computer-based simulations attempt to re-create an actual process or activity. In Chapter 3, we described how Lonnie Yandell used simulations for his cognitive psychology course at Belmont University. Although most simulations were provided in the in-class, lab portion of the course, others were available online. (You can see some examples of this type of simulation at the site for Purdue's Coglab; go to **http://coglab.psych.purdue.edu/coglab/** and sign in as *guest*.)

In Yandell's class, students were asked to post online their answers to a series of questions based on the simulations. Two examples were "Indicate the independent variables and the operational definitions in this simulation" and "Overall, rate this simulation in terms of helping you understand the material presented in the text."

Many web sites provide simulations that can be used in a class. For example, NASA has a Solar System Simulator (**http://space. jpl.nasa.gov/**) that would allow a student to look at Jupiter as seen from Earth and compare that view with Jupiter as seen from Uranus. The University of Toledo College of Engineering offers a gas turbine simulator that students can manipulate: (**http://mem slab.eng.utoledo.edu/~jreed/jgts/JavaGasTurbineSimulator. html**). Students could be asked to observe and note the results of their manipulations, or they could be tested on what they learn from the site.

Peer Editing and Peer Evaluation

Peer editing and evaluation are marvelous activities from the standpoint of workload management, enabling an instructor to provide students in a large class with additional opportunities for feedback. These activities are also intrinsically beneficial to students, for at least two reasons. First, they require students to view the criteria for an assignment with fresh eyes. This helps them critically review their own work. Second, students get the benefit of a perspective other than the instructor's, and sometimes that can provide added insight.

Whether on the ground or online, peer review activities are most effective when instructors provide specific questions or defined criteria to use in evaluation and editing. For example, an evaluation rubric sets the criteria for each grade designation, explaining what "100%" or "5 points" or "B+" indicates. If a student is evaluating an essay, the rubric may state that 5 points are to be awarded only if the essay contains certain specific elements; if two of these elements are lacking, the essay rates only 3 points. Similarly, a series of guideline questions, coordinated with the original guidelines for the assignment, can focus the peer reviewer's attention: "Did the paper summarize the main thesis of the article? According to the author of the paper, what evidence was given in the article that supports the conclusions of Dr. X?"

For peer review to be most effective, students should be graded as much on their work as reviewers as on their classmates' reviews of their work. Students often worry about being unfairly appraised by the inexpert eyes of their fellow students. But if they are graded on how well they review others, students will exercise more prudence and care in their reviews, and they will be assured that at least one portion of this peer assignment is receiving the attention of the instructor.

Student Activities Involving Guest Speakers

You can bring in a guest "speaker" for a period of several days or a week, during which time he or she will post some material and be available for questions. Or you can simply post the material from the speaker in the asynchronous class forum. The material may be plain text, or it may take the form of a Power-Point lecture or audio presentation.

In some cases, a guest speaker may be available only for a live, real-time chat experience. Because chat is at best a fast-paced activity that demands quick thinking, you should make sure that students are familiar enough with the speaker's material so that they can make informed comments and frame relevant questions. We recommend that you ask the guest to submit some materials in advance, for you to post before the chat date. Students can then read the materials and prepare themselves for the chat. On the basis of this asynchronous posting, you may also wish to ask students to submit questions to convey to the guest prior to the chat date.

During the chat, in addition to introducing the guest speaker and setting some ground rules, you may want to act as moderator. We recommend, too, that you save and post the transcript of the chat for the benefit of students who cannot attend. Then, if it's possible for the guest to make himself or herself available later for a set period of time, students can pose their questions in the asynchronous discussion forum and have the guest reply to them there.

Generally, then, the keys to making guest appearances serve as valuable learning experiences are

1. providing an asynchronous channel for questions and answers, as well as for the presentation of the guest's main material.

2. budgeting adequate time for students to prepare themselves for any real-time activities.

Jennifer Lieberman, a trainer with the Illinois Online Network, comments on the advantages of providing a guest speaker: "This activity gives my participants a chance to hear an insider's story . . . they can ask the guest questions . . . the guest will bring a new perspective different from mine into the course." After the guest has submitted a lecture or other presentation, Lieberman provides discussion questions. "Course participants are encouraged to answer these questions and to pose more questions to the guest." The guest will then log on for a period of three days to communicate with the students asynchronously.

Summaries

A very uncomplicated but effective online activity is to ask students, either individually or as a group, to summarize some aspect of a course's activities, discussions, or readings. This process reinforces the material and provides additional perspectives from the students themselves about the course's themes and foci. It also serves to help students synthesize the discussion and topics of study in a busy online classroom. This can be particularly important in a classroom that is highly interactive, one that has many students, or one in which students are divided up into smaller groups for a portion of their work.

When you have an online class with fifty or more students, it's usually necessary to divide it up for discussion. But students need to know what transpires in the rest of the class, as well as what they can learn from their own group activities. Having small groups of students present their summaries to the entire class forum allows students to analyze and then synthesize a wide variety of material. It permits students to feel involved in the larger class while maintaining the interaction and focus of the smaller groups.

A variation on this procedure is to ask each small group to appoint a spokesperson who not only will present a summary of findings to the entire class but also will lead a discussion. Or one person from the group can present the summary while another from the group responds to questions and comments from the rest of the class.

Cross-Cultural Exchanges

When a course involves students from two or more countries, it can be an exciting learning opportunity. Naturally there are also many barriers to overcome.

First, assuming the countries have different languages, which language will be used to communicate? If one is chosen as the common language, will the students for whom that is not a native language be able to receive some assistance when communication is not clear? At each principal site, it is helpful to have an instructor or assistant who is bilingual and who can intervene or redirect conversation when communications become garbled or strained.

A related issue is whether the main texts will be available in one or both languages. Even when one group of students is fairly proficient in speaking the other's language, it may be a strain for them to keep up with the pace of reading challenging texts in that language.

Gerda Lederer, a political psychologist who has taught online for the New School's DIAL program since 1995, has team-taught a series of online courses with instructors in Germany or Austria. Although the common language used in all these courses was English, a few occasions arose when students needed some clarification of communications. In these cases, it was helpful that both instructors were able to translate. Lederer also points out that she and her co-teacher chose texts that were available in both German and English, putting students on an equal footing as far as the assigned readings were concerned.

Another potential challenge relates to cultural patterns of learning. If students are used to an instructor-centered classroom where there is little student-initiated participation, they may need specific guidelines about when and how to volunteer their comments and questions. In some cases, students' habits of learning may not be readily apparent until the course begins. You may need to rely on your co-teacher to play the role of informant for his or her culture.

It may be best for organizers or leaders at each site to develop a set of guidelines for both instructors and students, covering communications in the classroom as well as expectations for written assignments. The latter would involve guidelines for writing as well as rules about plagiarism and originality. For example, in many Asian countries, modeling one's work on that of an authority or expert has long been a traditional study method, whereas in Western countries this might be interpreted to some degree as plagiarism. To avoid misunderstandings, you can develop mutually agreed-upon policies that are posted for students to read.

Make sure, too, that the forums for discussion are clearly established and that file exchange methods and file formats are all made explicit. Place, time, method, and the rules of engagement should be clearly delineated in every online class or online component of a class, but these are even more crucial for classes involving two different countries.

Cross-Cultural Teams

In cross-cultural courses, one question that often arises is whether to form teams composed of a mixture of students from both countries or to have each country's students form their own team. The latter setup is easier to organize, but the former may lead to better cross-cultural exchanges and greater opportunities for new perspectives.

Gerda Lederer found cross-cultural pairs easier to handle than groups of three or four. It's hard enough, she points out, to achieve true collaboration in a group of two; with the addition of even one more person, coordination becomes significantly more complicated. She also notes that the instructor's evaluation of students is facilitated by the pair arrangement—that is, it's easier to discern the individual contributions when there are only two members in the group. This was important in Lederer's case, because she and her co-teachers gave students the option of communicating within their own designated asynchronous discussion areas or using private e-mail. Private e-mail was often more appropriate for the initial stages of projects, which involved many interpersonal exchanges that seemed to thrive on the relative privacy of the e-mail communications. However, if there had been more than two students involved in each exchange, these private communications would have reduced the instructors' opportunities to assess individual contributions.

In the course Lederer team-taught with Albert Lichtblau of the University of Salzburg in 1999, "The Third Generation Looks at the Holocaust," students from the United States and Austria had to interview someone close to them, such as a grandfather, about that person's experiences during World War II. Each pair of students then dovetailed their two interviews and their findings to present a collaborative report to the entire class. In this case, private e-mail correspondence helped some pairs get to know and understand each other in the early stages of collaboration.

If you choose to create teams that mix students of different countries, do prepare specific guidelines about times and frequency of communications. Remind students about the time differences. Ask your counterparts about details such as ease and frequency of Internet access. Students in many countries have only limited Internet access at the campus site, and Internet service providers and phone connections in many countries are not stable. Find out how often students are likely to suffer broken Internet connections midway through their work. If Internet connections are unreliable, you would want to avoid scheduling many real-time activities, and you should probably build in more time for asynchronous activities to be coordinated.

Another potential difficulty arises when students in another country observe different religious and secular holidays than those at your site. Lederer points out that the German and Austrian students in her course not only observed a number of extended religious holidays but also were unable to access their university computers during these periods. In addition, few of these students had Internet connections or even computers in their homes.

Rewards of Cross-Cultural Courses

Even though cross-cultural international courses present complex issues, the rewards can be enormous. Lederer feels that the full potential of online education is exemplified by courses like hers. The benefit, Lederer points out, is the ability to gain access to another culture *on its own terms.* When we meet an exchange student studying in our country, she notes, our understanding of his culture is naturally colored by his being in our own environment. But, if we contact him "in his own home environment, surrounded by his culture and supported by those values, it's an entirely different sort of experience." To get the most out of a cross-cultural course, Lederer urges us to choose our subject matter carefully to take full advantage of the online medium.

The Experience-Based Practicum or Lab Assignment

The online class that includes a practicum or similar activity can not only provide all the advantages of traditional field-based exercises but offer some additional benefits as well.

A practicum by its nature involves the organizing and accomplishment of an individualized plan of action. Even though the practicum may rely mainly on the student's performing some activity in the real world, the online environment allows opportunities for peer review and exchanges with classmates, to help the individual reflect on his or her experience. The feedback might occur in response to obligatory weekly or monthly reports. Or students involved in a practicum could make occasional postings whenever they needed feedback from the instructor or from classmates.

In an education course, for example, a practicum or field-based exercise might involve the student's observation of a classroom situation, the creation of a lesson plan, an internship situation, or the conducting of an interview. Reports of that experience might then be shared with others in the online classroom, and classmates might be asked to critique or pose questions to the presenter.

In Linda Zimring's "Practicum in College Counseling" course, which forms the capstone of an online certificate program in college counseling offered by UCLA Extension, students choose projects such as helping to prepare a high school's College Night program, interning with a nearby college's admissions office, and observing the college counseling process with a high school counselor. Students voluntarily post regular weekly reports on their progress for their classmates to read and discuss, which adds a group dimension to what would otherwise be an individual project experience.

Lab work presents unique challenges to instructors who are teaching online classes. In introductory classes in particular, some online instructors devise lab kits that students can use to do simple experiments at home. Others arrange for students to work in labs at nearby campuses or to use videoconference hookups to observe lab experiments. Still others rely on a combination of these methods along with videotapes and computer-based simulations. Whatever the methods used to integrate lab work into the online classroom, the lab component needs to be carefully thought out and arranged well before the course begins.

Some of the teaching strategies we have mentioned might be enhanced by the use of online multimedia—graphics, animation, sound, or video. In the next chapter, we will introduce you to some of the tools you might use to produce these elements.

Resources

Cooperative Learning and Case Study Methods

Instructional Innovation Network. **http://bestpractice.net/**

At this site sponsored by Arizona State and Cal Poly Pomona, follow the links to the Cooperative Learning Homepage and the Case Study Homepage, which contain explanations of each method, along with teaching materials and resources. Linked articles explain the difference between group projects and true cooperative learning.

Learning Styles

Addressing Diverse Learning Styles Through the Use of Multimedia. **http://www.vpaa.uillinois.edu/tid/resources/montgomery.html**

A paper by Susan Montgomery, University of Michigan, based on the use of multimedia in an engineering class.

DVC Learning Style Survey for College. **http://silcon.com/~scmiller/lsweb/dvclearn.htm**

Prepared by Suzanne Miller of Diablo Valley College in California, this site explains various learning styles and offers a survey to determine your preferred learning style.

Learning Styles and the Online Environment. **http://illinois.online.uillinois.edu/model/learningstyles.htm**

This Illinois Online site offers a short explanation of learning styles and a collection of links to other resources on the subject.

Online News Sources

CNN. **http://www.cnn.com/**

The Economist. **http://www.economist.com/**

The New York Times. **http://www.nytimes.com/**

Salon. **http://www.salon.com/**

Web Resources

Educational Object Economy. **http://www.eoe.org/**

Follow the links to the EOE Learning Community and then to Learning Objects and the educational Java applet library.

Internet Scout Project. **http://scout.cs.wisc.edu/index.html**

An annotated and continually updated site reporting on selected educational web resources.

Web Search and Evaluation

Advanced Web Searching. **http://www.atl.ualberta.ca/
articles/web/advance.cfm**

*Kenton Good of the University of Alberta explains how to get
the most out of using a web search engine.*

Evaluating Web Resources. **http://www2.widener.edu/
Wolfgram-Memorial-Library/webeval.htm**

*Jan Alexander and Marsha Ann Tate at Widener University's
Wolfgram Library offer checklists for evaluating sites and
teaching modules on related subjects.*

Search Engines. **http://illinois.online.uillinois.edu/
ionpointers/ionpointers.html**

*From Illinois Online Network's "Pointers and Clickers" tech-
nology tips (October 1999), a succinct explanation of the differences among types of search engines.*

Thinking Critically About World Wide Web Resources. **http://
www.library.ucla.edu/libraries/college/instruct/web/
critical.htm**

*Esther Grassian of UCLA College Library provides a checklist
of questions to ask in evaluating a web site.*

Webhound. **http://www.mcli.dist.maricopa.edu/webhound/
index.html**

*This Maricopa Community Colleges site offers tutorials on
web searching skills, as well as links to other guides and tutorials. See especially the link to "What a Site!" (**http://www.mcli.
dist.maricopa.edu/show/what/index.html**), which focuses on
how instructors can find and integrate web resources into student activities.*

Creating Courseware:
When Low-Tech Is
High-Tech Enough

Sooner or later, you're going to have to face "the wall." This is the mythological barrier separating those who plan from those who execute, those who serve their students from those who only stand and wait. In other words, those who make web pages from those who don't.

Not everybody has to make web pages, of course. Some institutions provide templates for their faculty to use. With a template, you merely fill in the form boxes with the text you want and point to the image on your hard disk that you want to use, and then the template "makes" the web page for you and displays it online. An example of such a form can be found in Figure 7.1. Other institutions "outsource" their web work to firms like eCollege, which will create web pages from content supplied by instructors. Such firms contract with colleges to create the web interface and format the content in return for a fee (often a percentage of what the student pays the institution).

Most instructors, however, are pretty much on their own. Support is minimal, if it exists at all. If you are one of these, then making a web page is your primary means of expression, the method by which you can publish your syllabus, lectures, or assignments on the Web. If you're more than just a text-and-print person (the pedagogical equivalent of cut and paste), you may want to create web pages that link to other web sites or that are enlivened with relevant graphics, tables, or charts. If you're even more ambitious, you may want to create animation or a

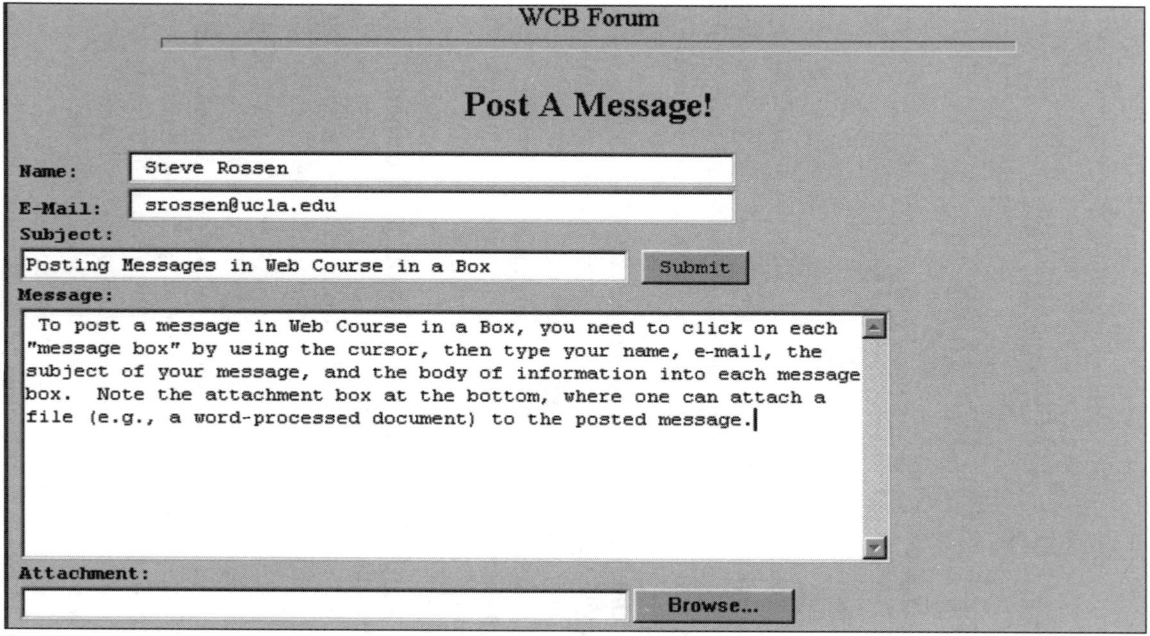

WCB Forum

Post A Message!

Name: Steve Rossen

E-Mail: srossen@ucla.edu

Subject:

Posting Messages in Web Course in a Box

[Submit]

Message:

To post a message in Web Course in a Box, you need to click on each "message box" by using the cursor, then type your name, e-mail, the subject of your message, and the body of information into each message box. Note the attachment box at the bottom, where one can attach a file (e.g., a word-processed document) to the posted message.|

Attachment:

[Browse...]

Figure 7.1 Form Box in Web Course in a Box, a Course Management System. By clicking on the empty space, an instructor can type messages directly into the form box, avoiding the necessity of creating a separate web page or converting a word-processed document into a web page.

narrated slide show with the sound of your voice synchronized to the display of images.

Is this all beyond your reach? Many instructional designers and programmers would have you think so. They would tell you that creating "really good" web pages requires a working knowledge of HTML, the ability to create web pages with frames, or knowing how to use Adobe Photoshop filters to doctor a photo you've scanned. Friends in the know will mention such programs as Macromedia's Director to make really cool web pages, the ones with text flying around like swarms of locusts and colors undulating like northern lights.

Don't listen to them. They're only feathering their nests. Ninety percent of the time, you won't need to know any of that. After all, you aren't creating an e-commerce site on which to sell designer clothes. You're trying to communicate information so that you can teach your course. And the great news about software is that every year it becomes easier and easier to use. In fact, there are a number of so-called low-tech tools that cost very little, or even nothing at all, that are easy to learn, easy to use, and easy to remember when you use them again a month or so down the road. Better still, much of what you may need to do can be accomplished using software you already own, such as your word processing software. In fact, Netscape Communicator has a built-in function called Composer that lets you create web pages while still browsing the Internet (we'll talk more about that later in the chapter).

Let's look at some of your options, beginning with the simplest.

Creating Text for Web Pages

To write text for your web page, you can work either in a standard word processing program or in a more specialized web page editing program.

Creating Web Text in a Word Processor

To create a syllabus or assignment page to post online, you can type it out in Microsoft Word, WordPerfect, or Filemaker's

HomePage, click the Save As function in the File menu, choose HTML as the file type, and, voilà, you've created a web page.* No programming, no special language, no mumbo jumbo of any sort. The only thing you need to do then is to hand-carry your web page on a floppy to your web site or to your web site manager (also known by that medieval job descriptor "webmaster"), or send it to him or her as an e-mail attachment, and your web page can now be displayed online.

Of course, there are a few drawbacks to making web pages this way. For example, when you convert a document into a web page using Microsoft Word 97, the web page will sometimes contain extra spaces between lines that did not exist in the original (this glitch has been rectified in Word 2000). In order to get rid of them, you have to edit them in a web page editing program like Netscape Composer, deleting the extra spaces one by one. But this seems like a minor bug compared to the ease and convenience of using your favorite word processor to produce and save the files that you need.

Creating Web Text in a Web Editor

Another low-cost, low-tech, and more reliable way to produce a web page is to work directly in a web page editing program. The two most popular web browsers offer their own web page editors. Netscape Composer is a complete, what-you-see-is-what-you-get (WYSIWYG) web editor built into Netscape Communicator. Similarly, Internet Explorer provides FrontPage Express, another WYSIWYG page editor. If FrontPage Express is on your machine, you will be able to find it in the Internet Explorer folder (on a Mac) or through the Start menu (on a PC).

To illustrate how WYSIWYG editors work, Figures 7.2 through 7.7 demonstrate steps in creating a web page with Netscape Composer. When your Netscape Communicator browser is open, you can find Composer by clicking on the Communicator option on the menu bar at the very top of the screen. A drop-down menu will then appear, one of whose choices will be Composer (Figure 7.2).

---

* In Microsoft Word, this will work only if you have installed the optional "Web Authoring" component.

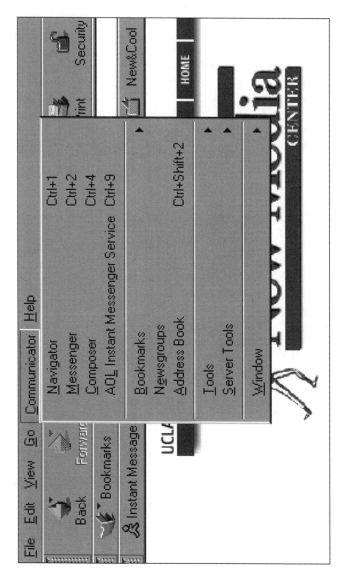

Figure 7.2 The what-you-see-is-what-you-get editor, Composer, is part of Netscape. You can find it by clicking on the Communicator button on the menu bar and looking for it in the pulldown selection box.

When Composer opens, you will see a mostly blank page topped by several rows of tools displayed as little graphic icons. Running your cursor over these icons slowly, one by one, will reveal what their function is. A small label will appear just below them, identifying them as the tool you use to create a numbered list, or to make a line into a headline, or to create a hyperlink to another file on the Web. You can find many of these same icons in your word processing program as well. Netscape Composer, however, is a what-you-see-is-what-you-get program. Whatever you make with it will be exactly reflected in the web page you display on the Web.

You can type text in the blank area of the Composer screen (Figure 7.3). You can also choose various tools to modify and format the text, as shown in Figures 7.4 through 7.7.

Designing Web Text: A Few Tips

- Keep the background simple. The fact that you *can* add a background color or design doesn't mean you ought to. Your students are visiting your page in order to get information they need. What's important to them is seeing the information clearly. So, if you must use a background, make it very light so that dark text will contrast with it.

- When choosing fonts, don't overdo it. Too many fonts, sizes, or colors confuse the eye rather than guide it. Look at any published book and notice the relative simplicity of the layout. One size of font (generally between 10- and 12-point type) defines the body text. It is usually a font with serifs—the fine strokes at the tops and bottoms of letters—because serifs help make a visual connection between one letter and the next. Headings tend to be printed either in bold or in a sans serif (that is, nonserif) font. Sans serif fonts tend to look stolid and important—or so our brains have been trained to think.

- Never use light text against a light background, such as yellow text against a white background. It's usually unreadable. Always use very light against dark, or very dark against white.

- Don't force your readers to scroll down the page to follow the text. Reading on a screen isn't the same as reading a printed page. Most

(cont.)

people don't like to read too much text from the screen, because of eye fatigue or the unfamiliarity of the medium. On the other hand, it isn't particularly enjoyable to follow links from one short page to another short page. Usually, the best compromise is to create one long page and then provide some way, other than tedious scrolling, for your reader to navigate through it. This means creating a table of contents somewhere (usually at the top of the page) with links to "anchors" you set up on the page. For information on how to do this, see Chapter 9.

- Don't stretch your text completely across the page. Leave a little white space on the left and the right. The white space contains the text and makes it easier to read on the screen. The easiest way to achieve this format is to create a table with two columns. Type in the right column and leave the left column blank. Format the table so that it has no lines defining the columns. Using a table, in fact, is one of the most effective and efficient ways to format both text and graphics on a web page and to make sure they will display evenly no matter what the resolution and size of the monitor on which they appear.

- Don't overload your page with web links. Your students are visiting *your* page; they should be able to see or get to the information they want to find immediately. Even links to other pages within your own site can easily be overdone. Try to make it easy for students by listing the main topics on the front or main page, with links to related pages. On the related pages, make sure you provide them with a way to get back to the main page. That way, your students can move back and forth with ease.

Adding Graphics to Your Web Pages

OK, you say, that's all very well and good—I can create a web page by simply typing and saving my work. But what if I want to display some pictures? Don't I need to know Adobe Photoshop or take a course in graphics?

The answer is no. Placing graphics in a web page is a simple process. Figures 7.8 and 7.9 illustrate how you would do it in

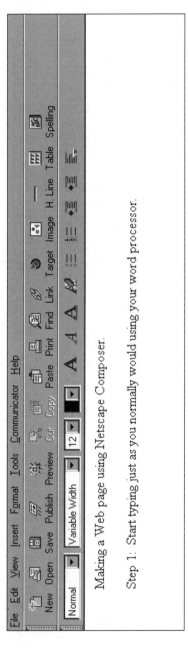

Figure 7.3 The Screen in Netscape Composer. This is what you will see when you first select Composer. Notice the row of functions across the top, most of which are similar to what you might find in a word processor. If you run the cursor over the icons, a little label will appear to tell you what each icon is. To begin, start typing in the blank area of the page as if you were typing in a word processor, as we've done in this example.

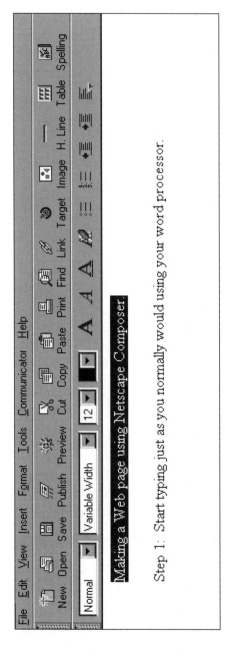

Figure 7.4 To change or reformat something you've typed in Netscape Composer, you have to select it. By holding the mouse button down and running the cursor over the word or words you want to select, you will cause the line to be darkened. When it is dark, it has been selected.

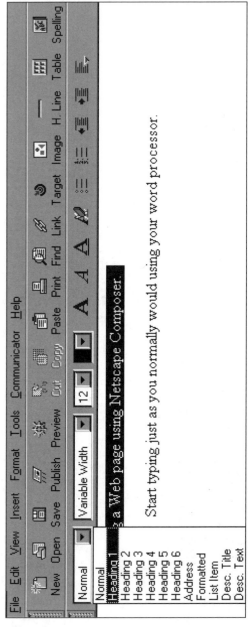

Figure 7.5 Clicking on any function along the bottom menu row in Netscape Composer will cause something to happen to the word or words you've selected. In this case, we've decided to convert the selected line into a heading.

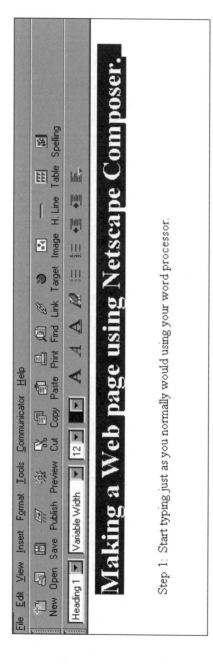

Figure 7.6 This is what the heading in Figure 7.5 looks like after we change it.

Figure 7.7 Using Netscape Composer, you can insert images, link to web sites, create tables, even check your spelling. The functions are all listed across the menu bar at the top of the page. Try them out and experiment. Use the Preview button to test your work and see what it will look like on the Web.

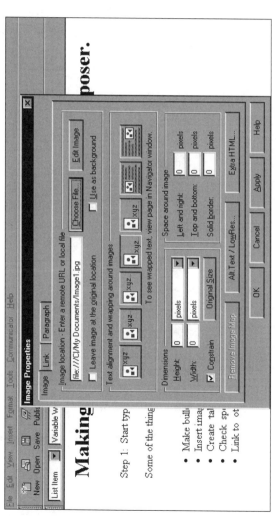

Figure 7.8 This is the dropdown box in Netscape Composer for inserting an image. To insert a graphic onto your web page ("insert" is technical lingo for putting or pasting an image into the page), click on the Image icon on the menu bar. Once you do, the dialogue box shown here will appear. Click on the Choose File button and find the image you've saved on your hard disk. You don't have to fill in all of the fields shown in this dialogue box, but it's nice to know that you can tell Netscape Composer how you want text to align with an image (the seven buttons in the middle of the dialogue box) and whether you want some text to appear when the mouse travels over the image (the Alt. Text/LowRes button near the bottom of the dialogue box). The latter option is especially important for visually impaired students who access your web page.

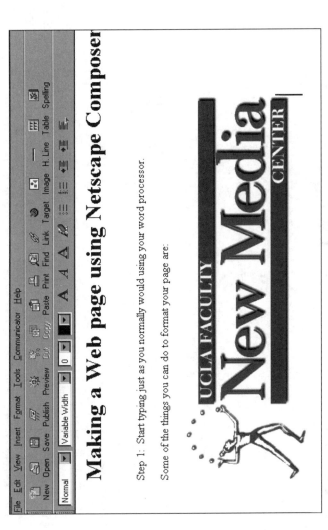

Figure 7.9. Here is our sample Netscape Composer web page with an image inserted. In this case, it was an image we downloaded from the Web.

Netscape Composer, using a graphic image that you've saved on your hard drive.

But what about acquiring and saving such a graphic image—isn't that complicated? Again, no.

Important! *Collecting, scanning, and saving graphics for use in a web page can be accomplished using very simple software, some of which you no doubt already own.*

For example, you can save almost any image you find on the Web by clicking on it once, and then (if you're on a PC) right-clicking your mouse or (if you use a Mac) just holding the mouse button down. Immediately you will be greeted with a little pull-down dialogue box (see Figure 7.10), which will permit you to save the image on your hard disk. Once you do, you can go back to your word-processed document or to the page you were working on in Netscape Composer, and insert the image into your document, as shown in Figures 7.8 and 7.9.

What if you want to scan an image from a printed source or touch up an image that isn't quite right for your purposes? For those purposes, you do need access to some additional hardware or software, but once more, the process isn't difficult.

Scanning Images

No matter how many images you can find searching on the Web, you can't find everything. Many of the graphics you may need still reside in your college library's books or magazines. To display these images on your web site, you will have to **scan** them. Most universities and colleges have scanners you can use. If yours doesn't have one you can use, and you can't afford to

> **scanning** Converting printed material (whether graphic or text) into a format a computer can read—those mystical 1s and 0s that make up the mathematical language of computing. Once a computer can read the material, you can put it on a web page to display to your class.

purchase one yourself, you can always try the local copy shops. Very often, for a fee, they will let you use theirs.

Copyright for Web Graphics

An image that you have downloaded from someone else's web site doesn't belong to you, and if you're going to use it on a public web site, you will have to get permission from the image's creator to do so. The same rule applies to any text, sound, animation, simulation, or video that you might find on the Web, as well as to any material you scan from a copyrighted book or periodical. Similarly, material that *you* create is deemed your intellectual property and is also protected.

There is a set of generally accepted guidelines known as the Fair Use Guidelines for Educational Multimedia. These specify reasonable amounts of material that you can "borrow" and use as part of your online class. In other words, you *can* use material that does not belong to you; you just have to use it correctly. For a detailed discussion of this issue, please be sure to read Chapter 8.

But is it difficult to scan documents? Do you need to purchase special software or possess special skills? The answer to all three of these questions is no.

The actual act of scanning is similar to using a copy machine. You lay the book or newspaper face down on the scanner (Figure 7.11). Then you find the software program that runs the scanner (you may have to ask someone for help locating it on the hard disk). That software program will present you with a little control panel with which to make the scan (Figure 7.12). Although the design of the control panel may vary from scanner to scanner, the functions remain essentially the same. You can preview the work you're scanning, decide which part of it you want to scan, and usually define how large the final image will be once it is scanned. Then you can save the image file on a floppy or on your hard disk, and insert it into your web page.

Size and Resolution Getting the size and resolution right when you scan a graphic can save you a lot of time down the road. There are many software programs that will help you "fix up" a graphic once it has been scanned, but if you scan it correctly in the first place, you may not have to use them at all. The basic trick in getting the size and resolution right is knowing how large you want your graphic to be on screen.

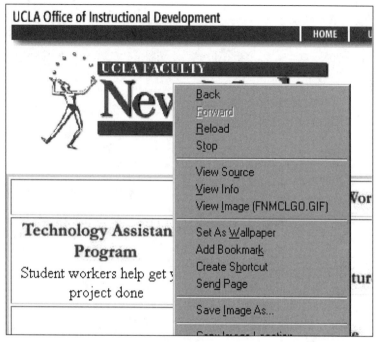

Figure 7.10 Saving an Image from a Web Page. In this case, the image is the icon of the juggler and the logo. When we right-click on the image (or use a regular click on a Mac, holding the mouse button down), a pulldown box appears. Note the line second from the bottom: Save Image As. By selecting that function, you can save the image to your hard disk.

A computer monitor displays images as a series of colored dots, or **pixels.** For example, most monitors can display an image that is 800 dots per inch (dpi) wide by 600 dpi high. Many monitors can display more dots per inch, but it is probably best to design your graphics for the lowest common denominator. That way, you can be sure that all your students will be able to see the graphic well.

> **pixel** Short for *picture element*, the individual dots that make up images on an electronic screen. A screen's resolution is defined by the number of pixels in a given area, usually expressed as dots per inch (dpi).

Figure 7.11 A scanner is like a copy machine. You lay the document you want to scan face down on the screen, close the top, and then use software to control the scanner.

Now look again at the scanning software shown in Figure 7.12. Notice on the right that the resolution is set for 100 dpi. The bottom left tells us that the image scanned is 8.46 inches wide and 11.04 inches high. Will these settings produce an appropriate size and resolution for your students' monitors?

To find out the size of the scanned picture in Figure 7.12 in dots per inch, you would multiply the width (8.46 inches) by 100 dpi, to get 846 dpi. Similarly, for the height, you would multiply 11.04 inches by 100 dpi, to get 1,104 dpi. Thus, if you saved the picture at that size and then displayed it on a computer monitor set at 800 × 600 dpi, it would be larger than the size of the screen. You would have to scroll sideways and downward to see the whole picture. Large images like this one also take a long time to download when viewed online. So you wouldn't want to make an image as large as this example, at least not for display on a web page, particularly for students viewing it from home.

One option would be to choose a smaller image to scan—for instance, a detail of the picture shown in Figure 7.12. Say your detail measured approximately 2 inches square in actual size. In that case, you could even increase the dpi setting from 100 dpi to 200 dpi, so that the detail would appear twice as large when displayed on the screen.

Another option would be to scan the entire large image, but then edit it in a graphics editing program. Figure 7.13 shows how you could easily adjust the image size to make the graphic appropriate for a low-resolution monitor. Now let's look at some other things you can do in an editing program.

Editing Images

Some scanned images need a little help. Some look dark and dreary, and others, such as those gleaned from magazines or newspapers, seem tinted, grayish, or full of dots. More common still, the image you scanned is upside down or tilted.

It's fun to fix up these images, but to do so you're going to need some sort of image-editing software. There are many programs available. The venerable monarch of all image-editing programs is Adobe Photoshop. This is the program you would want to use if your goal were to show a politician standing next to a beautiful young woman he had actually never met. In other

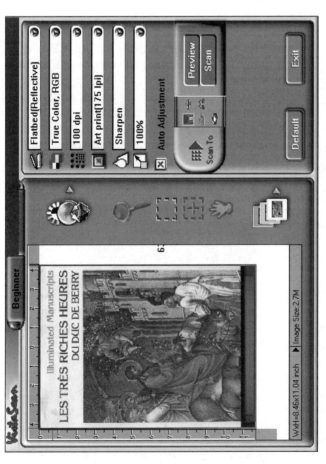

Figure 7.12 Scanning Software (VistaScan). On the left, an image has already been scanned. At the bottom of the scanned image, note the information about the size in inches as well as in bits. On the right is a series of pulldown boxes that let you make adjustments to the image.

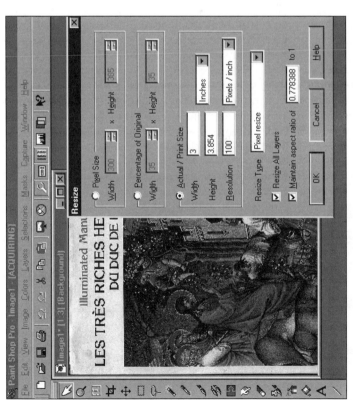

Figure 7.13 Using Paint Shop Pro. The image size of the scanned picture is being reduced to 3 inches × 3.85 inches.

words, it's pretty sophisticated—and expensive. In our view, for most faculty members such a program amounts to software overkill. It has so many features and special effects that remembering them after two weeks or so is a considerable feat.

The lesser-known image-editing programs are often a better choice. Paint Shop Pro and LView Pro for Windows and Graphic Converter for the Mac are good examples. These programs are far less expensive than Photoshop—LView Pro, for example, sells for about $50—and don't have all of Photoshop's functions and special effects. But they are easier to use and to learn and will let you do almost all of the things you need to do to fix up your images. A list of web sites for some of these programs may be found in the Guide to Resources at the end of this book.

No matter which program you decide to buy, they all let you do the same basic things: make images brighter (or darker); increase the contrast (or lessen it); rotate the image; or crop it down to size. All of them will let you save your image in a format you can use for display on the Web.

A Graphics Editing Example   Figure 7.14 shows some typical problems with a scanned graphic that call for the use of a graphics editing program. In this case, the picture is skewed to the left because it was not laid perfectly straight on the scanner when it was scanned. In addition to the tilt, the graphic contains an unnecessary white border and caption.

Figure 7.15 shows how the tilt can be fixed with Paint Shop Pro. Finding the Rotate function (there's one in every program, although not necessarily in the same place on the menu bar), we rotated the image 1 degree at a time to the right, until it looked straight, just as you might do if you hung a picture on your wall.

We then clicked on the cropping tool (Figure 7.16). This icon is practically universal. Holding the cursor down, we defined a rectangle around the graphic information we wanted to keep. Letting go, we double-clicked inside this defining box to confirm our selection, and the image was cropped to its proper size.

Saving Images

Now that you've fixed up your image, the last thing you must do is to save it in a format you can use on the Web. Fortunately, there are only two common choices for this purpose.

Figure 7.14 A Typical Situation After Scanning an Image. The graphic is skewed to the left, and there is unneeded lettering and white space. You can edit this graphic in a graphics editing program.

If your image is an artist's illustration or a piece of line art, then the file format you should use is **GIF.** It was developed by CompuServe, an Internet service provider, some years ago as a way to send or display graphics on the Web. At that time, most monitors could display only a limited palette of colors (generally 256 colors), and the GIF format was particularly adept at compressing colors into that format. Now, even though monitors typically display millions of colors, GIF remains an excellent choice for an image with relatively few colors.

Figure 7.15 Here, we are rotating the image 2 degrees to the right, using Paint Shop Pro. We arrived at 2 degrees by trial and error. The goal is to keep rotating it until the image looks straight.

Figure 7.16 Cropping. Using the cropping tool (the fourth tool down along the left of the page, outlined by a black circle), we defined what we wanted to see, clicked twice, and cropped the image down to size.

If, however, the image you are saving is a photograph, GIF is not an appropriate format. You should save a photograph as a **JPEG** file, a format developed specifi-

> **GIF** Graphics Interchange Format, a compression format useful for graphics files with a limited number of colors.
>
> **JPEG** A compression format useful for photographs; the acronym stands for Joint Photographic Experts Group.

cally for this purpose. Photographs typically contain millions of colors, and JPEGs are very adept at compressing them while retaining sufficient clarity. JPEGs aren't so good, though, for simple line art with just a few colors; with that type of art, the JPEG format often smudges lines or makes them look ragged.

Tips and Techniques for Working with Graphics

- ***Compressing graphics.*** If you really want to alienate your students, create a long page of text that stretches from side to side and has embedded in it five to ten graphics. Such a richly embellished page will take forever to download, and, by the time it does, your students will no doubt have lost all interest in viewing it.

  There are several ways to reduce the download times of web pages with graphics. One way is to control the size of the graphics by cropping them and saving them at a manageable size. We recommend a size of approximately 260 x 140 dpi, that is, about one-quarter the size of a low-resolution monitor. If it's important to have images appear bigger, try putting them on a separate page and linking to them from "thumbnail" portraits embedded on your main web page. Then, if students don't want to see a particular graphic, or have already seen it and don't want to see it again, they can move on without wasting precious download time.

  Another solution is to compress the graphics with either an image-editing program, such as Paint Shop Pro or Photoshop, or an image compression program, such as Macromedia Fireworks or Ulead SmartSaver. The latter programs can take a photograph you've scanned and saved in JPEG format, and compress it to one-quarter the original size without noticeable loss of quality. The former programs, Paint Shop Pro and Photoshop, will let you reduce the number of colors, and even bits, that your graphic contains, thus

  (cont.)

reducing file size. But compressing your images in that manner does require some expertise.

- *Placing graphics properly.* If your web page has text describing a graphic image, you should place the graphic and text adjacent to one another. Most web page design software (including Netscape Composer, Adobe PageMill, and Macromedia Dreamweaver) will permit you to place your graphic either on the left, on the right, or at the center of the page and decide how text will flow around it.

- *"Bleaching out" the background.* When using a graphic as a background for your web page, make sure to "bleach out" the graphic as much as possible by reducing contrast and increasing brightness. You can do this in a graphics program such as Paint Shop Pro, or even in a word processing program that permits images to be edited, such as Microsoft Word. Fading out the background makes the foreground text much easier to read.

Adding Sound and Other Streaming Media

So now you have a web page with images that you've down-loaded or scanned and fixed up in an image-editing program. What else can you do to liven up your page?

How about sound?

Sound is a much-overlooked element on web pages. But it can do a lot. You can search for sound files on the Web and per-haps discover a radio show that is relevant to your class. Or you can tape-record an interview with a colleague in your field, make the recording available on your web page, and then ask your students to comment on what your colleague said.

But what do you need in order to listen to the radio show online? And how can you convert a tape recording into a file your students can "play" on the Web?

It used to be that, if you wanted to play a sound file you found on the Web, you had to download it first. That was often a tedious process. A sound file one minute in length might take ten minutes to download. If the file was particularly important (such as a clip from Kennedy's inauguration speech), you might accept the inconvenience. But for anything else . . . well, you had to think about it.

Suddenly, however, all that has changed. With the advent of **streaming media** technologies, as mentioned in Chapter 2, you no longer have to wait for the *entire* file to download in order to hear it. Now it will start playing, and continue to play, within fifteen seconds or so of your making the request. That's what "streaming media" means: Information is fed in a continuous stream, rather than in one huge hunk, to your computer.

There are three major types of streaming media (and a number of lesser ones): QuickTime, RealNetworks, and Windows Media Technology. By "types" we mean formats, that is, the methods by which visual or audio information is assembled, compressed, and delivered. Each type has a "player" of its own—a piece of software residing on the user's computer that can "play" the multimedia file once it arrives from the server via the Internet.

Without getting too technical, it's safe to say that the most popular player as of this writing is the RealPlayer produced by RealNetworks (the current version is called the G2). This player, which can be freely downloaded from RealNetworks' web site **(http://www.real.com/),** works on both Mac and PC platforms, installing itself into whichever browser you normally use—Netscape Communicator or Internet Explorer. It works as a **plug-in;** that is, once installed, it will auto-

> **plug-in** An application that supplements a web browser, automatically activating itself when it is needed.

matically go into action whenever you click on a link that connects to a RealNetworks streaming media file. Most Internet radio shows, for example, use RealAudio files, and when you click on the link that accesses such a program, the RealNetworks player will begin to play the sound.

Not only does RealNetworks offer the most popular player, it also happens to produce a number of free production tools that permit you, as only a novice user, to create some highly sophisticated streaming media products. With no more than an average computer equipped with a sound card and an inexpensive computer microphone, you can produce sound files that you can put on your web site and stream to your students anywhere in the world.

What Kind of Microphone Should You Get?

To make sound recordings to use with streaming media, you'll need a microphone. The best microphone you can buy is one with a headband that allows you to situate the mike to the side of your mouth. That way, your hands are free, and the recording will not have a "pop" whenever you say a word with a *p* in it.

One manufacturer that produces such microphones is Labtec, whose web site can be found at **http://www.labtec.com/.** The Labtec mikes we've purchased have cost less than $30.

An Example of Streaming Audio

One of the tools RealNetworks makes available is called RealProducer. It can be downloaded at no charge from RealNetworks' web site.

With RealProducer, you can create a sound file using a prerecorded tape or a microphone. For example, you might use an ordinary tape recorder to interview an expert or colleague in your field. Then you could play the tape back by connecting the tape recorder to your computer's sound card input plug. RealProducer would then convert the interview into a streaming sound file that you would place on your web site. Your students could listen to the interview on the Web and reply to it using the course discussion board. RealProducer will also accept direct input from an audio CD or a VCR.

RealProducer uses a set of prompts known as a "wizard" (for the medieval sage); that is, it prompts you as you go along. Figures 7.17 through 7.19 show some of the choices you must make before recording your file (there are only a few). You need to specify what kind of recording device or file you are using to make your sound file; what kind of file it is (voice, music, voice with background music, stereo music); and what kind of modem your students will be using to listen to it.

Following these prompts, you can then begin recording—either speaking into the microphone, playing a tape, or recording directly from a CD or VCR (Figure 7.20). Once you've stopped, RealProducer will create a web page for you with your sound file already embedded (that is, surrounded by the proper HTML tags

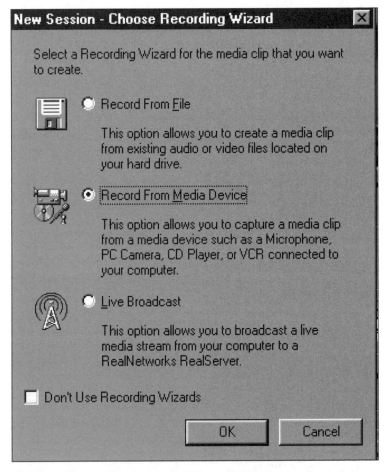

Figure 7.17 The First "Wizard" Screen in RealProducer. This screen prompts you to tell RealProducer the source for the sound file. In this case, the selection is Record From Media Device, because the input device is a microphone.

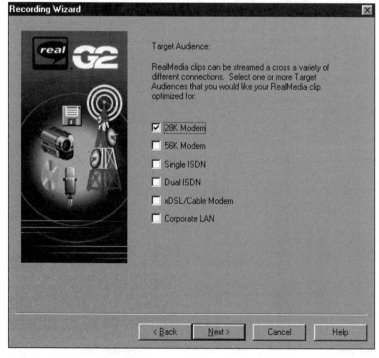

Figure 7.18 Selecting Modem Speed. In this dialogue box, RealProducer wants to know what sort of modem will be receiving the streaming sound file. It is usually best to choose the slowest modem speed (28K) to make sure that all your students will be able to hear the sound file clearly.

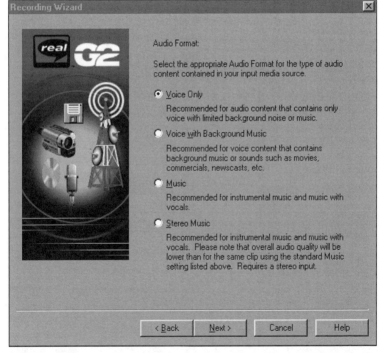

Figure 7.19 Another Screen from the RealProducer "Wizard." By selecting Voice Only, you're telling RealProducer how large a file it needs to create in order to transmit the file to your students effectively. A file containing stereo music, for example, will be much larger, and thus harder to transmit, than one containing only the sound of your voice.

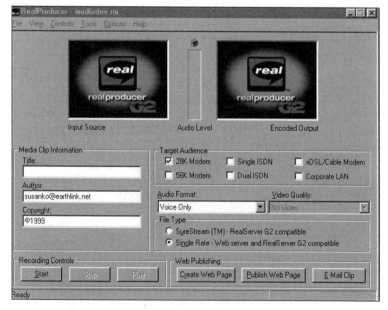

Figure 7.20 The Final Recording Screen in RealProducer. By clicking on Start on the lower left, you can begin to record. Once you stop, you've automatically created a streaming audio file. Using some of the choices on the lower right, you can create a web page with your sound file already embedded, "publish" your web page to a web server (if you know the correct URL, or web address), or send your creation as an e-mail to a colleague or friend.

so that it will play). You can also publish this file to your web site or attach it to an e-mail you're sending to a colleague or a friend.

Not bad for a piece of freeware.

Narrated Slide Shows

So now, for a minimal cost, you have the ability to make web pages, insert graphics (which you've scanned and fixed up), and create a link to a streaming audio file that you've made yourself. Though we don't want this to sound like a sales pitch for miracle kitchen devices, there is more, much more.

Not only can you make an audio file that will stream to your students, you can make a narrated slide show containing images, text, and the sound of your voice. A narrated slide show can be a very useful tool for any instructor. With it, you can take a series of slides—say, for a biology instructor, pictures of a cell dividing—and create an illustrated lecture in which you talk to your students directly, explaining the significance of the images they are seeing.

Until recently, producing such an application was the province of skilled programmers using complicated and expensive software and hardware tools. But here again, the landscape has changed. Now there are several free or inexpensive software programs you can use that will permit you to make these files with little effort at all.

The three most popular of these programs are RealSlideshow (from RealNetworks, **http://www.real.com/**), QuickTime (from Apple, **http://www.apple.com/**), and PowerPoint 2000 (from Microsoft, **http://www.microsoft.com/**).

Of these three, only RealSlideshow is free. As of this writing, though, RealSlideshow works only on a PC. QuickTime is quite inexpensive (about $30) and works best on a Mac. PowerPoint 2000 comes with Office 2000 or can be purchased separately (prices vary, but it isn't inexpensive).

An Example Using RealSlideshow   With RealSlideshow you can assemble a narrated slide show using scanned graphics and a microphone. You can even add some background music, with dissolves and other special effects between the scenes, and the slide show will remain perfectly in sync.

Scripted Versus Unscripted Slide Shows

There are two ways to narrate a slide show: scripted and unscripted. Scripting—that is, writing out what you want to say in advance, word for word—is effective for those instructors who are dealing with complex or detailed material and don't want to make a mistake. Unscripted narrations, with the instructor speaking to the students from notes or from memory, replicate more of the classroom experience.

Unscripted narrations tend to sound more personal when transmitted through the impersonal medium of the Internet. The ad-libbed quality, with the occasional error, creates a sense of intimacy between instructor and student. On the other hand, the ad-libbed narration may ramble on too long. Some of the newer slide show software (RealPresenter G2, for example) makes it easier to redo the sound narrations for individual slides, permitting the instructor to make necessary edits.

Creating a slide show is fairly straightforward. First, of course, you assemble the graphics, downloading them from the Web, scanning them, or creating them in a graphics editing program such as Paint Shop Pro.

Then you open RealSlideshow and insert the images (Figure 7.21). You click on each image and, one by one, add the sound narration (Figure 7.22). You can insert a CD into the CD player and record some background music (Figure 7.23). To assemble the slide show you've designed, you then click on the Generate button. RealSlideshow will create all the files you need. You can then either "play" the slide show or "send" it. The latter choice means sending it to your departmental web site.

If you don't have permission to upload your files to your departmental web site this way, you can always save the files on a floppy or a **Zip disk** and hand-carry them to your webmaster. Better yet, you can

> **Zip disk** A portable hard disk that allows you to store and retrieve files.

use one of the online hosting services now available.

Online Hosting Services   Online hosting services are relatively new. Such a service permits you to leave material on a server for

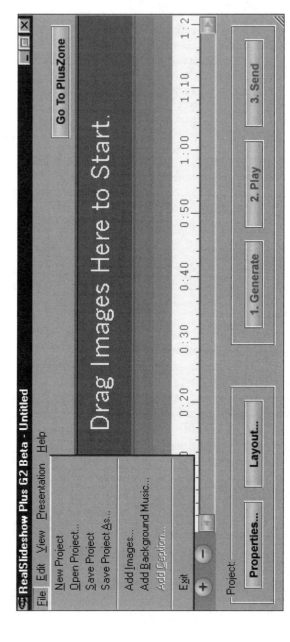

Figure 7.21 Beginning a Narrated Slide Show Using RealSlideshow.
The dropdown File menu contains choices for saving the project so that files
can be edited at a later time. Note the Add Images and Add Background
Music selections.

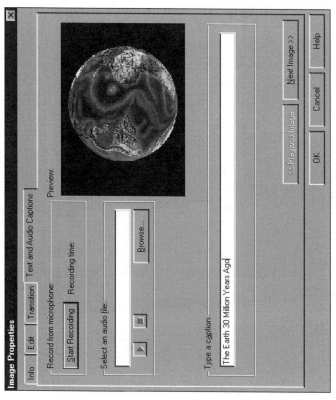

Figure 7.22 Recording a Voiceover. By double-clicking on one of the images in RealSlideshow, you cause this dialogue box to appear, permitting you to record your voiceover narration. This slide show is about the evolution of Earth over time.

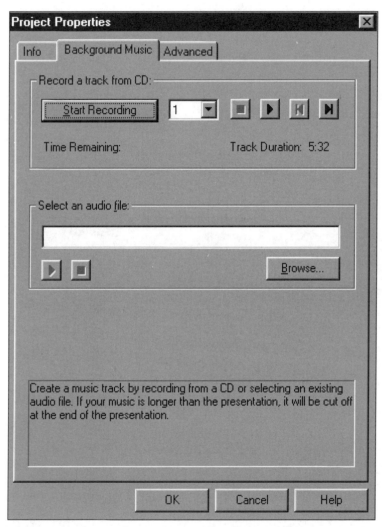

Figure 7.23 In RealSlideshow you can add background music to your presentation from a CD. You insert the CD into the player, choose a track, and play. The music will continue to play underneath the voice recording. Of course, to use it on an open web site, you would have to have permission.

others to see. What the provider gains from this free service is web traffic, and web traffic means revenue from advertisers online. You, on the other hand, gain a free storage area and the use of powerful server software.

One such service that we have used is PhotoPoint (**http://www. photopoint.com/**). PhotoPoint will permit you to register online. The only information you need to provide in order to register is your e-mail address. Then, when you're "sending" your RealSlideshow, you can choose PhotoPoint as your destination (Figure 7.24). It is one of the choices built into RealSlideshow. Using PhotoPoint as your online server, you can publish as many slide shows as you want without having to bother your computer support personnel. When your students link to the slide show (PhotoPoint provides you with a specific URL), they can use their RealPlayer plug-in to see and hear the slide show you've made.

There are other ways to create narrated slide shows. We've already mentioned QuickTime and PowerPoint, and new software is being developed all the time. What's important to know is that the ability to create and use slide shows is now within the reach of everyone. The tools are becoming easier all the time, and the price of admission is steadily going down.

Animation

Some instructors seem to think that a good web site is one that looks like Times Square, circa 1955, with great smoke rings wafting into the air and giant, neon-green olives plopping into blue martini glasses. Although this sort of animation can be decorative, it doesn't really have anything to do with teaching and, more often than not, diverts the eye, increases download times, and ultimately annoys anyone visiting your site for a second time.

But animations can be effective when illustrating processes or phenomena that change over time, such as cell division or the movement of planetary objects. Some fine examples of educational animations can be found on a web site maintained by Ed Stephan at Western Washington University (**http://www.ac.wwu. edu/~stephan/Animation/animation.html**). Stephan has created animations dealing with everything from the march of

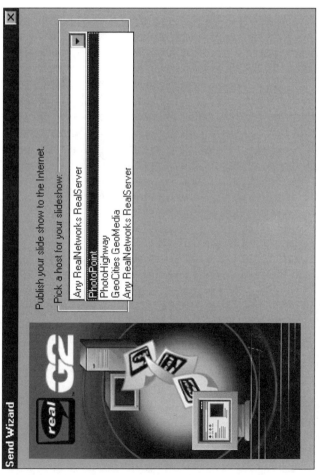

Figure 7.24 Publishing Your Slide Show to the Web. If you have permission to do so, RealSlideshow allows you to send your narrated slide show, complete with all the necessary files, directly to your web site. You can also use one of the commercially available (and free) web hosting sites, such as PhotoPoint, as shown above.

Alexander the Great across the Near East (Figure 7.25) to the mechanics of Ted Williams's swing.

Creating animations can be fun as well as instructive, but be forewarned that it can also be time consuming. Most of the software programs available for making animations use cells or frames. Usually, you create a cell by drawing in it or importing a graphic into it. Then you copy the cell to create a new cell, either moving the object slightly or adding something new, so that when you play your animation, the cells will appear to move, much as if you riffled a pack of cards.

Most animations on the Web are saved as GIF animations. They can be imported into a web page just as any GIF graphic might be, and they automatically begin playing when the web page you've created is downloaded by one of your students. GIF animations tend to be quite large, so before you import one into a web page, it is probably best to compress it, using a program like Ulead SmartSaver or Macromedia Fireworks.

Some more sophisticated animation software packages, such as Macromedia's Flash and Apple's QuickTime, require special plug-ins for users to see them, but they have the added advantage of incorporating sound and interactive buttons into their design. They also cost more and are somewhat difficult to use.

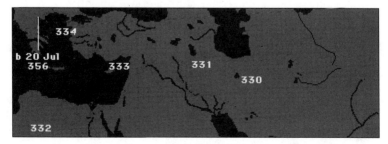

Figure 7.25 Animation Created by Ed Stephan. This animation shows the route and dates of Alexander the Great's conquests in the Near East. As the animation progresses, the dates appear in chronological order, and the route lines are traced on the screen.

Using Multimedia: Why and When Is It Worth It?

Having discussed some of the software packages and techniques for creating multimedia, we want to conclude this chapter by considering when the use of multimedia is worthwhile and when it isn't.

When to Use Multimedia

If you teach art history, then using graphics of an artist's work will seem a self-evident reason for employing multimedia. But if you teach mathematics or philosophy, the need to enhance your pages with graphics, sound, animation, or video may not seem quite so obvious. Such subjects are traditionally taught with nothing more than plain old text. So why would an instructor choose to spend the extra time and effort to use multimedia?

Here are some possible reasons:

1. *To illustrate the mechanics of how things work.* Often, instructors in seemingly abstract subject areas are called upon to describe the process of how things work. An economics instructor may need to illustrate how demand affects cost, or an electrical engineer may want to demonstrate how digital information flows through logic gates. These needs call for multimedia. Sometimes the process in question can be illustrated with a graph or with a series of illustrations. At other times, an animation showing the process in motion is preferable.

   Figure 7.26 shows how a Chinese language instructor combined sound and calligraphy to illustrate Chinese characters. The student can select a RealAudio sound file just beneath each character to hear the word pronounced. Or the student can view an animation (in the upper right-hand corner) to see how the character is drawn.

2. *To clarify or emphasize abstract concepts.* Complex abstract concepts are often difficult for students to sort out or remember. Often, graphics can serve as memory jogs for students who are attempting to keep a host of such con-

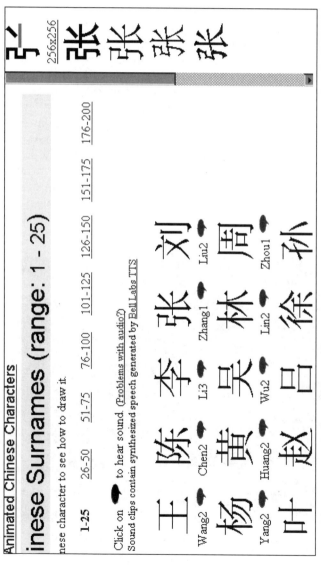

Figure 7.26 Chinese Characters. These characters include sound files and animation illustrating how each one should be pronounced and drawn.

cepts straight. For example, a history professor dealing with the Spanish Civil War used posters to help students keep track of the seemingly bewildering array of acronyms for the anarchists, trade unionists, socialists, communists, and other political groups involved (Figure 7.27).

3. *To enliven or illustrate unfamiliar material.* Whether you're dealing with historical or geographical contexts (poverty in nineteenth-century London, the ecology of Central American rain forests), the identification of organisms or structures (spirochetes, postmodern architecture), or the way things function (human ambulation, a four-cycle engine), the use of graphics and animation can greatly enhance your students' comprehension. A major value of textbooks is the profusion of illustrations, graphs, and tables they provide. The Web provides a vehicle by which individual instructors, using comparatively inexpensive tools, can "publish" their own textbook-quality material and make it available to their students.

Figure 7.27 Spanish Civil War Posters. An example of the useful images you can post on a web site for students' reference.

4. *As the basis for an assignment.* Illustrations can be powerful and fascinating stimuli for an assignment. Newspaper articles, advertisements, photographs, even articles, scanned and displayed (following copyright prescriptions), can provide the basis for an assignment requiring students to critically evaluate the material and post their analyses on an electronic bulletin board. Students can also be asked to collect information in the field, convert it into digital form, and display it online as part of an assignment, assuming, of course, that they have the means to do so.

As you saw earlier in this chapter, you can interview an expert by telephone and, with his or her permission, tape the interview, convert it into a streaming audio file, and present it online for students to comment on. This often makes an excellent type of assignment. You might supplement it by asking the expert to host an online discussion on your bulletin board for a week or two, allowing your students to converse with him or her directly.

When to Avoid Multimedia

Putting together a site enhanced by graphics, animation, or video poses an immediate problem: How much is too much when it comes to the time and effort involved in creating and assembling these multimedia elements?

For those fortunate enough to work at an institution that provides ample financial, administrative, and staff support, this question may be moot. However, for the majority of instructors, the burden of putting together such materials falls squarely on their shoulders. How can you gauge in advance whether creating a graphic or an animation is worth the time you will need to produce it? Here are some factors to consider.

1. *Institutional support.* Some institutions encourage innovative teaching by rewarding faculty members with either merit promotions or release time. Other institutions provide support through labs, media centers, or paid student assistants. In such situations, taking time to enhance your web site with multimedia makes sense.

If, on the other hand, your university will regard your extra work with indifference, putting in the extra effort becomes strictly a question of how much experimentation with new forms of expression means to you personally. It *does* take time to assemble a web site with significant multimedia elements. Even an advanced user needs a few hours to put together a PowerPoint presentation, for example, or to scan and reformat some graphics or text. If the effort cuts into your ability to do your own research, and if your institution offers no compensation for your endeavors, then obviously you will want to use discretion before embarking on anything too ambitious.

2. *Relevance of the material.* It may seem that using an animation or video will encourage your students to dig into the material you are presenting. All too often, however, instructors sacrifice relevance to convenience, using a graphic that almost, but not quite, expresses the concept or the subject they are trying to illustrate. In these cases, students are often more confused by the material than aided by it. In such situations, it would be better not to produce the material at all.

3. *Availability of the material elsewhere.* Before you create a multimedia presentation, make sure that the material doesn't exist on another publicly accessible web site. Spend some time searching online. If you find what you're looking for, create a link from your web page to the site, thus saving yourself the considerable time and effort to create the material from scratch. Don't forget to ask the site's owners for permission to add your link to the site.

4. *Accessibility of the material.* Before embarking on the production of a complex multimedia element, consider whether your students will be able to view it easily from a home computer using an unsophisticated modem. For instance, if you're creating a digital video enhanced by a sound narration, do you or your institution have the expertise and equipment necessary to stream it? If you're linking to another site that has videos or animations, will your students have the necessary software to view it? Is the material you're planning to produce so complex or dense that viewing it online may be more tedious than helpful?

These considerations can help you decide whether making a given piece of multimedia is worth your time.

Resources

Web Page Composer

Netscape Composer. **http://www.netscape.com/**

A useful composing tool included in the Communicator web browser.

Multimedia Software and Hardware

Labtec. **http://www.labtec.com/**

A manufacturer of computer microphones and other peripheral equipment.

QuickTime. **http://www.apple.com/**

Apple's streaming media software.

RealProducer and RealSlideshow. **http://www.real.com/**

RealNetworks' software that allows you to create streaming audio and video, and narrated slide shows.

Web Hosting Service

PhotoPoint. **http://www.photopoint.com/**

A web site that allows free storage of photos and slide shows.

Animation

Animation Projects. **http://www.ac.wwu.edu/~stephan/Animation/animation.html**

This page by Ed Stephan offers a sampling of his animations.

8

Copyright and Intellectual Property

This chapter deals with two related issues of import to the online instructor. Essentially they are two sides of the same coin.

1. *Copyright and fair use.* Do you have the right to use other people's materials in teaching your course?

2. *Intellectual property.* What happens to the intellectual material that you create once you've posted it online? Do you still own it? What can you do if an unauthorized person makes use of it?

Copyright and Fair Use

In Chapter 7 we wrote about gathering materials, particularly multimedia materials, for use in your online course. We noted, however, that to use them correctly you need to heed the copyright law. Specifically, you need to know what material you can use, under what circumstances you can use it, and when you are breaking the law.

The simple answer to all of the above is that copyright law, as it is presently written, states that, if you're using material that belongs to others without their permission and the material you're using is freely accessible (either on your public web site or via a CD you've distributed to your students), then you're probably breaking the law and thus vulnerable to a suit by the material's rightful owner.

But, because you are an educator, the powers that be (a consortium consisting of representatives of industry, publishing, education, and other areas, convened to advise Congress on the creation of a new or amended copyright law) have made a few grudging exceptions. If you are teaching in a classroom or online, you may make use of materials that you don't own, as long as you do *not* make them freely available for distribution and the amount you use does not exceed certain fixed limits. These exceptions have been collected in a document known as the Fair Use Guidelines for Educational Multimedia. They are "guidelines" rather than legal code because no formal amendment to the basic copyright law has yet been adopted. Nevertheless, an educator adhering to the Fair Use Guidelines is probably immune from liability in a suit.

But how do you determine if what you're using falls within the fair use criteria? The copyright law itself specifies four overall determining factors:

1. What is the character of the use? Put simply, is it for commercial or noncommercial purposes? Noncommercial use is much more permissible. If you are a teacher at an educational institution, you will have no problem satisfying this criterion. But if you are assembling courseware for distribution—say, via a CD—you may not qualify for the fair use exemption because you have copied information that does not belong to you and made it available outside the confines of your classroom.

2. What is the nature of the work to be used? If the work is in the public domain—that is, out of copyright or never copyrighted—then, of course, you're fine. If the work is copyrighted, the "nature of the work" may include how original or creative it's considered to be. Original or creative work often requires the permission of the owner. Strictly factual material is less likely to require permission.

3. How much of the work will you use? Large amounts—and large percentages of the original work—do not qualify as fair use.

4. What effect would the use have on the market for the original work? Use that would significantly damage the work's market

value does not qualify as fair use. This is the key provision for online educators. If you are teaching via a password-protected site, to which only students or other invited guests may gain access, you probably qualify under this part of the fair use rules. In essence, your site may be deemed the equivalent of a traditional classroom bounded by four walls. But if your class is accessible by anyone on the Internet, you are, in effect, making the work available for anyone who wants it, and this presumably damages the work's market value.

To these four original factors, the consortium that developed the Fair Use Guidelines for Educational Multimedia added the following stipulations:

1. Students may incorporate portions of others' works into their multimedia creations and perform and display those creations for academic assignments.

2. Faculty may incorporate portions of others' works into their multimedia creations

   a. to create multimedia curriculum materials.

   b. to teach remote classes where access and total number of students are limited and where technology makes copying impossible. (If materials can be copied, they may be made available over the network for only fifteen days and then must be placed on reserve for on-site use only.)

3. Faculty may demonstrate their multimedia creations at professional symposia and retain them in their own portfolios.

4. Time limit on fair use by faculty: two years from first instructional use of the multimedia work.

5. Copies limit: Generally only two copies are allowed, but joint work creators may each have a copy. In an electronic sense, a copy is a file you have saved on a disk.

6. Portion limits:

   a. Motion media (including video and animations): up to 10 percent of the original work or 3 minutes, whichever is less

   b. Text: up to 10 percent of the original work or 1,000 words, whichever is less

   c. Poems: up to 250 words, but further limited to

      i. three poems or portions of poems by one poet or

     ii. five poems or portions of poems by different poets from a single anthology

7. Music (including lyrics and music videos): up to 10 percent of the original work or 30 seconds, whichever is less

8. Photos and images: up to five works from one artist or photographer; up to 10 percent or fifteen works, whichever is less, from a collection

9. Database information: up to 10 percent or 2,500 fields or cell entries, whichever is less

Is Anyone Really Watching?

Some readers may find the foregoing fair use guidelines somewhat excessive. After all, you might argue, with so much material available on the Web, who could possibly monitor it all anyway?

Think of the matter this way: It is just as easy for those who own material to find it on the Web as it was for you to secure it in the first place. Sophisticated search tools now exist, and are continually being improved upon, for tracking down pirated material. As the market for distance education grows, so do the economic incentives for people to protect any material that rightfully belongs to them.

Thus, you must be especially conscientious about materials you post on the Web. If you aren't, the institution you work for will no doubt encourage you to revise your behavior, because it is usually the institution that bears the heaviest liability in a copyright suit. But you personally are not immune.

What to Do If You Aren't Sure

So what should you do if you think the work you are using does not qualify for the fair use exemption? You should write the owner and ask for permission.

State who you are, what you plan to do with the material, and when you plan to remove it from your course site. (See the box "A Sample Letter Requesting Permission.") Keep a copy of all your correspondence, whether by letter or by e-mail. If no one responds to your request, you can then probably use the

A Sample Letter Requesting Permission

The following general template was composed by CETUS, the Consortium for Educational Technology in University Systems **(http://www. cetus.org/).** You can adapt it as necessary when you need to secure permission to use someone else's work. In the paragraph where you explain your intentions, be sure to note the key features of the proposed use, such as who will have access to the site and how long the material will be made available.

[letterhead stationery or return address]

[Date]

[Name and address of addressee]

Dear [title, name]:

[If you called first, begin your letter: This letter will confirm our recent telephone conversation.] I am [describe your position] at [name of institution] University. I would like your permission to [explain your intended use in detail; e.g., reprint the following article in a coursepack for my course].

[Insert full citation to the original work.]

Please indicate your approval of this permission by signing the letter where indicated below and returning it to me as soon as possible. My fax number is set forth above. Your signing of this letter will also confirm that you own [or your company owns] the copyright to the above described material.

Thank you very much.

Sincerely,

[Your name and signature]

PERMISSION GRANTED FOR THE USE REQUESTED ABOVE:

_____

[Type name of addressee below signature line]

Date

material, relatively secure that you have made a good-faith effort to contact the author and secure his or her permission.

In most cases—probably about 95 percent of the time—you will receive permission to use the material without having to pay any fee or royalty. In those rare cases in which you are not given permission free of charge, you can either pay the fee or use other material instead.

Finding the Rightful Owner

Ascertaining who is the rightful owner of copyrighted material can sometimes prove quite complex, particularly when ownership may have changed hands several times since the work was first published.

There are a number of ways to track down authorship using the Web. Services such as the Copyright Clearance Center can help with searching out the ownership status of a given piece of material. The University of Texas also maintains a very extensive and useful web site that lists a number of methods by which you can locate a property's true owner. If you are especially fortunate, your university or institution may hire a staff member to handle the copyright searches for you. In the Resources section at the end of this chapter, we cite a number of web sites you can consult for more detailed information about this complex subject.

What About Links?

Linking to someone else's public web site, whether as part of a course assignment or as an addition to a page of course notes, does not contradict the copyright strictures. However, as a matter of courtesy, it is advisable to let the owner of the page know that you are linking to the site, particularly if it is housed on a host site, such as GeoCities or EarthLink. Such web sites incur additional costs if more than a prescribed number of visitors "hit" the site. Very often, when you notify the owner this way, he or she may return the favor by letting you know when the URL for the site has changed.

Intellectual Property

I t's one thing to borrow someone else's work to help teach your class—you know your intentions are good—but it's quite another thing if someone borrows your work. Among instructors who are leery of using the Web, one persistent fear is that their intellectual property will be stolen by some enterprising student or—worse still—by another educator.

This fear is not unfounded. Students do reproduce course notes and even sell them, often supplementing them with notes they have written themselves. This practice has been going on since long before the advent of the Web (surely no one has forgotten the dreaded copying machine). But the practice is significantly easier when lectures and other course materials are posted online, because all one needs to do is to copy the materials electronically and save them as a file.

A more sinister scenario involves other educators, or even for-profit publishers of educational material, "borrowing" your lectures and using them for their own purposes, either reworking them or reformatting them to suit their own needs. In a world in which tenured positions are becoming less commonplace, and many instructors find themselves teaching for various universities at one time or another, intellectual theft of this sort may not be as rare as you suppose.

Let's look first at your legal rights and then at some practical steps you can take to protect your work.

The Legal Status of Your Work

Believe it or not, legal ownership of material you create is a very gray area at most institutions. Most faculty members are under the impression that the intellectual work they produce or publish automatically belongs to them. Not so. It is simply the accepted custom of most universities, particularly those involved in research, to cede rights to such intellectual property to their faculty members, because the administrators realize that work thus produced will bring the institution revenue in the form of grants. But institutions do not *have* to cede these rights. They merely choose to.

The same has been historically true for course content, including syllabi, lecture notes, and course outlines. Departments, however, often retain copies of these materials to make available to new instructors or TAs who are teaching the course for the first time. Of course, in this situation the new instructors are expected to *adapt* rather than copy the original syllabus. A departing instructor is also usually free to take his or her courseware to a new institution.

Teaching online often means creating original material in the form of web pages enriched with multimedia elements such as graphics, sound, video, and animations. Instructors who create such material may assume it belongs to them, but when a university or other institution is intent on marketing its courses and programs online, ownership of said materials may not be quite as clear-cut. From the institution's point of view, such material may not bring in revenue in the form of grants, but it can help create revenue in the form of increased tuition. Hence the institution may be less willing to cede rights to the instructor.

It is a good idea, therefore, to find out—in writing—your institution's policy with respect to online materials you've created to teach your course. If there is no established policy, come to some agreement with the administrators about your material. This is especially important if you're a nontenured adjunct or lecturer and expect to use your courseware at several different institutions, either online or as part of a hybrid course.

If you can't secure clear ownership rights to your own material, you can always copyright the material yourself before making it available to your institution or class. Although most faculty members aren't aware of this, you automatically hold the copyright of your intellectual property the moment you commit it to paper or to disk. If it came to a court case, however, you would have to prove the date you created the material. One way to do this is to send yourself a registered envelope or package with the material inside and then keep the package unopened. A second way is to submit a claim for copyright to the Library of Congress.

As online instruction becomes more lucrative for universities and private institutions alike, the question of who owns the rights to material and who benefits from revenues derived from it will become more and more important. The field of copyright law and intellectual property is rife with legal experts. We do not pretend to a special expertise. What we do suggest is that you take nothing for granted when it comes to material you have created, and that you make the effort to learn in advance the specific policies of the institution you are working for.

Practical Steps for Protecting Your Work

A copyright notice prominently displayed is like a scarecrow in a field. It will scare away some of the crows, but some will come pecking all the same. So it pays to be both vigilant and practical.

Various instructional materials are pilfered from ordinary classrooms every day, and the Internet makes it even easier to steal material and repurpose it. With a little care, however, most instructors who post material online can avoid serious problems.

Begin with common sense. Say you have an essay you've been working on. It hasn't yet been published, but you'd like your class to read it. If you're fearful that one of your students may copy it or send it to someone else, then post an abstract or description of it instead.

There are also some technological strategies you can use to help ward off potential thieves.

Technological Methods   The first, and probably the most obvious, technological stratagem to reduce theft is to use a password-protected web site. Most course management systems, such as WebCT and Blackboard CourseInfo, possess encryption tools that prevent unwanted visitors from viewing the course. If you aren't using a course management system, tools exist that will permit your computer support personnel to password-protect your web site with various computer programs written in Perl or C. Even if you're essentially on your own, with no support, a number of easily accessible programs will allow you to password-protect your site (refer to the web sites listed in the Resources section at the end of this chapter).

There are also some technological methods for protecting unlawful copying or downloading of your work. Some software programs permit you to limit the way your work can be copied by others online. Take the case of a lecture you have created using Microsoft Word. If you save this document as an HTML file, or post it to your web site as an attachment, your students will be able to open it or download it exactly as if they had copied it from your hard disk. What you might do instead is to use a program such as Adobe Acrobat. This is the program that permits you to create the Acrobat file format that you see everywhere on the Web, and it provides options that can help limit unauthorized use of your material.

Using Adobe Acrobat

With Adobe Acrobat, you can use any program you normally would to format your material: Microsoft Word, QuarkXPress, FrontPage Express, PowerPoint—any program that permits you to print. When your document is ready, you "print" it in a format known as PDF (Portable Document Format). You can then make this PDF file available via your web site, permitting any student who possesses the ubiquitous Adobe Acrobat Reader to read, download, and even reprint your file exactly as you originally formatted it without having to own the software program that created it.

However, if you do not want your students to reprint your material or save it, Adobe Acrobat permits you to restrict how the material is used. You can remove the ability to reprint text and graphics or even to select and copy them once they reach a student's home computer. You can further restrict use by means of a password (see Figure 8.1). Similarly, assuming you are operating according to the fair use guidelines, you can copy articles or material culled from other sources and "print" them as PDF files, then limit your students' rights to repurpose them by taking advantage of the features just mentioned. Once Acrobat is installed, the PDF option appears as one of the printers available in the print setup box (Figure 8.2).

Another way to protect your intellectual property is to convert it into streaming media format, particularly when it involves the use of multimedia. Streaming media, such as narrated slide shows and recorded audio files, are housed on the server and streamed to the user. They exist in temporary memory on the user's computer. A particularly clever student hacker might figure out how to retrieve this material from the cache, or temporary memory, but most users will neither want to nor know how to. Thus sending out information in this format is like building a fence around your fields. It will keep most, although not all, intruders from pillaging your crops.

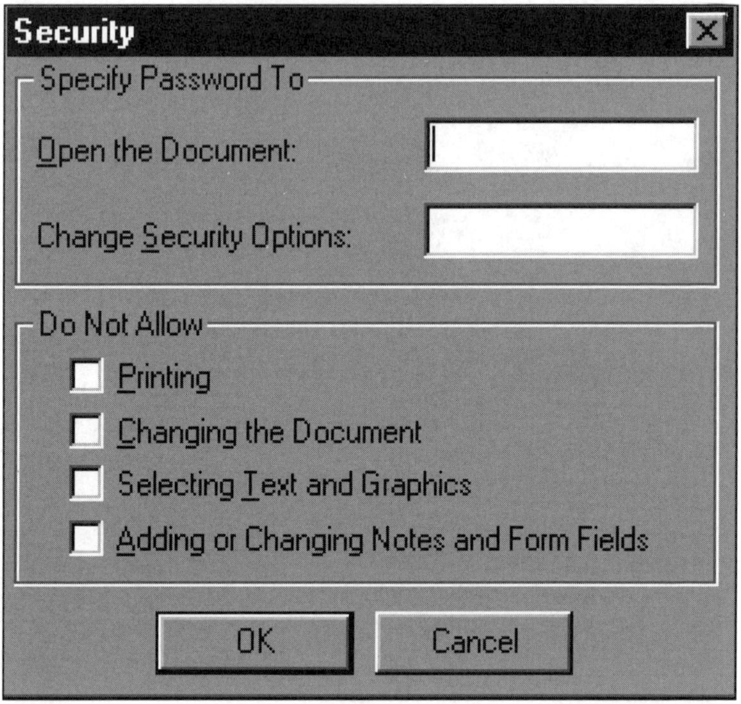

Figure 8.1 Security Features Available to Users of Adobe Acrobat. When saving a PDF file, you can specify a password for opening the document. You can also prevent or allow printing, modifications to the document, selection of text and graphics for eventual copying, and changes to notes or form fields.

Checking for Unauthorized Use   Finally, if you are worried that your intellectual property is being stolen, or even if you are just sensibly concerned, try conducting an online search every six months or so. Choose a unique sentence or phrase from one of your lectures and use one of the search engines such as AltaVista, HotBot, or Ask Jeeves to search online. If the phrase pops up, and it looks like it was borrowed from your notes, drop the author of the offending page a warning note.

This technique is also useful for instructors who suspect that the elegantly worded phrases they suddenly encounter in their students' essays may have been borrowed from something the

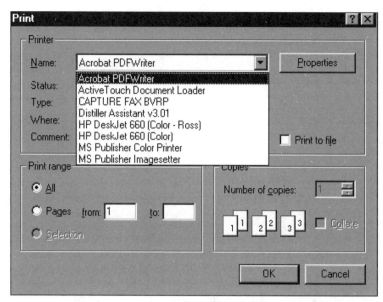

Figure 8.2 The Acrobat PDFWriter appears as one of the printer selection options whenever a user prints a file. At any time, the user can choose to create a PDF file by simply "printing" to the PDFWriter. The software then creates the file.

students discovered online. A quick search will often produce the same phrase, word for word. In such an eventuality, you should keep careful records of both the students' original work and the citations you have found, for later use in any dispute.

Resources

General Information on Copyright and Intellectual Property

Copyright Clearance Center. **http://www.copyright.com/**

One of several online services that will help you find a copyright owner and secure permission to use material.

Copyright Considerations. **http://twist.lib.uiowa.edu/resources/fairuse/index.html**

Sponsored by the University of Iowa, this is a well-thought-out selection of links dealing with various issues of copyright, fair use, and intellectual property.

Distance Learning: Intellectual Property. **http://distancelearn.about.com/education/distancelearn/msubip.htm**

Kristin Hirst's unique compilation of links to sites dealing with various issues of intellectual property.

The UT System Crash Course in Copyright. **http://www.utsystem.edu/ogc/intellectualproperty/cprtindx.htm**

Provided by the University of Texas, this is another well-designed and comprehensible site dealing with copyright and intellectual property. The "crash course" is extremely useful.

Password Protection Software

The following two popular online technological portals offer tutorials, articles, and links to help you understand and implement password protection software. With the search mechanisms on these sites, search for "password protection" to get directly to the information on this subject.

About.com. **http://www.about.com/**

Webmonkey. **http://hotwired.lycos.com/webmonkey/**

III

Teaching in the Online Classroom

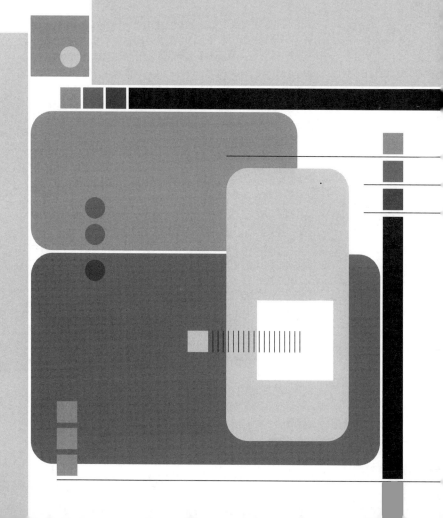

9

Preparing Students
for Online Learning

Learning online can be as exasperating for the student as for
the instructor, particularly for those taking a course for the
first time. Suddenly thrust into a world in which independent or
collaborative learning is heavily stressed, students accustomed
to traditional classroom procedures—taking notes during a lecture, answering the occasional question, attending discussion
sections—must make unexpected and often jolting adjustments
to their study habits.

In addition to these pedagogical concerns, students must
contend with varying web site formats requiring special equipment or software. Indeed, it isn't unusual for students at the
same university to encounter two or sometimes three different
course management software systems during a single semester.
With unsophisticated equipment and busy schedules, perhaps
unsure whether they should communicate by e-mail or by posting queries on discussion boards, students often feel frustrated,
abandoned, or confused.

Students' problems fast become those of the instructor as
well. Instead of teaching their course, posting information, and
responding to legitimate queries on the discussion board,
instructors often find themselves trying to troubleshoot technical queries for which they have minimal expertise. Tussling with
why a student using AOL can't see a given web page, or why
another is unable to install a program on her home computer,
instructors expend too much time and energy providing support and maintenance while struggling to keep up with the normal duties of teaching a course.

This chapter will address these and related issues concerning preparation of students for the online learning environment. The key is to identify and be forewarned about potential problems and to learn some effective methods for handling them.

Problems That Students Typically Encounter

A student logging on to a course web site for the first time has a lot to contend with. To begin with, there's the terminology. Those neat rows of icons, either along the side or across the top or bottom of the screen, meant to guide students to the course material, often bear names, captions, or titles the users have never seen before. For example, a button might say "Course Notes," "My Course," "Course Information," or "Main Page," all of which generally mean the same thing. The icons under which such captions appear may look like an open notepad, an owl reading a book, or a blackboard.

Similarly, an area set aside for students to post information about themselves, including a small digital photograph, might say "Course Information," "Student Home Pages," or "Biographies." Most variable of all is the button or caption leading to the conferencing system. In WebCT, for example, it is called the "Bulletin Board," while in Web Course in a Box it is called "Learning Links." Elsewhere it might be called "Conference Board," "Discussion Area," or "Electronic Message Board." Tests are sometimes called quizzes, sometimes assessments, while the areas where students collaborate on projects may bear names like "Group Pages" and "Student Presentations."

Often these mysteries of nomenclature and icons are just the beginning of the puzzles a student must solve. There are also technical problems and communication difficulties.

Technical Problems

When they begin a course, students may find themselves unable to view the web pages properly, either because the browser they're using is too old or because they haven't installed the necessary plug-ins. An instructor using Microsoft's PowerPoint 2000, for example, may have posted a slide show he has created, complete with sound narration and animations, unaware of the fact that his students can't view it properly unless they're using Microsoft's own browser, Internet Explorer. Another instructor may have assembled a web page with a link to an animation created using Macromedia's animation program, Flash. Unfortunately, for the students to view this page they must install the Shockwave plug-in, an add-on that enables their browsers to "see" the file. Downloading such a file may prove either burdensome or bewildering, or both.

Another common experience is not being able to share word-processed documents. Some students use Microsoft Word, while others may use AppleWorks (known as ClarisWorks in earlier versions) or WordPerfect. Even if students are using the same program, those with earlier releases may not be able to read documents created by classmates or instructors with more current versions.

Problems Related to Learning Style and Online Communication

Far more significant, perhaps, is the variance in learning styles required of those learning online. Students used to instructor-directed learning may feel somewhat lost in an environment that relies heavily on individual initiative and independent learning.

Even though the requirements of the course are clearly outlined in the syllabus and in the class announcements, the effect isn't the same as seeing an instructor glare severely at the class and announce that the essays are due the following week, *without fail.* Assignments are completed at home, often in solitude, and submitted through the click of a button, without that warm feeling students sometimes get when they pass in their blue books or hand their essays over to their teacher in person. Indeed, without the discipline and structure imposed by the requirement of physically sitting in a classroom, students often feel cast adrift.

The complicated mechanisms of human expression—facial expressions, voice intonation, body language, eye contact—are also no longer available. In their place are the contextual and stylistic conventions of the written word, a mode of communication that favors verbal over visual or kinesthetic learners, thus leaving some students curiously unsatisfied. Learning how to modulate their own speech is also a concern for online students. Most of us rely on body language to deflect the impact of what we say; we convey our true intentions through gestures and vocal intonation. The absence of these conventions sometimes causes students real distress.

The asynchronous nature of most online communication adds a further dimension to this problem. We are all used to instant feedback: Susan says something, and Steve responds. Online, Susan may still say something to which Steve responds—but the reply may come a day later. This spasmodic flow of communication takes some adjustment.

None of these problems is beyond the reach of a dedicated instructor. Dealing with them effectively can save both the student and the instructor valuable time, reducing some of the tensions inherent in learning something new. The key is to understand the need to prepare students adequately for what they are about to encounter, and to provide them with the necessary tools to get through the course. These efforts will complement the work you put into designing your course and syllabus.

Preparing Your Students

To address the kinds of problems we've been describing, the most successful online programs offer student orientations as well as continuing technical support and resources. But instructors who are left mostly to their own devices can also find effective ways to meet their students' needs. In the following pages, we suggest approaches for both the individual instructor and the institution as a whole.

Orientation Programs

Ideally, your institution should devise a student orientation program that will take care of major issues such as these:

- Equipment and browser requirements
- A general introduction to the software platform and its major features

- Instructions and links for downloading necessary software plug-ins
- Information about issues that arise in an online class—perhaps in the form of a checklist about what one can expect as an online student

Lists of frequently asked questions (FAQs), referral e-mail addresses, and toll-free numbers for reaching support staff are other useful features often included.

Many institutions or their hosting and delivery partners have created such orientation programs. Most are simply self-paced series of web pages, some interactive and some not. Many incorporate self-assessment surveys that seek to help students identify whether they are suited for online learning. Others test knowledge about computers, the institution's procedures, and so forth. Some orientation programs contain an element of human supervision and feedback, so that students must complete a few tasks in order to "pass" the orientation and be admitted to the classroom (the New School's DIAL program and OnlineLearning.net's orientation for UCLA Extension are examples). These requirements are particularly effective in ensuring that students have the minimum skills, resources, and knowledge for an online course.

Having well-prepared students will mean that you as the instructor can concentrate on teaching rather than on resolving extraneous problems. There's enough for you to do once your online course has begun without having to divert attention to these preparation issues. Effective student orientation is also beneficial to the institution, because it makes a significant difference in the retention rates in online programs. Students who start off with a good orientation are most likely to have a positive experience and to return for further courses.

Preparing Your Own Orientation Program   What if your institution hasn't yet made arrangements for an adequate student orientation? What should you do?

Two methods will resolve your dilemma. First, you can devise a simple orientation of your own, one that will satisfy at least the minimum requirements. Second, as noted in Chapter 4, you can include in your syllabus clear directions for dealing with documents, as well as explicit explanations of how and where you will handle material and activities in the classroom.

Before you begin creating your own orientation, you may want to take a look at some of the information and orientation pages that other institutions and institutional partners have set up. The following offer useful examples:

- SUNY Learning Network's "Getting Started" pages, accessed from **http://sln1.esc.edu/admin/sln/original.nsf**
- OnlineLearning.net's "How Online Learning Works" pages, accessed from **http://www.onlinelearning.net/**
- The University of Central Florida's "Learning On-Line Orientation Course," accessed from **http://reach.ucf.edu/~coursdev/learning/orient/**

Samples from Online Orientations

One typical feature of orientation pages is a list of answers to common questions raised by students who are new to the online environment. For example, to the question "I worry that I'll miss the face-to-face contact of a classroom. Will I be able to communicate with the instructor or other students?" OnlineLearning.net offers this answer:

A lot of people mistakenly assume that they'll feel isolated in an online course. To their surprise, most find that online courses actually provide a high degree of personal contact. Not only will you and your instructor communicate directly, everyone in the class will be involved in many group and individual discussions. Far from being an impediment to communication, the online format facilitates and enhances it in ways that would be impossible in other situations.

Some orientation programs address the issue of basic computer skills. The College of DuPage **(http://www.cod.edu/Online/exper.htm)** provides the following advice:

You should have some experience and familiarity with navigating and using the Internet as an information and communication resource. Knowing how to download files, attach document files to e-mail, [and] use word processing software are necessary skills to achieving academic success in an online course environment. . . . You may find help on using the Internet by visiting Newbie University and reviewing the sections on P.E.G., the Web, and e-mail.

Elements of an Orientation   If you create your own student orientation, there are several elements you should consider including:

1. *General introduction, including your expectations for online students.* A general introduction can be made available to students even before they enroll in your course. Anita Reach of Kansas City (Kansas) Community College developed such a document for the first running of her online class. She kept it casual and simple, calling it "Note to Students Taking Online Classes."

> The decision to take a class online as opposed to an onground class should be carefully considered before enrolling. It is true that online courses allow a student to be free of time and place. Class occurs when the student logs on to the computer at his or her convenience. It doesn't matter if it's 6:00 P.M. in the computing lab, Sunday afternoon at the local library, or 3:00 A.M. at home. The class will be there when the student is ready. That's a wonderful advantage to those with full time jobs, full time families, transportation problems, special needs or interests.
>
> However advantageous online courses appear to be, please consider the following:
>
> Online courses require extreme self-discipline. One must log on and be prepared to read through many pages and comments. It must be done regularly (3–5 times per week). You must plan to spend 4–6 hours per week reading, preparing, and submitting assignments.
>
> A great deal of time is spent visiting web sites, reading articles, dealing with technical problems. Technology is unreliable. The plan to submit homework at the last moment can be defeated with a busy or down server.
>
> Sometimes the cyberdog eats your homework. That is no excuse for not submitting homework. You should always have a copy saved to a disk so you can resubmit. Failure to do so leads to more work.
>
> Most people who have taken online courses will tell you that it is more "labor intensive" than onground courses. It just takes more time. In an online course every student contributes to the discussion.
>
> Online classes tend to be accelerated. That is, material is covered at a faster pace. It would not be uncommon for an online

class to cover in 10 or 12 weeks what an onground class covers in 16. This may not always be the case but it is possible.

If you are not highly motivated, disciplined, and patient, online courses are not the best option. There are other forms of distance education that may be more appropriate for you.

If you are still undecided about whether online courses are for you, please contact me.

Anita Reach, Instructor

As Anita's program evolved, so did the comprehensiveness of the instructions, but the basic principles remained.

2. *Requirements for computer equipment and software (other than the platform being used).* State these as simply as possible. Realize that many people don't actually know the "numbers" for their computers, such as how large the hard drive is. However, they can easily identify their modem speed and the version of their software and browser, so be specific about these; for instance, "Must have Internet Explorer or Netscape 4.0 or higher" or "Should have at least a 28.8-speed modem connection." You can also devise your own "tests" of certain requirements. For example, if students need to be able to access audio in your course, give them a sample to test—either on your own site or elsewhere on the Web.

Many institutions can make a common word processing program available to your students, or they have site licenses for other software. But if your students don't have access to a common program supplied by your institution—and this is usually the case for continuing education students—you will need to stipulate how documents will be shared. You might ask students to save all documents as Rich Text Format (which a majority of students will be able to read) or to use a specific **freeware** or **shareware** program. Or, to avoid the com-

> **freeware** Software available free of charge.
>
> **shareware** Software available for a free trial period, with the stipulation that a fee (usually small) be paid if use continues beyond that period.

patibility problem altogether, you might want students to paste their documents into text boxes provided in your course management software.

Gather information about the software possibilities ahead of time, and let students know whom they can contact for technical support or to obtain software. Include links on the Web where students can download any free programs, such as Adobe Acrobat Reader and Microsoft Net-Meeting, that you intend to use in the classroom. Don't overload new online students with many different references; instead, choose a few carefully evaluated resource links that will meet the students' needs.

3. *Computer skills needed.* Depending on your student audience, you may want to suggest a computer skill set necessary for taking your course. In most cases, this is fairly simple: "Students should know how to cut and paste, how to e-mail and send attachments, how to use a browser, and how to download from the Web." Refer students to web sites for Internet neophytes (such as the ones mentioned in Chapter 1), which can help those who are unsure about their basic skills. Urge them to check their skills *before* entering your classroom. In some cases, you may be able to refer students to on-campus workshops as well.

4. *Introduction to the course management software or other programs you will use to teach the class.* Some course management software companies have already put together a general introduction, student manual, or classroom demo for their software. Whenever possible, refer students to such premade resources. For example, IntraKal and WebCT offer student manuals or guides to the major features of their software (see **http://www.anlon.com/techsupport/** and **http://www.webct.com/v2/guide/**), while Web Course in a Box offers students a sample classroom (see **http://www.madduck.com/index.html**) as well as a student guide.

You may also be able to find examples of software introductions at the sites of other institutions that use the same software your institution does. For example, Illinois Online features a tutorial in WebBoard (**http://illinois.online.uillinois.edu/online/webboardtutorial/starthere.htm**), and George Mason University has a list of sites offering student guides to WebCT (**http://www.irc.gmu.edu/WebCT/ default.asp**).

5. *A first assignment that requires students to demonstrate some familiarity with the software being used.* This might be combined with one of the icebreaking activities described in Chapter 6. Typical of such assignments (depending on the software features available) would be these:

- Write a short self-introduction and post it in the discussion forum.
- Take an orientation quiz using online testing.
- Fill in the template of a basic web page with some biographical data and an optional photo of yourself.

Providing FAQs

Take a good, hard look at your syllabus and ask yourself if anything you're requiring your students to do will require special additional skills or equipment. For example, if you've devised an exercise that entails using the Web to gather information, go through the steps of completing it and jot down whether or not you used a search engine, saved a graphic, or copied the address of a URL. You may think that some of these operations are commonly known, but you'll be surprised to discover how many students don't understand them. If you don't provide some way for students to readily find out, you may spend an inordinate amount of class time filling in the blanks.

One approach is to gather all these possible sticking points into one FAQ file. You can compose it using a word processor, then copy what you've written into Netscape Composer or FrontPage Express and save it as an HTML page, as described in Chapter 7. In this FAQ you should list each procedure your students may encounter and provide a short explanation of what they need to know to complete it. The web convention for composing such FAQ pages is to list all the possible questions at the top of the page and then create a link to each one with a bookmark (in Word or WordPerfect) or an anchor (in HTML), thus permitting your students to find the question they want answered without having to search the entire document.

Creating an FAQ Page in Netscape Composer

Figure 9.1 shows a typical FAQ page created in Netscape Composer, with the questions at the top of the page and the answers below. To allow students to jump directly from a particular question to its answer, you create an anchor (the HTML equivalent of a place marker) next to the sentence or paragraph containing the answer. In other words, instead of linking to another address somewhere on the Internet, you create a link to a spot on the same page.

The process is simple. First you select an answer, defining it as the Target, as shown in Figure 9.2; then you select the original question to specify the Link (Figure 9.3). A nice added touch is to create a backward link to the top of the page so that the student can return quickly to the list of questions.

Introductory Techniques

Your initial postings in the discussion forum, your first messages sent to all by e-mail or listserv, or the greeting you post on your course home page will do much to set the tone and expectations for your course. These "first words" can also provide models of online communication for your students.

Your introductory remarks should reinforce what is contained in your syllabus, your orientation, and other documents students will encounter as they commence their online class. For example, for Richard Rains's online astronomy course at Mission College in California, the opening description posted on the course home page includes the following words:

> The format of the course is totally online, which means that your grade will be determined a little differently from what you're probably used to. You will not only be taking tests and quizzes online, but will be doing research on the Internet, writing reports, communicating with other students, and generally expressing yourself in terms of your increasing comprehension of the Universe. The mechanics of the course, and what you will need to do, are described in detail below.

Online Learning Works

Frequently Asked Questions

What Are the Advantages of Online Learning?
What's the Difference Between Online Learning and Traditional Classrooms?
How Do I Manage My Time When Learning Online?
How Do I Know Online Learning Is for Me?
Where Can I Read More About Distance Education?

What Are the Advantages of Online Learning?

Small class size means one-on-one instructor guidance and personalized communication. First of all, our online courses are just like traditional "on-the-ground" classes. You take your course with a group of other students (maximum class size is rarely more than 20). Your instructor is an experienced professional in his or her field. And, throughout the course, you have ongoing, individual and group dialogues with the instructor and the other students.

What's the Difference Between Online Learning and Traditional Classrooms?

The big difference is that there's no classroom to go to. There's no commute. You'll never have conflicts with family obligations, business travel or vacations. There's no chance of arriving late or missing a class because of illness or lack of child care. You

Figure 9.1 Creating an FAQ Page Using Netscape Composer. This material was composed in a word processor, then copied and pasted into Netscape Composer. Questions, in italics, are listed at the top of the page. Below, the questions appear as headings (again in italics), followed by the answers. (Text adapted from OnlineLearning.net's "How Online Learning Works: Overview," **http://www.onlinelearning.net/**).

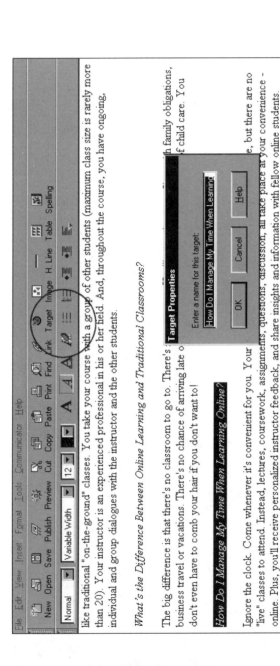

Figure 9.2 Creating an FAQ Page Using Netscape Composer (Continued). To add an anchor, you scroll down the page and find the heading you're looking for. Select it, as shown here, and then click on Target (outlined by a black circle on the menu bar). This will cause the Target Properties dialogue box to pop up, as pictured. The title you have selected will appear as the name of the target. By clicking OK, you will make this heading a *linked* target. See Figure 9.3 for the next step.

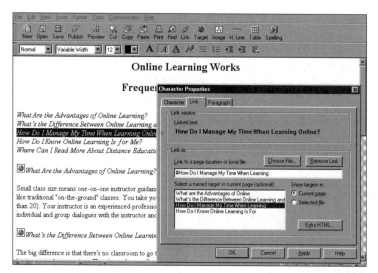

Figure 9.3 Creating an FAQ Page Using Netscape Composer (Continued). To complete the process begun in Figure 9.2, you return to the top of the page and select one of the questions (in this case, "How Do I Manage My Time When Learning Online?"). To connect the question to the anchor you've created on the page, click on the Link tool (on the menu bar, to the left of the Target tool). The Link Character Properties box will appear, as pictured here. Note that all the anchors, including the one you're looking for, appear in the box. By selecting the correct anchor, you will allow your students to go directly to the answer they're seeking, without having to scroll. Note the two anchors already visible on the left of this figure.

Nancy Levenburg opens her course "Marketing Principles and Practices" for UCLA Extension with a posting for all to read. Her subject line is "Hello!"

> Hello!
>
> You have enrolled in a course which will be taught in an online computer learning environment. This will offer some unique opportunities and also some challenges that you should know about as you begin the course.

She goes on to say:

> At first, you may feel that this format is uncomfortable; however,

students typically adjust rapidly to this environment and soon you will probably not feel that this is an inhibitor. There are some differences between classes delivered online and "traditional" face-to-face classes in the way that communication "flows." The following points will help you to anticipate some of the differences, and allow you to have an optimally positive experience in the classroom.

1) Benefits to participating in your online class:

   a) This has been called the "communication environment of the future" and participating in this type of class will help you prepare to communicate effectively in this environment.

   b) Because the course is delivered asynchronously (time- and location-shifts), you choose when and where you want to "attend" class. This means that you can have a full-time job, a full schedule, and other life responsibilities and still pursue new learning.

   c) You will have the opportunity to work with "cutting edge" learning resources, and participating in this course will provide you with access to the most up-to-date information and technologies.

   d) The possibility of re-reading and reviewing key lectures or presentations exists. You will be able to evaluate course material at your own pace and then respond in a thoughtful and constructive manner.

2) Challenges faced by students in online classes:

   a) Students may be asked to perform certain simple operations such as accessing web sites or downloading software from the Internet. However, students will receive instructions and guidance, and will not be put in difficult or awkward situations or "graded down" for a lack of technological expertise or experience.

   b) You will need to participate regularly as part of the overall learning experience; in fact, most students access their e-mail five to seven times each week.

   c) The interaction of an online class is intense and can be intimidating to some students. Your classmates' backgrounds and experiences are varied, and the willingness to share and support each other is much greater in an online class. You will find that you will receive feedback from not only the instructor but also your classmates.

If you have questions about this class, please get in touch with me via either e-mail or telephone. My phone number is listed on the syllabus. I truly believe that you will find the experience interesting and enjoyable once you have adjusted to the differences between your experiences in the "virtual classroom" and those existing in a "traditional" one. Please do not hesitate to ask any questions and/or to make your needs known as the semester progresses.

Sincerely,

Nancy Levenburg

The last thing we would like you to remember is that you must establish a presence and rapport in your classroom that are evident to students as soon as they walk through the classroom door. Even though this would seem to be a matter of instructor preparation, it is an important part of what you can do to foster your students' readiness to begin the learning process. A well-organized course, with signs that you have anticipated the students' problems, plus a welcoming attitude apparent in your first communication, conveys your appreciation of student concerns. Your initial efforts set the tone, and when these are followed by a responsiveness to students throughout the course, they will go a long way toward instilling student confidence in the online learning process.

Resources

Sample Orientation Programs: General

DIAL program, New School University. **http://www.dialnsa. edu/stdsrv5a.htm**

OnlineLearning.net. **http://www.onlinelearning.net/**

Choose the tab for "How Online Learning Works."

SUNY Learning Network. **http://sln1.esc.edu/admin/sln/ original.nsf**

Follow the link for "Getting Started."

University of Central Florida. **http://reach.ucf.edu/~coursdev/ learning/orient/**

Sample Orientation Programs: Specific Software Platforms

George Mason University's WebCT Resource Page. **http://www. irc.gmu.edu/WebCT/default.asp**

Illinois Online's WebBoard Tutorial. **http://illinois.online. uillinois.edu/online/webboardtutorial/starthere.htm**

IntraKal. **http://www.anlon.com/techsupport/**

An instruction manual can be downloaded.

Web Course in a Box. **http://www.madduck.com/index.html**

WebCT Student Guide. **http://www.webct.com/v2/guide/**

10

Classroom Management: General Considerations

Classroom management, as we use the term, includes all the organizational and procedural measures that keep a class moving along. Like any class on the ground, an online class can get out of hand if you don't manage it properly. In this chapter, we'll look at record keeping, class communications and participation, and arrangements for team teaching. Chapter 11 will deal with special issues, such as student behavior problems.

Your classroom software, whether a full-scale course management program or simply a set of web pages and discussion boards, will have an impact on your classroom management alternatives. We urge you again, therefore, to become familiar with your software in advance, so that you can exploit its capabilities and compensate for its shortcomings.

Record Keeping and File Management

Teaching online can be a nightmare for record keeping. By the end of a course, there may be thousands of postings and e-mails from students. Where and how will you save this information? How will you organize it?

Begin by finding out what the rules are for the server on which your course is housed. Will material be left on the server after the course is over, or archived in a way accessible to you? Even if you're lucky enough to have such an arrangement, it's a good idea to prepare a system for saving material on your own computer. Moreover, if you intend to save any discussion

materials, it's important to do so at intervals during the course
rather than trying to sort through them all at the end.

Tips for Record Keeping

Here are some suggestions for setting up your record-keeping
system:

1. When you compose major pieces of information, do so first
   in your word processing program rather than directly in
   your online classroom. If you are writing online and your
   connection is interrupted, you may lose all or part of your
   material. Also, if you start out in your word processing program—and save your work there—you will already have created an instant "archive" of your material.

2. On your computer's hard drive or on a **Zip disk,** create a
   series of folders
   that parallel the   **Zip disk** A portable hard disk that allows
   divisions of your   you to store and retrieve files.
   course. For exam-
   ple, if your course is organized by week, create a folder on
   your computer for each week and then subfolders for "Discussion," "Lecture," "Exercises," and whatever other components you may have.

3. Create folders for student work on your computer and make
   sure that you've set up folders for student assignments in
   your e-mail program. If possible, don't leave students'
   assignments in your e-mail program only, but download
   and store them along with the other classroom folders.
   Some instructors like to house all Assignment #1 papers
   from students in the same folder, while others keep all
   assignments from an individual student in a sort of portfolio
   set aside for him or her alone.

   You may also find it useful to take notes on the contributions of individual students while you read postings in the
   discussion forum, particularly in a large or active class. This
   can be done with simple paper and pen, in your word processing program, or even by copying and pasting represen-
   tative snippets of a student's postings into a folder for that
   student. Any measures that help you build up a profile of

individual students will assist you in following their progress and evaluating their work.

4. Make sure that all student e-mail is sorted automatically or manually as it arrives at your e-mail address. One of the greatest organizational perils is e-mail from students that becomes commingled with e-mail from other sources. This results in misplaced assignments and late responses to communications.

   If you're working from a business account or a personal e-mail account, you may want to consider establishing a separate e-mail address for your class communications. There are many free e-mail services available on the Web. However, be certain to ask whether the service includes the ability to send and receive attachments, because you will need that option.

5. As noted in Chapter 4, make sure you specify how students should use the subject line in e-mail communications with you. For example, you may want to specify that the subject line consist of *student's first name + last initial + number of assignment.* Gently remind class members if there are lapses (and there will be) during the progress of the course.

   Extend this system to students' attachments as well: Make sure that students put their name and assignment number in the body of the attached text itself. Often, attachments are downloaded and saved separately from the e-mails that delivered them. In this case, if students remember to affix their names and assignment numbers, you will be able to print out assignments, if you wish, without having to guess who authored each paper!

   Relabel assignments and e-mails if necessary before saving them to folders. Keeping the nomenclature uniform will enable you to sort quickly through your students' contributions. This is a valuable time saver.

Electronic Files Versus Hard Copy

In contemplating the multitude of online activities and student assignments, you may be wondering how much you need to read online and how much you should download and print out.

This is really a personal choice. However, don't feel somehow less "cyber-expert" if you want to print out and read most assignments or even some discussion offline. It can be very hard on the eyes to read a great deal online. Some instructors print out and read *all* assignments offline, preferring to make their notes in the paper margins while on the train, at the coffee shop, or lying in bed. Others read the papers offline but make their notes in word-processed documents, which they then copy and paste into their e-mailed correspondence with their students.

The same issues apply to record keeping. If you want to keep paper records as well as electronic ones, that's fine. In any case, always keep a backup copy—either on disk or on paper—of your gradebook and any other important class records. You may want to have a paper chart that you use while online, to tick off credits for student participation as you read. This may save you the time and bother of having to toggle back and forth between the classroom and your word processing program. You may also want to keep a paper journal of events in your class.

You may have to experiment to find out which system works best for you. The factors to balance here are flexibility, economy of time, security of records, and the health issues related to total time spent online.

Managing Communications

Not surprisingly, many online classroom management issues involve communication—between you and your students, and among the students themselves. Designing an effective communication system and monitoring it are key steps in teaching online.

Creating a Uniform Announcement Area

You need some area within your course where students know they can receive the latest updates and corrections. If you cannot easily update a web page area linked to the course's home page, consider using a mailing list to e-mail students your updates. If you have a discussion board, you can also choose that as your venue: Let students know from the first day of class that, each time they log in, they should check a particular area for the latest announcements.

It's a good habit to make regular announcements on a weekly or biweekly basis—to keep students on task, even if there are no special changes or updates to announce. Simply give an overview of the week ahead or of upcoming due dates for assignments and exams.

Here are a few examples of the types of information that might appear in announcements:

1. Reminding students about upcoming due dates and stages of the course:

   > As we start week 5, all of you should now have chosen your topics for the final essay. It's a good idea to start outlining your ideas now for the rough draft that will be due at the end of week 6.

2. Offering a preview or overview of the week's activities to reinforce the students' attention to tasks:

   > This week we will be focusing on the romantic poets. Be sure to visit at least one or two of the recommended web sites for additional background information before taking part in the discussion about the readings.

3. Taking stock of progress and encouraging students:

   > We are now entering the seventh week of the course. I am pleased that so many of you are participating in the weekly discussion forums and that the quality of those conversations is so evident. Nearly all of you have turned in your journal entries for week 6. You can expect to receive your grades and comments from me during the next week. Feel free to e-mail me if you have any questions about how I determined your grade.

4. Noting problems in computer access:

   > Our server experienced a shutdown this morning from 8:00 A.M. to 9:00 A.M. EST. If you tried to access the classroom at that time, you would have received an error message.

5. Updating, clarifying, or changing the syllabus or schedule:

> Please note the following change in the reading for this week: pages 10–25 in White (not 110–125 as recorded on the syllabus). Quiz #2 will be postponed until after the holidays—therefore, it has not yet been posted. Also, there will be no on-campus meeting this week, due to the holidays. However, I will be holding live online chats throughout this week, by prior e-mail appointment only. Student groups who hoped to meet on campus are encouraged to use the live chat as well.

6. Reminding students about special events or introducing speakers:

> This week we are fortunate to have as our guest Dr. Basstone. I have posted Dr. Basstone's lecture in Unit Three. He will be available on Tuesday and Thursday of this week only to answer your questions in Discussion Forum Three.

Setting Rules for E-Mail

One key to handling the e-mail problem—the potential deluge of e-mail you may receive—is to divert individual e-mail, as much as possible, into the common classroom space. This prevents your having to make the same response over and over again, and it also has the positive effect of promoting students' consciousness of the online classroom as a shared space, not simply an assemblage of web pages. If you make your presence felt primarily in the online classroom and only secondarily in the private e-mail realm, your students will look for you in that public space. When you receive an e-mailed question or comment that isn't really private in nature, praise the student and encourage her or him by requesting that the student post the item in the classroom—or offer to do so yourself.

Joan Morris, an associate professor of sociology at the University of Central Florida, in her web page "Scaling Up Class Size in Web Courses" (**http://pegasus.cc.ucf.edu/~jmorris/resources/ScalingUp2.html**), suggests developing a protocol for asking questions in large classes. For example, she suggests that you can encourage students to pose a question first to their discussion group before e-mailing you about it. Another recommendation from her web page is that you establish a forum for the purpose of asking questions about the class; after posting a question in the forum, students would be expected to wait twenty-four hours for an adequate answer before separately e-mailing you with the question.

These modes of behavior will not evolve among students on their own—you must set the rules and procedures early in your course and carefully consider how to structure the channels of communication.

Encouraging Participation and Managing Your Workload

Most instructors would like to promote as much interaction as possible in an online class—not only between instructor and students, but student to student as well. Instructors who run large, lecture hall, on-campus courses with an online component would perhaps like to use the online environment not only to replace some of the lecture time, but also to give students additional opportunities for discussion, presentation of projects to their classmates, and other forms of participation that are difficult to manage in a large classroom meeting. In Chapter 6, we discussed the variety of activities you can set in motion to engage students. Here we want to take a look at how you can promote participation in these activities. At the same time, we will examine how the choice and design of activities may affect your workload.

Two factors determine the level and quality of participation and interaction in a class—your design and student dynamics. The second part of this formula, student dynamics, is really no different online than in the on-campus classroom or discussion seminar. Students will bring their own expectations and work habits to your online classroom. To some degree, you will be able to shape and influence their behavior, but in other respects it's the luck of the draw. Experienced instructors can fairly quickly identify the core group of students who are active participants (perhaps including obnoxious students as well as the most delightful), and these can be enlisted to get the classroom dynamics moving. Here, though, the factor of course design comes into play as well: Instructors need to design the course so that other students are drawn into the orbit of the core group and begin to participate, even if in different ways and to a lesser degree. The trick is to get enough of the reluctant or shy students to be active in the classroom, at least occasionally, to make the class more diverse and interesting for all.

The Effect of Class Size

The way you use classroom design and organization to promote student participation will probably depend on the class size. As in the handling of e-mail, your own workload can become an important factor in your decisions. Let's look at the issues involved in an online classroom or online component for classes of various sizes.

Classes of 10 to 30 Students   If you have a class of only 10 students, your major problem will be how to encourage participation and student-to-student interaction. Given that, in a class of 10, perhaps only 3 to 5 students will have a tendency to be very active, while the others will be nearly inactive or only moderately active, that group of 3 to 5 may become discouraged, fatigued, or bored if it spends most of the course carrying the load for the entire class. While you can give each of your students more individual attention than in a larger class, you presumably would like to avoid having the course become a de facto independent study class. So you have a real incentive to encourage student-to-student participation.

With a class of 20, you may have several active coteries of students, and if even half of the students are active in discussions, they can potentially generate hundreds of messages for you to read—not to mention homework or exercises. You need to achieve a balance of energy between relating to students as individuals and relating to groups of students. This means not only getting students to talk to one another, but also apportioning your assignments and activities so that at least a few are group efforts or involve peer contributions.

In a class of 30, your potential problems are your workload and the risk that students will disappear into the corners of cyberspace. In a class of 30 on the ground, you can see the rows of students and generally keep track of them visually. Online, you really do have to remember the names and check your records and notes to keep track of all of them. At this level, group work and presentations become a necessary part of your course design. You'll want to create smaller groups for the purposes of at least some discussion topics and projects. This arrangement will give shy students a more comfortable environment for airing their views and asking questions. It will also allow students to form social connections with other students and build up a sense of camaraderie. In any class of more than 20 students, you will probably also want to use some type of self-assessment or an automatic assessment vehicle such as online testing.

Classes of 40 to 100 Students (or More)   Beyond 30 or so students, you will find it difficult to operate without the assistance of a TA. In our comments we will assume the addition of teaching assistants or else an arrangement for team teaching with other instructors.

In a class of 40 or more students, even with a TA, you must interact more with groups of students than with individuals. In such classes, if possible, you should use online testing with automatic grading for at least one-third to one-half of your assessments, and you should have students working in groups and making presentations to the entire class.

In such a large class, discussion forums can be established for groups of 10 to 15 students. You and your TA can then observe the groups, noting the interaction and responding when necessary. You can think of this as the party-host model. You and your colleague circulate among the various groups of guests, joining in on conversations at times and making sure there are no wallflowers sitting by themselves.

In order for students to benefit from ideas and questions that arise in groups other than their own, you should set up dual levels of the classroom—one for the entire class and the other for the group level of organization. Establish a forum where students can ask general questions about the course; this will prevent your having to answer these questions in each group. But also establish discussion areas where student representatives from each group can address the topics of discussion with the entire class.

The Debate About Class Size

Most instructors are aware that class sizes of totally online courses have become an issue on many campuses. Often overlooked in this discussion are the basic assumptions about the instructor's role in the online classroom, the nature of the course, and the design considerations that are appropriate for the course.

Some suggest that the real discussion should focus on what is happening in on-campus courses. In other words, is the lecture hall of 300 students, followed by the once-a-week small discussion section, a model that we want to continue? It's certainly one of the most economical arrangements as long as you have the physical plant to support it. It has proved effective for many students, though for others it generates only apathy and poor results.

We will state one point quite emphatically here:

Important! *You can't have a high level of individual student-instructor interaction in an online class of 40 or more students.*

One instructor should not be asked to handle such a class alone unless the course is designed to be merely lecture with automatic assessment and mainly student-to-student interaction. Some institutions have applied the same rules to online courses as to their on-campus versions—for example, one TA for every 20 to 25 students if a class exceeds 40 students.

Applying such equations is generally a good start. However, the cut-off point for the "average" class served by one instructor should be lower for a completely online class than for an on-campus version. From the experience of those who have taught in both formats, it appears that one instructor in an on-campus class can comfortably handle a class of 30 to 50 by herself, whereas the equivalent online is closer to 15 to 30 students, with the latter number dependent on the level of instructor-student interaction desired in the class.

Some instructors who have taught online would put the number even lower—say, 15 to 20 students for one instructor. Although this estimate may come from a heartfelt reaction based on their experience, it cannot necessarily be applied to all cases. Our observation is that many who teach online automatically fall into a pattern of very intense instructor-generated activity and a great deal of one-on-one interaction. In fact,

(cont.)

the workload issue is usually the number one complaint of first-time online instructors, whether they have 15 students or 25.

The very seductiveness of the online environment, with its seemingly endless avenues of communication, can cause an instructor to become far more interactive online than he or she would be in a regular on-campus class. Student expectations also play a role here: Online students tend to be more demanding and to need more affirmation and attention than their on-campus counterparts. Further, the fact that one can see and review one's interactions with students may make an instructor acutely self-conscious and eager to respond more often and more elaborately than in an on-campus class.

While this high level of instructor responsiveness may be a desirable thing in itself, it may not be practical for some programs to have classes small enough to make it feasible. Programs should ideally base such decisions on the type of course. For example, if the course involves many assignments that must be manually graded and requires lots of one-on-one supervision and criticism, 15 to 20 students is a realistic number. But many courses that seem ideal at 15 could be redesigned to comfortably fit 20, albeit with some loss in the instructor's interaction with individual students.

For example, in week 3, if students are discussing the chapter reading assigned on the French Revolution, you might have students meet first in their groups to discuss and summarize the main ideas of the chapter on Robespierre or to reach some conclusions about the dominant causes of the Revolution. You would set a time limit for these group discussions to conclude. Then you would post the same discussion question or assignment in the discussion forum for the entire class, asking the student spokespersons for the various groups to exchange and discuss their groups' ideas.

When there are individual assignments for a large class, you can choose examples that typify the responses and the problems encountered, then post these anonymously (without the student's name attached) for all students to view. In this way you can create a lesson by means of your comments. This method works best for courses with much factual or objective material—

computer science, math, and so forth. For courses that involve more subjective responses, you can spotlight those you think are full or good responses. Some instructors do this by creating presentation pages, while others use the discussion forum areas for this purpose. To comment on problems the students may be encountering, you can derive principles and illustrations from the poorer student work without actually posting individual examples.

Finding a Balance Between Student-Centered and Instructor-Centered Activities

No matter what the class size, most students appreciate a balance between student-centered activities and those that focus on the instructor. In other words, they want the instructor to contribute something unique, something they can't "get from the book," but they also respond well to an environment that asks them to be active participants in their own learning.

In a class of 15, you might wish to do away with the formal lecture mode and simply provide a segmented lecture as described in Chapter 3: a running commentary of short paragraphs that offers the initial material—the thread topics—on which students can base their discussion. But in a larger class, you will want to provide a more structured presentation of instructor-generated materials. Students would quickly lose their way if they had to find the tidbits of lecture material hidden among hundreds of discussion topics or anecdotal comments.

Your ideal mix of instructor-generated and student-based activity depends on the number of students; the length of the course (for instance, whether there is enough time for several projects and how long students will have to get organized for group efforts); the number of TAs you have (if any); and any matters related to the level or type of course you teach. We recommend that you include some calculations for your ideal mix in the planning stage for your course.

Some General Guidelines for Student Participation

One of the most effective ways to promote student participation in an online class is to make it required and graded. As explained in Chapter 4, this should be clearly stated in your syllabus, and the criteria must be defined.

Participation online ranges from "attendance"—defined as logging on and (presumably) reading in the online classroom—to actually posting messages in discussion forums and taking part in small group activities. It is not possible to gauge pure attendance unless you have tracking features in your software that monitor the opening of files or time spent in a particular portion of the classroom. These tracking capabilities, as we said in Chapter 5, can help give you a clearer picture of a student's activities, but they are generally not sufficient for assessment purposes. For example, they may tell you that a student opened up a particular document and kept it open for a period of time, but not whether the student actually read the document. So it's best to think of the information you gain from these features, if you're lucky enough to have them, as merely a small piece in the puzzle.

To be an effective goad to activity, participation grades for a completely online class should constitute somewhere between 10 and 40 percent of the student's overall grade. If you include a separate category for contribution to small group activities, you might end up with 50 percent of the grade in the "participation" category. For an online component in a face-to-face course, we recommend that at least 10 percent of the total grade for the course be reserved for online participation.

You may want to establish criteria for both quantity and quality of participation. For instance, one-third of the participation grade might be based on the student's meeting a minimum quantity level (say, posting a comment or question in the discussion forum once a week), with the remaining two-thirds based on the quality of participation. Or, if your course involves lots of teamwork, you might divide the participation grade between individual accomplishments and contributions to the group.

Depending on your course objectives, presentations—either group or individual—may be an essential part of student participation. You might define participation to mean completing all weekly classroom exercises, taking part in discussions, *and* presenting a project to the class. The use of presentations—either group or individual—fosters interaction among students, but it is most effective if you emphasize that student comments and questions about their classmates' presentations are counted in participation grades or are separately graded.

Important! *However you choose to define "participation," make sure that the greater part of the grade depends on what the student does in the shared classroom, not simply on the completion of assignments submitted to you alone.*

So think about how you can structure opportunities for student-to-student interaction—it's not something that will necessarily happen without your deliberate effort.

Tips for Fostering Asynchronous Discussion

In Chapter 5, we discussed the impact that a particular discussion software structure may have on the way you organize your discussions. However, no matter how your software may be organized, there are techniques you can use to foster greater participation and clarity among your students.

1. *Start the major topic threads yourself.* It's a good idea for the instructor to start all major topic threads. If you wish to (and your software permits), you can allow students to contribute additional threads as they feel the need. This arrangement should be considered with great care, however, because students often tend to create new topics without real necessity, and your discussion area may soon be overwhelmed with too many threads on duplicate topics.

2. *Narrow down topics.* A good discussion needs pruning and shaping. An overly broad topic thread—say, "The French Revolution: What Do You Think of It?"—will often result in very fragmented discussion. This is especially true in an introductory class, in which most students know little about the subject. If you divide up broad topics into logical subtopics—say, "Economic Conditions on the Eve of the Revolution" or "The Execution of the Royal Family"—you can prevent the discussion from going off in too many directions. In an introductory class, you may want to provide even more guidance. For example, a discussion based on

specific readings in the textbook, on a focused web site visit, or on assigned exercises, coupled with your guideline questions, will likely be more productive of a fruitful discussion than simply pointing students to the forum and expecting them to find their own direction.

A short series of closely related questions can allow students to jump in on any one of the points and still find themselves "on topic." In our example of the French Revolution, a topic thread might contain several questions about the economic conditions: "What were the land-holding patterns? How important was foreign trade? Had the average well-being of the citizens improved or worsened in the years leading up to the Revolution?"

However, Tisha Bender, who was a trainer for SUNY Learning Network and the New School's DIAL program and who has been an online instructor for many years, reminds us that a factual question for which there is only one answer (such as "When was the Battle of Waterloo?") can't be expected to generate a discussion. She suggests that the best discussions arise from questions that may not have only one answer. She also points out that instructors can set guidelines so that students know they can go against the prevailing opinion as long as they can substantiate their views.

The shaping of discussions takes some genuine forethought. You might think of this task as similar to creating chapters in a book or long article you are writing. Threads will stay of manageable length if you keep topics specific and allow a place such as a lounge or question-and-answer forum for off-topic conversations.

Sometimes, of course, a thread goes off on a digression that is so valuable and interesting in itself that you don't want to curb it. The pruning and organization of threads is for the purpose of sustaining discussion, not stifling it. Allow students to digress, but if you think that the new direction in the conversation calls for an entirely new thread, you might create one or suggest that a student begin a new topic message to explore the subject further.

3. *Organize forums and threads to reflect the class chronology or sequence.* The organization of discussion forums should

complement the class structure but also provide some reminders of the course chronology and sequence. For example, if forums are the outer level of your discussion structure, creating one for each week or unit of the course helps students know at a glance where they should be looking for that week's activity. Even if you don't have an outer forum structure, you can designate all the threads for a particular week under the rubric "Week 1" or "Unit I."

If you have a general forum area for ongoing questions about the course, you might want to divide this up by week so that students can more easily find questions that pertain to a particular week's activities.

4. *Key the thread topics to appropriate activities.* Keying thread topics to the assignments, readings, projects, and exercises for a particular week will help keep students on topic in their discussions and also provide an obvious place to discuss anything that occurs in the course during that week.

5. *Establish a pattern of frequent response.* Students tend to follow instructor expectations for online participation, and these expectations are communicated not only by the declarations of the syllabus but also by the instructor's behavior. During the first week or so, if your class size allows (this would be in a class of no more than 30 students), greet all students individually in the classroom as they arrive and engage as many as possible in discussion. Then make an effort to respond to a diverse group of students each week—not just to the same one or two individuals. If you have a large class, you will find yourself rotating your time among all the small groups, as well as tending to any all-class forums.

Rather than engaging in long, concentrated visits to your classroom, it is best to establish a pattern of short but frequent activity. When students see you "poke your head into" the classroom (that is, see your postings), it makes them feel that you are truly present and actively responding to the class. In contrast, when students see that an instructor only rarely engages with them, they are discouraged from posing questions and comments aimed even indirectly at the instructor, and they may also conclude that the instructor will be unaware of what is going on in the classroom.

Think in terms of three to five short periods of logging on each week, rather than the one or two sessions you may be used to in your on-campus courses. If you have only four hours to devote to the classroom in one week, spend an hour for each of four days in the classroom, rather than two hours twice a week. This will allow you to keep up with the flow of student discussions and will also reinforce the impression that you are responsive and on the scene.

If you are teaching a primarily on-campus course that meets once a week and also has an online component, you will have to decide how important student discussion online will be in your class. If you really want students to make use of this venue, then you, too, must actively attend to it. The discussion forum is a great place for you to continue conversations you started in class or for the TA to extend the weekly discussion section. Initiate topics on a weekly basis and require some weekly participation from students in the online forum. This is also the best place to update the class on changes and errors, to pose and answer questions, and to help students review material. Again, unless you are actively "showing the flag" in this area, students will quickly learn that they can ignore it with impunity.

6. *Facilitate and build on participation.* Don't try to respond to every posting in the classroom. Even in a class of 20, this will quickly overwhelm you. Also, you want to encourage students to interact with each other, not only with you. So make comments that address a whole train of thought—responding, for example, to five or six related messages in the thread rather than to each of the five individually. In this way you will do your part to encourage participation as well as interaction among students.

Think about jumping in or tending to the conversational fires at critical junctures, working as a facilitator to help move the discussion forward and keep the fire going. Tisha Bender remarks that your experience in the on-campus classroom should provide some cues for you online as well: "Base your behavior on what you normally would do in a classroom discussion. Make your point where you would normally feel it's appropriate to do so."

Don't merely post friendly expressions of affirmation. You should also contribute comments that summarize what students have posted, as well as follow-up questions that stimulate further discussion. In some cases, it might be appropriate to invite students' responses to their class-mates' ideas: "Anyone else want to comment on Tom's observation?" "Did anyone reach a different conclusion about this issue?"

If a class is fairly quiet, it may seem that it's a good idea to jump in and reply as soon as someone finally posts some-thing. The truth is, instructors feel uncomfortable when nobody's talking. But Tisha Bender reminds us that "it's not only about your own comfort level." Sometimes, particularly in the beginning when the group dynamic is just becoming established, "you need to hold back and let it happen rather than pouncing on a single response."

There are also times when there will be a lull in conversa-tions because students are working on a major assignment. Some instructors may even schedule a "quiet time," such as a few days during which students are encouraged to devote most of their time to a project.

7. *Be aware of cultural patterns as well as differences in per-sonal styles in discussion.* If you have a classroom that includes students from another country, be alert and request information from informants (rather than making assumptions) about the best way to ask questions. For example, a group of students from China or Taiwan may not respond very well to questions and topics that call for volunteered responses. In this case, a question like "Anyone want to comment on this?" is better altered to "Please post your response to this question by Wednesday afternoon."

Be aware, too, that not all students respond well to the same approaches to discussion. For example, some stu-dents respond poorly to a question that asks them to share personal experiences, while others are not at all shy about divulging information about their background and prefer-ences. We think it's important to respect these differences and not make students feel boxed in by the way you frame a question. A way around this problem can be to split the question in such a way as to offer an alternative: "Can you relate this to your own experience or one you have heard or read about?"

Tips for Establishing Effective Synchronous Communication

The most common form of synchronous communication available to instructors is text-based chat. Voice-enhanced and video-enhanced chat are becoming more widely available, but at this point they aren't often used in online classroom situations.

You should carefully consider any requirement that students participate in chat as a graded assignment. When students live on campus, chat arrangements are not a difficult problem, but if your group includes working adults or students from other time zones, chat can be a real impediment to their full participation in the class. In such cases, you will have to be very flexible about scheduling times for chat. As mentioned in Chapter 3, it is best to offer some variety in the choice of times. If possible, too, you should copy the chat to post asynchronously for the benefit of those who cannot attend. If you are supervising group work, request that groups post their chat transcripts in a group asynchronous area or e-mail it to all the group's members and to you.

Here are some further tips for organizing an instructor-led chat with more than one student:

1. Try to limit group chats to four or five participants.

2. If you must have a group of more than five students, establish a system for granting turns to speak. If your chat software includes a crowd-control function (the equivalent of raising hands to be recognized), then you should definitely make use of it. If your software doesn't have such a built-in system, you can design one: for instance, a question mark, asterisk, or some other sign that, when typed, will appear next to the student's name, allowing you to recognize him or her to speak.

3. Allow some time at either the beginning or the end of the chat for students to ask off-topic questions and to socialize.

Chat: Benefits Versus Drawbacks

Let's be honest about the shortcomings of chat communication. Chat is often productive of disjointed or widely digressing conversations, sloppy or impressionistic responses, bad spelling, poor grammar, and flippant attitudes.

The lines of communication are often out of sync. While you're typing your response, the others may already have moved on to other questions. An instructor-led chat with more than five people quickly becomes difficult to follow. In fact, real-time chat is probably the most exhausting, intensive activity an online instructor will ever encounter. Your attention must be attuned to rapid-fire comments and questions from several students; you must respond quickly, and, if your typing ability isn't the best, you may struggle to keep up with more nimble-fingered students.

Given all these shortcomings, why use chat at all? And when is it most appropriate or effective? Here are some answers:

1. One use of chat is to provide reinforcement and immediate feedback for students. When there are no face-to-face meetings in the course, chat can provide a forum for such communication.

2. Virtual office hours and personal consultation can be provided by chat. It can serve in lieu of an e-mail or phone conversation, or provide clarification for communications by those methods. For example, you may have a student who writes cryptic e-mails with key information missing. You may be able to clarify his questions via a real-time chat. If a whiteboard feature is available as well, you might be able to assist a student with a problem that requires more hands-on demonstration. You might also want to schedule individual chats with students for the purpose of asking follow-up questions about their work.

3. The social aspect of chat may be one of the most important uses. Students may appreciate the opportunity to use chat among themselves without its being an official class activity. It can help students form bonds with others in the class. Whole-class or group chats may add to the sense of cohesion among group members. Some students miss the spontaneous interaction common to on-campus classes, and chat may provide a suitable outlet for humorous exchanges, social chatter, and team-building conversations.

4. Chat may be used in conjunction with asynchronous group areas for group project meetings and discussions. Typical reasons for holding a chat are brainstorming and finalizing unresolved issues.

(cont.)

5. Chat may be used to bring in a guest speaker. This is best done in conjunction with an assigned paper or lecture by the guest, and it may follow the guest's participation in an asynchronous discussion for a period of a few days. This technique is most effective when you adequately prepare students for the guest chat. You should time the chat to coordinate with associated activities and give students an interval to formulate questions they can pose to the guest.

Announce this before the chat or at the opening of the session. Budget an extra two minutes as well, just for greetings and goodbyes.

4. Limit each session to approximately forty-five minutes and announce the time limit before the chat. A forty-five-minute period allows for the social niceties that smooth the way, as well as some spontaneity, but also provides a substantial period of time during which all can focus on the preannounced topics.

5. Prepare students for the chat by posting the topics or agenda, assigning readings or activities, or giving them questions to consider before the chat. Ask them to keep these questions or notes at their side while chatting. Have ready your own notes or outline so that you can keep track of all the items on the agenda. In some chat software, students entering late can't read anything that was said before their entrance. In such cases, strongly emphasize in advance that students should appear on time. You won't have time to keep recapitulating the "plot."

6. Whenever possible, preface your response with the name of the student to whom you are replying, or include bits of the question or comment to which you are responding. Using student names is particularly effective when you answer two students in one reply.

> Joe, I think reading the book before seeing the film would be best. No, Elsa, Exercise 1 is not due the day after tomorrow.

Including bits of the question also helps pinpoint the object of your response. This is often necessary when several comments have been made in rapid succession.

Joe, book before film is best, but, as Linda reminds us, there are some films that are merely loose adaptations of books.

7. Remember that students can't hear you thinking or typing. They are often impatient in chat, trying to keep alert and anticipating your answers. So, in a fast-paced chat with more than one or two students, break up any long responses into two or three parts. This will let students know you're actually formulating a reply, not ignoring what they've said:

First response: Joe, book before film is best, but,

Second response: as Linda reminds us, there are some films that are merely loose adaptations of books, while

Third response: at the same time it is true that some books are created after the fact, to capitalize on interest in a movie.

This technique can also help you set the pace of the chat. Students automatically slow down, knowing that you're still sending your response. A similar slowdown tactic is to type just the student's name with a comma and send that, and then send the rest of the message in your next segment. As students see "Joe," they will await the remaining phrase, "book before film is best."

8. Have a backup plan in place, in the event that you or some of the students lose the Internet connection. For example, note all participants as they come in, so that you can e-mail everyone in the event of a break in your own connection. If you have twenty-four-hour technical support, make sure the phone number is available, in case students who are cut off cannot access their e-mail.

Team Teaching Online

Team teaching, whether online or on the ground, presents some unique challenges as well as opportunities. Students can derive the benefit of the multiple perspectives and teaching styles brought by two instructors, while instructors may appreciate the intellectual stimulation of the collaboration as well as the prospect of sharing some of their duties and workload. However, instructors who have experience with team teaching know that being half of a two-member team doesn't necessarily mean doing only half the work. Moreover, the difficulties involved in coordination can be legion.

Important! *Team teaching online requires even more advance planning than its on-the-ground counterpart.*

Even though you and your colleague aren't together in a physical classroom setting, you are very much occupying the same online classroom space, and you can easily trip over each other there as well! Once teaching begins, differences in teaching style and approaches will invariably appear, so it's best to discuss your pedagogical approach as well as practical procedures before the course begins.

Avoid team-teaching a course with fewer than fifteen students. Tisha Bender notes that, in her experience, the presence of two instructors can easily overwhelm a small group of students, dampening all participation, while a larger class can really appreciate the added instructor attention.

There are three basic models you can adopt in team teaching: shared responsibility, division of labor, and primary-secondary. Let's look at each of them in turn.

The Shared Responsibility Model

In the shared responsibility model, both instructors do everything; that is, each of you shares the responsibility for all activities in the class. Online, this means that both of you read and respond to all discussions and assignments. Students will know which instructor is which in the discussion forum, because your name will appear next to your comments.

Assignments can be graded by consensus (very time consuming if you're communicating with each other only online) or by averaging. However, unless you have an online gradebook, one of you will have to take charge of notifying students of grades and passing along the corresponding comments by e-mail. If you wish, you can sign both names to the grade and add comments.

One risk in this form of team teaching is that students may not know whom to address with a particular question. Students may also become confused by the two instructors' different teaching styles and approaches. No matter how much we instructors like to imagine that we have a student-centered classroom and an antiauthoritarian style, students do tend to adjust themselves to the prevailing classroom mode that we set.

This model of team teaching also presents some of the same problems encountered by two parents. You want to be two individuals, offering different opinions, but you don't want to contradict or undermine each other. You must also avoid being played off, one against the other, by students.

A further risk of this model is that neither one of the instructors may have the course firmly in focus. Areas of the course can become relatively neglected if no one takes responsibility for them. Finally, this model can be exhausting for instructors because not only are they responsible for teaching the entire class, but they also must spend additional time coordinating with the other member of the team.

Nevertheless, in some situations you may decide that the shared responsibility model is the best approach for you. If so, here are some tips on making this "everything" model work:

1. Ask students to send any e-mailed queries to both instructors.

2. Each instructor must assiduously read all discussion threads in the class. If one instructor has more comments than the other on a particular topic, that's fine, but the other should make at least a few responses to the same topic.

3. In your syllabus or introductory messages, clearly state the procedures for students to contact you and to submit assignments.

4. For grading and evaluating student work and participation, work out a procedure that you can easily follow. If you're meeting with your co-teacher online, you'll need a way to smoothly exchange any e-mailed assignments and to maintain record keeping as well.

The Division of Labor Model

The division of labor model involves just what the name suggests: The two instructors divide their responsibilities according to a prearranged plan. Like the shared responsibility model, division of labor also requires a great deal of planning and coordination, but it is generally easier to implement.

The division of labor may be arranged by weeks (Joe for week 1, Mary for week 2); by topics (which may overlap with weeks); by types of class activities (Mary handles the research project, and Joe supervises all group reports); or by a combination of these factors (Joe takes on the research project and weeks 2, 4, and 6 of the discussion, while Mary handles all individual presentations and weeks 1, 3, and 5 of the discussion). You may also want to have some activities handled separately by each of the two instructors, while other activities are a joint effort.

The biggest risk in this model is that one instructor may lose track of the classroom while the other instructor is taking his or her turn. Here are some tips for making the division of labor model most effective and least frustrating:

1. Make sure each instructor contributes something to the overall effort. This contribution should start with the selection of texts and planning of class activities.

2. Decide how you wish to divide up the classroom responsibilities, and state the arrangement in your syllabus so that students know who has the primary responsibility for any particular activity.

3. Make sure that your introductions during the first week of class, or your comments during the first topic of discussion, are carried out jointly with your co-teacher.

4. Ask students to **cc** the other instructor on any queries sent to one instructor. This will ensure that each instructor is kept "in the loop."

> **cc** An e-mail function that allows you to send copies of a message to one or more people other than the main recipient; the term, borrowed from old-fashioned business usage, was originally an abbreviation for *carbon copy*.

5. Even if you divide up the discussion responsibilities by week, make sure that the instructor not assigned to that duty in a particular week reads through the discussion. The "off-duty" instructor might want to make a comment as well, and he or she can best do so after the other instructor and the students have had their say.

6. Divide up grading of assignments as evenly as possible but in alternating cycles so that neither instructor loses track of students. In other words, Joe grades assignments 1 and 3, while Mary does 2 and 4. Each instructor should cc the other on any e-mailed evaluation comments to a student. Each instructor should have copies of all grades and comments. If there is no central gradebook online, the two instructors need to keep identical records. This may mean that, after each grading turn is taken, the instructor who did the grading e-mails a list of grades to the other.

The Primary-Secondary Model

In the primary-secondary model, one instructor assumes the primary or dominant role in managing the class. This approach is necessary when one instructor cannot participate in the class to the same extent as the other, yet is still making an active contribution. For example, one instructor may have less Internet access or more workload issues than the other, or one instructor may feel less expert in certain areas of course content.

Tips for making the primary-secondary model work include the following:

1. Make sure that each person is fully aware of the responsibilities he or she has agreed to take on. Work this out by going over the week-by-week activities of the course.

2. Try to balance the workload to each person's satisfaction. If one instructor cannot participate online as much as the other, for instance, let him or her take on more of the record-keeping duties or slightly more of the grading of assignments.

3. Clearly indicate to students the respective responsibilities for each instructor, but ask students to cc each instructor on any e-mail correspondence sent to the other.

4. If one instructor does not have as much uninterrupted web access as the other (this would be particularly true for partners who have no home access), set up a system so that the partner with good access does the posting. For example, if you need to post a message but lack ready access to the web page or discussion forum, you can e-mail the material to your partner, who can then post it for you. In this case, your name, as the instructor who wrote the actual message, should be typed at the top of the message itself (because the posting will automatically bear the name of the person who puts it online). Students need to be reminded about this practice to avoid confusion about the two instructors' contributions.

Resources

Keeping Online Asynchronous Discussions on Topic. **http://www.aln.org/alnweb/journal/Vol3_issue2/beaudin.htm**

This article by Bart Beaudin, from Journal of Asynchronous Learning Networks *3, no. 2 (November 1999), presents results of research into techniques used by instructors in managing asynchronous online discussion.*

Keeping the Thread: Adapting Conversational Practice to Help Distance Students and Instructors Manage Discussions in an Asynchronous Learning Network. **http://www.ed.psu.edu/acsde/deos/deosnews/deosnews9_2.asp**

In this 1999 article from DEOSNEWS *9, no. 2, Donald J. Winiecki compares the patterns of face-to-face and online asynchronous conversations and suggests some strategies for more effective communication.*

Scaling Up Class Size in Web Courses. **http://pegasus.cc.ucf.edu/~jmorris/resources/ScalingUp2.html**

Joan Morris from the University of Central Florida offers strategies for handling workload in online courses.

Classroom Management: Special Issues

In addition to the issues discussed in Chapter 10, several other issues may arise in conjunction with managing your online classroom. Some, such as student behavior problems, aren't unlike those that may occur in an on-the-ground classroom, except that the online environment may introduce further complications. Other issues, such as privacy concerns and the difficulty of confirming student identity, are unique to the online environment.

Privacy Issues

It's hard to argue that anything on the Web is truly private: Computers automatically make records, students may share their passwords, and so on. Password access to classrooms and discussion forums brings us some measure of privacy, but short of encryption and identification by eyeball, voice, or fingerprint, it is hard to ensure complete privacy or security. Perhaps, however, we can speak of "more or less private."

Beyond the security measures afforded by our software and hardware, there are other things we can do to protect privacy. For example, we must be careful about distributing student work, discussion transcripts, and e-mail outside the classroom without permission. It's surprising how many otherwise discreet and caring instructors will think nothing of posting student materials on an open web site for the entire world to access without permission or even notification.

Important! **What is said in the classroom is originally said in a defined context. Those later reading these words outside the classroom may not understand that context.**

Similar privacy concerns affect your own contributions. You can expect that students will copy and download your words for the purpose of learning. Do give some thought to what you wish to disclose about your private life and opinions in the classroom discussion. If you're concerned about students distributing your material, then make sure you state up front that words and materials are for class use only, not for distribution.

We recommend that instructors teaching completely online classes never give out their home phone numbers to students unless absolutely forced to by the program. If your institution requires some phone "office" hours each week, use either your campus phone or your work phone. It is also sometimes possible to work out an arrangement by which students who want to contact you by phone call your department, which relays the request to you via phone or e-mail. You can then return the student's call.

Most issues can be resolved in the online classroom or by private e-mail. This has the advantage of giving you a record of the communication with the student. It also means that the student has to think a bit about his or her question and perhaps has a greater opportunity to reflect on your answer as well.

Identity Issues

How do you know the real identity of the person you encounter online? The truth is, sometimes you don't. If students are registered with the university, we can assume with some degree of certainty that they are indeed the people they say they are. Presumably, they had to show an ID at some point in time. Yet in the continuing education classroom—and especially for students who live far away from campus—this authentication may not occur. Generally speaking, institutions are more concerned about identity confirmation when a student is enrolled in a state certification or degree program. In those cases, students may be required to take at least one live, proctored exam or to prove their identity when applying for and exiting the program.

In terms of our daily interactions with students online, we cannot always detect gender, ethnicity, age, and other characteristics that are often more easily detectable in a live classroom. This type of identity might be thought of as *social* identity. Some institutions may give you a roster with more than name and ID number and address, while at others you will have access to computer databases holding extensive information, but most instructors are unlikely to have ready access to more than the most limited details about students.

Although there may be clues—for example, a name that sounds Italian or references to foods and customs belonging to a particular culture—these are all merely guesses unless the student confirms our conjectures. Approximate age is sometimes easier to detect but also prone to error. Are those references to television shows of the fifties or music of the sixties the product of first-hand experience or a love of retro fashions?

We are particularly prone to mistakes about female students, because their surnames are often not those they grew up with, but instead represent new identities taken on through marriage. Immigrants may also take on new names that they think are appropriate to their new country. Students with names such as Pat, Dale, Sasha, Kim, and Ming may be male or female. Or your student's name may be in a language so unfamiliar to you that you have no way of knowing whether the syllables signify a particular gender.

You may ask for voluntary submission of photos, but even photos, short of the student's official ID photo, can be less than revealing of the truth. Is that your student in a photo taken ten years ago, or is that your student's handsome friend?

There's no point in trying to stop ourselves from imagining our students (and them from imagining us); our minds can't help trying to categorize. But be alert to the possibility that you may be dead wrong about the identity of your students. Avoid making statements and assumptions that aren't based on information actually provided by the student. The best policy is to allow students to self-identify.

Unless you think fraud may be involved (for example, one person masquerading as another to take a test or complete an assignment), we would advise you not to worry too much about such identity issues. Just keep an open mind and watch for clues.

Managing Student Behavior Online

In the online asynchronous discussion forum, listserv, or chat room, the range of student types remains pretty much the same as in the on-the-ground classroom. There are the quiet ones, the nurturers, the take-charge types, the class clowns, the disruptive ones, and the imaginative procrastinators. There are a few aspects of the online environment, however, that create new opportunities for the "usual suspects" to manifest their trademark styles.

Noisy Students

A noisy student in an online classroom, much like his or her traditional counterpart, spends much energy raising issues that are only tangentially related to the topics under discussion. One way this occurs online is that the student will begin new topic threads even when the comments he or she has to contribute actually fit in with preexisting threads. Such students often avoid replying to anything but the instructor's comments. And when they do join in the discussion, they generally ignore the direction of the conversation and simply pepper the thread with inane comments.

This type of student is actually easier to handle online, in asynchronous discussion, than in the regular classroom. There is more space and time in an online classroom for such students to perform without seriously affecting others. When they start a new thread on what is already an ongoing topic, most other students will simply ignore this detour in favor of continuing the more active and peopled conversation. In the interest of housekeeping and to prevent the area from overblooming with threads, you may want to drop this individual an e-mail note. Ask him or her to please reply to an existing thread if the aim is to participate in a conversation rather than to break out a true new topic. Treat the problem as a technical one. Remind the student of the difference between replying to a subject and starting a new one. Many students are actually confused by the differences in software response methods.

When the student peppers the existing conversation with inane comments, this isn't really as disruptive an influence as it would be in an on-the-ground setting. Classmates will read this student's inane comments but simply not respond to them and move on to the next message in the thread. Other than the moment required to read the inane comment, nothing is really lost. The noisy student hasn't forestalled the comments of others because the clock isn't ticking away in the asynchronous classroom, and no "air time" has been consumed.

A good way to deal with the noisy student is to give him or her some personal attention in the form of a personal e-mail. Sometimes a noisy student is just feeling a bit lost and anonymous, and wants some individual attention. Suggest that the student share some of his or her ideas with others in a lounge forum. In the public discussion area, acknowledge the student, but then steer him or her back on track: "What you say about X is interesting, Joe, but how would you respond to Ian's comment about Y?" or "This is an interesting point. We may be able to take this up later in week 5."

In the synchronous chat room, a noisy student can take up precious "real time," so setting rules and procedures for chat will make a major difference. Some forms of chat software will actually allow you to eject a student who isn't following the rules. While that is an extreme measure, it may be necessary if the noisy student crosses over the line to become disruptive. Other software permits you to call on students, supplying the equivalent of the raised hand. However, even if you don't have such software, simply requiring students to type an asterisk, exclamation mark, or question mark to be recognized before speaking will have the same regulating effect. The noisy student will have to wait his or her turn along with everyone else.

There are ways to deal effectively with the noisy student. Be gentle and remember that the noisy student may prove to be your salvation when the classroom discussion hits the doldrums and you desperately need someone to respond to your prodding!

Quiet Students

Quiet students can present even more of a problem online than in the traditional classroom situation, because you can't see them nodding their heads in assent or shaking their heads in disagreement. If the quiet student doesn't post anything, you can't readily tell if he or she is even in the room, occupying a virtual seat.

Two strategies can come into play here:

1. If tracking is available through your software, you can follow the quiet students to see if they are present, how often, and what they are reading.

2. By requiring a minimum level of participation by posting, you can probably coax a few contributions out of them.

You can also use private e-mail to gently urge quiet students back into the classroom discussion space. Send a message saying that you've noticed that the student has been accessing the classroom but not actually posting and that you wonder if he or she is having any technical problems. Or say that you wonder how the course is going for the student—does he or she have any special questions about procedures?

Often you can find a way to bring the student into the classroom discussion by virtue of his or her special talents or background—information you've gleaned from the biographical introduction. Sharon Packer, a psychiatrist who has taught online courses in psychology and religion for the New School's DIAL program, suggests that asking questions in the introduction phase, such as "What do you want to get out of this class?" (rather than the usual "Why are you taking this class?"), often elicits information that the instructor can later use to motivate students to participate. For example, in a comparative religion class, if Joe has mentioned that he lived half his life in Japan, you might address a question to him directly during the discussion of popular religious practices: "Joe, is there anything you can recall from your experience in Japan that relates to this type of folk practice?"

Also, once the student has completed an individual assignment, see if there is something worthy of note in it that you might ask him or her to share with the class. If the quiet student happens to send you an e-mail or reply to an inquiry of yours, grasp that opportunity to say that his or her presence is missed in the classroom. Emphasize that a good question is as valuable for discussion purposes as a brilliant comment, and that he or she should feel free to contribute in a casual tone to the conversation. Some quiet students are really just overly self-conscious about writing and posting their thoughts, imagining that anything seemingly "published" to the world in this manner ought to be perfectly expressed and articulated.

Disruptive Students

The disruptive student will attempt to take over your class by commandeering the discussion and questioning the major thrust of your course or some essential aspect of it in the public forum. He or she may answer questions addressed to you, contradict you, and in some cases become abusive. This is one of the worst situations an instructor has to face online. Few students will stage such behavior face to face, but more feel emboldened to do so online. The situation is considerably worsened by the fact that the comments will sit there for days, to be read by all.

At the extreme, when a student uses foul language or is abusive or threatening, you should immediately notify your administrator. Copy and save all posted or e-mailed communications with that individual. Although you may be moved to delete (or ask your administrator to delete) outright four-letter words and the like, knowing how to handle comments that don't sink to that level may be more difficult.

Some instructors post their own classroom codes of conduct at the beginning of the class to help set boundaries for students. Sharon Packer, whose classes concern the psychology of religion, history of psychiatry, and approaches to dreams, is particularly sensitive to discussions that might elicit personal or controversial topics. She recommends that instructors keep objective criteria in mind when formulating a code of conduct. These criteria often must be keyed directly to the type of course being taught. For example, in her courses she will include such guidelines as "There will be no discussion of personal use of illegal drugs" and "This isn't the place to discuss personal psychiatric history." She also urges that students maintain a cordial atmosphere and use tact in expressing differences of opinion.

Many instructors provide a link to, or an excerpt from, the text of their institution's honor code and emphasize that the code applies in the online classroom as well. Often, such codes are not specifically related to online education situations and may not be sufficient to provide all necessary guidance for your students. Nonetheless, in terms of issues such as plagiarism, cheating, and so forth, these may provide useful material.

Dealing with Disruptive Students

In dealing with disruptive students in particular, it's important to achieve a balance between asserting your authority in the classroom and overreacting to a student provocation. However, you must act quickly to prevent disruptive students from escalating tensions in the classroom, and you must take the lead in informing your department if students go over the line.

Following are some examples of different types of disruptive behavior and instructor responses, based on real situations we've observed or heard described. Please note that these are composite examples, not actual case histories.

Example 1: The Know-It-All   Midway through a course, one of the students, Joe, who had some real-world experience in the subject, began to answer questions that were addressed to the instructor in the asynchronous forum. At first this seemed fine, because Joe was contributing some good tips to the student questioners. The instructor simply acknowledged Joe's comments and then added her own remarks.

At some point, however, Joe began contradicting the instructor's information. Joe even offered his own web site information and suggested that students use it as their guide. The instructor checked her facts. She wasn't wrong, so she simply reaffirmed the information to the other students (and, by implication, to Joe as well) without responding directly to Joe's contradictory message. Her message was polite and generous, beginning with:

> Although there may be some disagreement by scholars in the field on the details, the general principle I enunciated remains sound and is the one I would like you to use in this course.

Joe wasn't directly mentioned, and he was able to save face; yet the instructor reasserted the primacy of her authority and refocused students on the objectives of the course.

Example 2: The Mutineer   The instructor's approach to the subject matter wasn't interesting to one of her students, Jerry. Jerry was a bright student and knew quite a bit about the subject. Therefore, he had already formed his own ideas about the way to approach it.

Jerry began to sound somewhat critical and condescending toward the instructor in the class discussions. But his first direct attack came in response to the instructor's comments on Jerry's public presentation. The instructor's comments were dry and very brief. Jerry commented in the classroom forum to the effect that the instructor had "not given me any constructive comments at all." Note that, at this point, the instructor had not responded in turn.

A few days later, in a private e-mail to the instructor, Jerry blasted the instructor's teaching methods and complained about the poor quality of the class. The instructor got angry, but instead of answering Jerry's more abusive private e-mail, she posted a public reply to his less strident public note:

> I believe I have given you constructive comments, and I don't appreciate your tone here or the way you expressed yourself in your recent e-mail.

This set Jerry off, and he began to post angry messages in the classroom, trying to enlist students to his way of thinking:

> I'm sure a lot of you feel the same way I do—this course is a gigantic waste of my time and money. I think we should ask the department for our money back.

A few students actually posted affirmative replies, such as these:

> I agree—am not satisfied with Professor X's responses.

> I feel that I was misled by the way this course was advertised.

Professor X was well on her way to losing control of this classroom. Jerry's original public posting about not getting constructive comments was sharp and somewhat rude but hadn't yet overstepped the bounds of decency. In responding publicly, the instructor would have been better advised to hold her criticism in check, merely noting the sharpness of Jerry's public message by implication.

> Jerry, I have been rather brief due to the constraints of time, and perhaps you did not get the full import of my comments. Any time students feel they need more feedback, I hope they will let me know via private e-mail. I will send you a private e-mail within a day or so that I hope will provide you with the additional details you have requested.

This response by Professor X would have had the effect of noting Jerry's complaint while ignoring the hostility behind it and addressing what she as a teacher could do to respond to the student's needs. She would also have succeeded in moving the conversation to the private sphere.

As for Jerry's private e-mail, she should have responded to it privately and firmly.

> Jerry, I'm glad that you have expressed these thoughts with me via private e-mail. I'm sorry that you don't find my approach one that is helpful to your study of the subject. Because it is too late to withdraw from the class, I suggest that you do the best you can with the material and activities. You have many good ideas, and I welcome your airing of alternative approaches in the classroom, as long as this is done in an objective manner and in the appropriate forums.

The subtext here is this:

> I did not appreciate the personal comment you made in the classroom; you should have withdrawn from the course when you could, but I will not penalize you for your opinions even though I do expect you to follow my syllabus. I appreciate that you are bright, and I will give you some opportunity to display your knowledge, but don't make any more personal comments in the classroom.

Note that, even if an instructor doesn't normally express herself in a formal manner in the classroom, this is a situation that calls for a certain degree of formality. Formality in online forums signifies seriousness, clarity, and firmness to students. It is particularly effective when it contrasts with an otherwise casual instructor tone.

Example 3: The Belligerent Student Who Hasn't Kept Up   Andy barely participated during the first part of Professor B's course, but he seemed suddenly to reappear, apparently angry that he was finding it hard to catch up with the class. He posted angry messages in the public classroom:

> What's this supposed to be about?
>
> I don't get it. What's the point of this assignment?

that reflected his very real frustration arising from his lack of understanding of what was going on in the class.

In a case like this, Professor B should ignore the emotion in Andy's comments in the classroom forum. The professor should post objective, concrete suggestions in reply:

> This concerns Lesson 5. You might find pages 10–25 the most useful.
>
> Andy, as I mentioned in my previous lecture, this assignment asks you to focus your attention on Problem 2. See the guidelines for Assignment #1 in the syllabus. All students: If you have any specific questions on this assignment, please feel free to post your questions here.

Professor B needs to back this up by e-mailing this student and being supportive, while still calling him to account.

> Andy, I have noted your expressions of frustration in the classroom and have responded. Since you were somewhat late getting started in the class, you may need to go back and review Lessons 1 and 2 and the guidelines. If you need further help, just e-mail me and I will try to assist you.

The subtext of this is:

> I can see that you're frustrated, and that may be due to the fact that you didn't keep up with the work. I think you can do it—go back and try again. Read the relevant material, read the guidelines. You aren't the only one who may have questions. If you really don't understand after making a decent effort, I'm here to help.

Example 4: The Belligerent Student on the Attack Professor Y teaches an online course in contemporary American politics, in which students are encouraged to explore their assumptions about American political parties and hot topics of the day. Professor Y does have a code for students to follow in expressing their opinions; however, she likes to keep the classroom as open and free as possible.

During a particularly heated argument about school vouchers, Tom attacks another student, Linda, saying, "You're a right-wing bigot!" Professor Y cannot track the readership of individual messages, but she assumes that many students have read this one, because it has been posted for two days and the record shows that many students have logged on during that time.

She carefully copies and saves a record of the online exchange. She then posts a response, without naming Tom:

> I would like to remind everyone to base your arguments on the issues. Please observe the code of conduct posted for this class, which asks students to refrain from personal attacks and labeling of other students.

At the same time, she writes a private e-mail to Tom:

> Tom, perhaps this was not your intent, but your remark to Linda seemed inappropriate and insulting. I hope you will apologize by private e-mail to her and then delete your comment.

But then Tom attacks Professor Y in the classroom forum:

> Who are you, the pope?! We should be able to say whatever we want to say.

At this point, Professor Y telephones an urgent request that her department head deal with this student and, if necessary, officially remove him from the class. She follows up with an e-mail that makes the same request but also includes a copy of all the online and e-mail communications. She sends a brief private e-mail to Tom, letting him know that she has referred his case to the department and warning him to refrain from any more personal comments; she forwards this to the department as well. She continues to monitor the situation and all classroom communications carefully until the matter is resolved.

There are a few particular things to note about this situation:

- Professor Y felt that she had to post a public response, but she wanted to avoid targeting Tom in public, so she posted a general reminder to all in the class about the code of behavior expected. She e-mailed Tom privately to give him an opportunity to make things right. If Professor Y had simply responded to Tom in the classroom forum with an equally personal remark, the situation would have rapidly degenerated.

- Even though Professor Y had the power to delete Tom's note, she felt it was better to ask Tom to delete it himself and apologize to his classmates.

- When Tom escalated the situation by posting a direct attack on her, Professor Y decided to let the department handle the matter. As a last resort, she was prepared to delete any more comments by Tom.

- Professor Y needed to back up her story and protect herself by forwarding a copy of the communications to the department. Otherwise, the department head might not have reacted quickly enough.

At this time, few institutions have sufficient guidelines in place for student conduct online, and even fewer have administrators who have first-hand familiarity with online classroom management. Although you should keep your department or other relevant institutional authorities in the loop whenever special issues arise—and protect yourself by keeping scrupulous records—you may find that you, as an online instructor, are often out there on your own. You must be proactive and quick-witted when dicey situations arise.

Other Behavior Problems

In addition to students who are unusually noisy, quiet, or disruptive, there are other behavior problems that may create problems in the online classroom. We'll comment on a few of them here.

The Controller   Sharon Packer notes that a student who e-mails you before the class begins, to request all assignments in advance, may not be the conscientious eager beaver you assume, but one who actually wants to control the class. By getting a head start on everyone else, this student can be the first to post responses to the discussion questions. Perhaps this student will post in such extensive detail that the entire discussion is squashed. Or perhaps this student wants to seem in control of the material because he or she actually lacks sufficient background for the class.

Naturally, there are students who request assignments in advance for valid reasons. Maybe they will be traveling during the first week of class, or they may have a disability that could slow their assimilation of the reading material. Some students just want to see the reading list to find out what they're getting into before committing to the class. These valid concerns can be discovered by simply asking the student his or her reasons for requesting all assignments in advance.

The Staller   Packer also suggests that students who delay logging on to the class (barring actual technical problems) may be unmotivated or stalling. These students may not want to become part of the group process and may fail to create bonds with others in the class. Some students of this sort simply like to work alone, and they may eventually access the class, absorb the material, and do all the necessary work; many more, however, are likely never to finish the course.

Another possibility is that such students are deeply insecure about their abilities or intimidated by the unfamiliar online environment, even when they've gone through an orientation. The strangeness of the online environment can make those who are normally competent and professional in their chosen fields fearful that they will look foolish or somehow lose control. An e-mail reminder to such students, to encourage their participation, can sometimes be the personal touch needed to bring them into the classroom. Technical problems are a wonderful face-saver: Even if they aren't the real issue, asking a student whether he or she has delayed logging on because of technical problems may elicit the actual reasons or at least cause the student to realize that he or she shouldn't delay any longer.

If you can use your tracking features and observation to keep track of student progress in the classroom, you may be able to intervene to encourage students who delay or stall. It's also important to keep a record of student "attendance"—how often and when the student was in the classroom—because being able to document a student's participation may be necessary in the event that a student challenges you about a grade. If attendance reports aren't available from your software, you should keep a manual record. Unfortunately, a small percentage of students imagine that they can more easily get away with a lack of participation in an online course than in a traditional classroom.

The "Must-Have-an-A" Student   Although the student who tells you early in the course that she or he "has to get an A in this course" is a familiar phenomenon, these students may be particularly drawn to distance learning and online courses. Some find it easier to assume a pose of invincibility and grandeur when they know they won't meet you in person; this type of adult student may even claim honors and credentials he or she doesn't really possess. Some students may simply find it easier to harass you about their grades by e-mail than they would by coming to your office.

In any case, those words, "have to get an A in this course," should definitely raise your antennae. Meet such declarations with firm, objective statements about your grading criteria and standards, combined with a mild rebuff:

> Thank you for your note. It is good to see that students are motivated, but there can be no guarantees that any particular student will receive an A in this class. This online course is a challenging one, no less rigorous than its on-campus version. See my grading criteria listed below. Students will receive further instructions about the requirements for assignments as the course proceeds.

Keep every scrap of correspondence with this student and be cautious in your e-mail to him or her. Be aware that this student will likely keep a record of everything you say.

A Final Word

The foregoing examples are offered to help you recognize and deal with potential problems. Naturally, each student presents a unique profile and must be responded to as an individual. Avoid jumping to conclusions, and don't hesitate to rely on those gut feelings derived from long experience in the traditional classroom to help you sort out one situation from another.

When in doubt, err on the side of softening your language in e-mails and postings. A "might" or "perhaps" in your advisory or disciplinary message can often provide the face-saving gesture needed to defuse a tense situation.

12

Integrating Online Elements in a Traditional Classroom

Although we've discussed "hybrid" classes throughout the book—classes that combine online and face-to-face activities—this chapter focuses specifically on them. How can you best integrate online elements into a traditional course you're teaching? What factors should you think about? Are there any pitfalls to avoid? To answer such questions, we'll try to offer helpful tips for integrating online tools in a variety of ways.

Many instructors who teach in traditional classrooms already have web sites of their own. Typically, such web sites contain a course syllabus, a schedule of required readings and assignments, a listing of the course office hours, and some hyperlinks to relevant web sites in the instructor's particular subject area. They may also include a link to a discussion board on which the instructor has posted the answers to a miscellaneous group of questions relating to the due dates for specific assignments or tests, problems with homework, and general concerns about the administration of the class. Most students visit the web site a few times during the term, usually at the beginning of the course and before the midterm and the final exam. Use of the web site is generally optional.

To us, the fact that students seldom look at the web site suggests that the instructor isn't using it to maximum advantage. If asked to provide a reason why their web sites are so lightly utilized, instructors will often cite their students' lack of reliable access to the Web. They may also say that, because of their own workload burdens, they don't want to spend more time creating web material. They may even express the fear that, if they use the Web more extensively, their students will no longer have a reason to come to class. In other words, instructors are asking why they should work more for the same pay, doing something that perhaps threatens their livelihood.

The ultimate answers to this question are beyond the purview of this book. Academic senates, institutional administrators, and union representatives must work them out. But we don't believe that using the Web effectively requires you to labor twice as long for the same pay. We do think that it can improve the way you teach your traditional course. To that end, this chapter will provide some practical suggestions.

Posting Lectures Online

The matter of online lectures is probably the biggest bugaboo teachers face when considering whether to use the Web. Why should students bother to come to class if they can simply read the lectures online?

Most lectures consist of a body of core material, factual or introductory in nature, followed by a discussion of more complex issues, proofs, or processes. The core material constitutes the meat and potatoes of the lecture. It's usually this material that students are expected to know. The other material serves as side dishes, which help differentiate the A students from the B's and C's. If the core material were posted online, enriched by graphics and charts (perhaps with a few links to other relevant material available online), students would be relieved of the chore of reproducing this material word for word in their notes. That would allow them to concentrate on the finer points of the lecture. In other words, posting the lectures online frees the students to concentrate on what is being said.

Yet that argument still begs the question: Why should most students bother to come to class?

The answer may have something to do with learning styles. Some students learn better by listening and taking notes. Others do better by reading rather than by listening to lectures, and a third group seems to benefit by doing specific assignments based on the material covered. In that sense, posting lecture notes online helps some, but not all, students.

But the answer goes deeper still. It involves the basic approach to lecturing.

A Revised Approach to Lecturing

Admittedly, an instructor who posts lecture notes *and* reads them aloud in class may be in danger of putting students to sleep. But if the lecturer alters what he or she does in class, relying on the fact that the material is freely available online, then the experience of attending class may have a different meaning.

Say that the assignment for the week is to read the core notes posted online, along with whatever textual material supports it. In that case, instead of spending the first twenty minutes or so reviewing the core or introductory material, the instructor can concentrate on a particularly knotty issue or complex concept, examining it, elucidating it, debating it in class. Those students who have read the material beforehand will gain a deeper insight into the concept. (Of course, those who have *not* read the material will have considerable difficulty following what's going on. One hopes they will get the message and come to the next session better prepared.)

Online lectures offer other advantages as well. For the instructor, posting lectures can be an aid in reevaluating older and possibly out-of-date course materials, improving organization, coherence, and comprehension. For the students, having the core portion of the lecture online provides an opportunity to review the material in its original form (rather than via their scribbled notes) or to catch up on material they may have missed because of illness or absence.

Important! *The point here is that using the Web to post lectures is neither a panacea nor a threat. It depends entirely on how effectively the web-based material is integrated into the class.*

How to Post Your Lectures Online

Posting your lecture notes online does add to your initial workload, particularly if you've never prepared them this way before. But once you've done it, you'll find it comparatively easy to update your notes the next time you teach the course. There are two basic steps:

1. *Convert your lecture notes to a web format.* If you've already written out your notes using your word processor, you can save your file as an HTML file, as explained in Chapter 7. Figure 12.1 indicates the simplicity of this process. Alternatively, if you've installed a copy of Adobe Acrobat, you can "print" your documents to the Acrobat printer, thereby creating a PDF (Portable Document Format) file, as shown in Figure 8.2 on page 191. A PDF file can be read using Acrobat Reader, which can be downloaded free from the Adobe web site.

2. *Preview the appearance.* Once you've saved your file as an HTML file, look at it by opening it in a browser. If it contains a few extra spaces between lines, edit it in an HTML editor such as Netscape Composer, as explained in Chapter 7.

You can post an outline of your lecture notes using the same technique.

An alternative method, which you might choose if you have a specially formatted web page template you like to use, is to highlight the contents of your word-processed file, choose the Copy command, and then paste the material into an HTML editor.

When you're dealing with a substantial amount of text, we don't recommend that you type directly into an HTML editor. If you do, save your work as both an HTML file and a plain text file so that, in the future, you'll be able to edit it in a word processor.

Once you have your lecture notes saved in a format appropriate for the Web, they can easily be posted on your web site, as explained in Chapter 7. If you customarily accompany your lectures with slides, you may want to post those as well; see the guidelines in Chapters 3 and 7.

Using a Discussion Board

Most classes, particularly smaller, seminar-style classes, involve discussions of some sort. Ordinarily, students prepare for the discussions through readings. In some graduate classes, students prepare "position" papers, which are then circulated to other students for their consideration before coming to class.

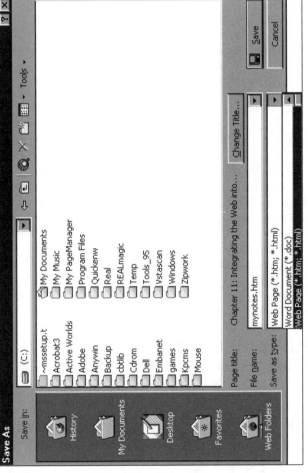

Figure 12.1 Saving Your Notes as an HTML File. When you save your lecture notes using Microsoft Word, you can choose to save them as an HTML file by selecting that option in the "Save as type" field. Be sure to preview the file in a browser to make sure that Word hasn't inserted any extra lines between sentences (a minor bug); you can delete superfluous lines using an HTML editor such as Netscape Composer.

Using the Web in conjunction with the work done in class can enhance any of these techniques. Take the case of the seminar. In order to present the topic properly, the instructor will generally introduce it with either a short lecture or an impromptu talk. The students will then offer initial reactions to the discussion topic, setting the stage for the eventual discussion. A half-hour or so may have elapsed before the discussion is really joined.

An alternative approach is to have the students post their initial reactions to a discussion topic online and read the postings on each topic before coming to class. Although this would require more work from the students, it would not increase the instructor's workload except insofar as he or she had to read the work posted to the web site. What it would require of the students is perhaps a more carefully considered appreciation of the discussion topic and a greater awareness of where they stand in relation to other students in the seminar. Presumably this would make for a livelier and more informed discussion, and it would elicit remarks from all the members of the class, rather than merely the most vocal.

A discussion board can be of use in large, lecture-style classes as well. For most students, "attending" such a class means finding a seat somewhere in an auditorium, staring at the back of someone's head, and listening to the instructor intone the lecture from a stage. Discussion in such a setting is usually fairly haphazard. The instructor pauses to solicit input from the assembled students. The more intrepid dare to raise their hands, while the rest sit quietly in the darkness.

Contrary to common wisdom, the Web can humanize such a class and permit students far more interaction with their colleagues and instructors than might otherwise be possible. An instructor can divide up the class into groups of twenty or so, depending on the number of TAs or assistants available. Students using the discussion board will thus have a work group composed of class members whom they might not ordinarily get to know, a considerable advantage in schools where a majority of students don't live on campus, or in large universities where most students know only their dormmates.

Instructors and students can use these virtual study groups for a number of purposes. Students can post and discuss questions related to the material covered in class. Or, having delivered a lecture in class, an instructor might post a follow-up question, requiring the students to formulate an appropriate response as part of their grade. These responses might then become the basis of a future class discussion or lecture. They might also serve as an archived resource for students reviewing the material.

An instructor can monitor the comments posted in the discussion groups and use them as the basis of a frequently-asked-questions (FAQ) page containing general answers to the students' more noteworthy queries and concerns. This will save the instructor the extra time of having to respond to the same question over and over again, either via e-mail or via one-to-one advising sessions. Finally, the discussion group postings can provide the instructor with valuable insight into how effectively the material in lectures has been conveyed.

Using Online Testing Tools

Another tool that can provide valuable assistance is the ability to construct self-grading quizzes online. Most course management systems contain this feature. They permit you to construct a quiz consisting of true/false statements, multiple-choice questions, one-word answers, multiple answers, matching answers, ordered answers, or short or long essay questions.

The last of these types—short or long essays—must be graded individually by you or your TA, but all the other types can be graded automatically. As we mentioned in Chapter 5, students taking the tests can receive immediate feedback. This feedback can consist of a simple "correct" or "incorrect" message, or a statement explaining in detail why the student got the answer right or wrong. Questions can include embedded graphics. They can even include sound or video files you've made, or links to such files that you found elsewhere on the Web. Figures 12.2 through 12.5 illustrate some of the steps involved in creating a quiz using Blackboard CourseInfo.

As with the preparation of lecture notes, creating quizzes can be time consuming at first and then save you a great deal of

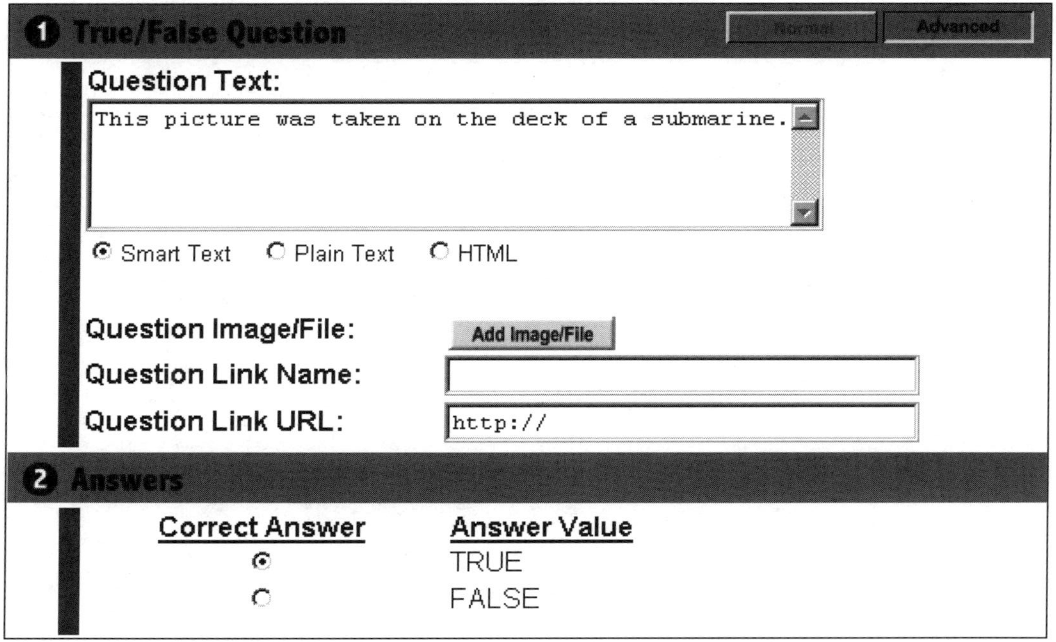

Figure 12.2 Preparing a Quiz Using Blackboard CourseInfo. In this instance, the instructor has chosen to create a true/false question. The text for the question is typed into the message box. By clicking on the Add Image/File button, the instructor can add an image or a sound or video file stored locally on his or her hard drive.

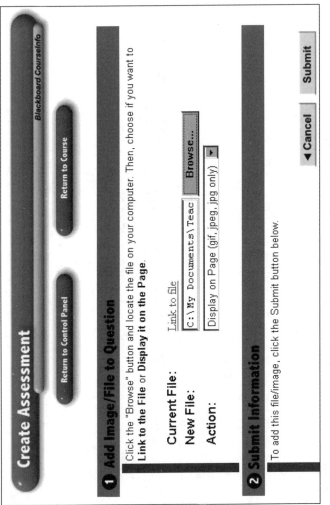

Figure 12.3 Selecting a Graphic in Blackboard CourseInfo. Again using Blackboard CourseInfo as the course management system, the instructor selects a graphic to display in the quiz and chooses whether to display it as part of the question or link to it if it's available elsewhere on the Web.

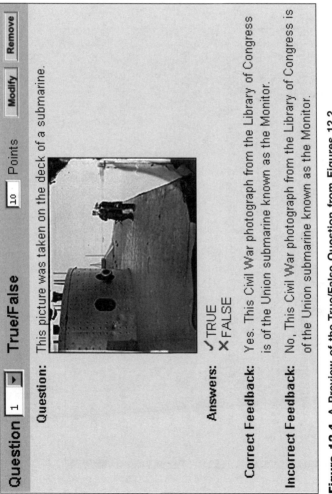

Question 1 ▶ **True/False** 10 Points **Modify** **Remove**

Question: This picture was taken on the deck of a submarine.

Answers: ✓ TRUE
✗ FALSE

Correct Feedback: Yes. This Civil War photograph from the Library of Congress is of the Union submarine known as the Monitor.

Incorrect Feedback: No. This Civil War photograph from the Library of Congress is of the Union submarine known as the Monitor.

Figure 12.4 A Preview of the True/False Question from Figures 12.2 and 12.3. The graphic can now be seen. Notice that the instructor has inserted the number of points this question is worth at the top. Note as well the feedback information for correct and incorrect answers.

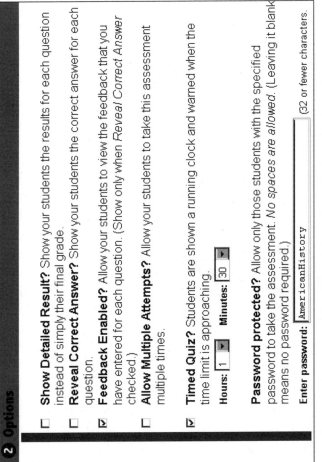

② Options

☐ **Show Detailed Result?** Show your students the results for each question instead of simply their final grade.

☐ **Reveal Correct Answer?** Show your students the correct answer for each question.

☑ **Feedback Enabled?** Allow your students to view the feedback that you have entered for each question. (Show only when *Reveal Correct Answer* checked.)

☐ **Allow Multiple Attempts?** Allow your students to take this assessment multiple times.

☑ **Timed Quiz?** Students are shown a running clock and warned when the time limit is approaching.

Hours: `1` ► Minutes: `30` ►

Password protected? Allow only those students with the specified password to take the assessment. *No spaces are allowed.* (Leaving it blank means no password required.)

Enter password: `AmericanHistory` (32 or fewer characters.

Figure 12.5 Options in a Blackboard CourseInfo Test. In Blackboard CourseInfo, the instructor can define when and under what circumstances a test can be taken. In this example, the test may be taken for an hour and a half, and the student must know the password "AmericanHistory" to take it.

trouble the second time around. One caveat, however: Be sure to save the questions and answers in a word processing file of your own. Sometimes institutions change their course management systems, and it isn't always possible to import a set of questions in one software system into another.

Even if your institution offers no access to course management systems, you'll find that several universities provide quiz-making services or software free of charge (see the box "Test-Making Software").

Proctoring the Online Exam

For many instructors, the prospect of online testing may raise the issue of plagiarism. How do you know which student is taking a test if it's taken online?

Generally, the answer is that you don't, unless you proctor the exam. In a school where computer labs are available, students can be directed to take the quiz in a lab, where you or a proctor you delegate can check student IDs. Typically, the testing soft-

Test-Making Software

In Chapter 2 we briefly mentioned two institutions that offer test-making software: the University of Victoria's language center and the University of Hawaii's QuizCenter.

The University of Hawaii (**http://www.motted.hawaii.edu/**) permits instructors to create their quizzes using the university's server, with a wizard template as a guide. The instructor provides the question, the answers, and the proper feedback. Students log in using a special password. Graded quiz results are e-mailed directly to the instructor.

The University of Victoria's system (**http://www.uvic.ca/hrd/ halfbaked/**) is somewhat different. It is a suite of software called Hot Potatoes (part of the Half-Baked Software line), which will run on either a Windows- or a Mac-based platform. Instructors download the software and install it on their school's server. The instructor can create a variety of quiz forms—everything from multiple choice to crossword puzzles. Students taking the quiz receive instant feedback and a percentage grade. They can take quizzes as many times as they like. This makes Hot Potatoes more suitable for quiz and review functions than for graded tests.

ware permits the instructor to designate a particular time or date during which the test may be taken, or specify a password that must be entered (see Figure 12.5). If the test is available only when a proctor is in a lab, the problem becomes one of simply making sure students aren't entering answers on a neighbor's keyboard. When two or more test-taking sessions are involved, as might be the case in a larger class, you can randomize the questions or even the question sets. Mixing up the order or content of the questions makes it difficult to pass on the correct answers to a student in one of the later test-taking sessions.

Where proctoring isn't available, online quizzes can still be a valuable resource for students. For example, instructors often post sample exams online for their students to use to prepare for midterm or final exams. Using one of the quiz generators, the instructor can provide both answers and focused feedback, so that those taking the trial exams can learn from their mistakes.

The problem of authentication—ascertaining the identity of the user—may soon be solved by biometric means. Researchers are devising methods by which online users can be recognized by computerized fingerprint or face recognition software. When such solutions are readily available, taking tests online will rapidly make the blue book a thing of the past.

Providing Advice and Support

Providing counseling, advice, mentoring, and support is part of the job of teaching. Instructors list their office hours in their syllabi and, once or twice a week, sit dutifully behind their desks waiting for someone to knock on their door. All too often, nobody comes, leaving the instructor to wonder about the utility of sitting in an office for two hours a week. For some, the meager trickle of students is an opportunity to catch up on paperwork. Some may see it as a testament to their pedagogical skills—a sign that students aren't having any difficulties. To others, however, the lack of office visitors is a warning signal that something may be wrong—either the allotted time isn't convenient or the students don't feel they are getting what they want from the course.

Using two of the online tools readily available to most instructors—e-mail and chat—can improve the flow of communication markedly.

Counseling Students via E-Mail

With e-mail, instructors can respond to student inquiries at a time and place of their choosing, leaving them freer to structure their activities during the day. Students can submit their inquiries as the need arises—for example, in their dorm room late at night when they're studying.

But shifting the counseling load to the Web has its obvious downside as well: It can significantly increase the instructor's workload if it isn't kept in check. To control your workload, we suggest the following guidelines, some of which we've recommended in earlier chapters:

- Set strict parameters for responding to e-mails and make them clear to your students in both your syllabus and your class. For instance, make sure your students understand that, although you will accept e-mails from them, you will *not* necessarily respond to each one personally, nor will you respond to each one immediately.

- Specify which kinds of problems you will respond to: for example, personal problems, requests, or issues; or difficulties comprehending the subject matter. Steer clear altogether of administrative issues, such as dates for upcoming tests or questions about homework. Such information is either available in the syllabus or more properly discussed in an online or on-the-ground discussion session.

- Insist that you will not respond to any e-mails whose chief issue isn't clearly identified in the subject line of the communication. This will save you the trouble of having to read through the entire e-mail to discover the problem at hand. It will also allow you to forward a student e-mail to a TA or assistant when appropriate.

- Respond by sending *one* e-mail to your entire class, or compile an FAQ page with your answers and post it on your web site.

Establishing Virtual Office Hours

Online chat software can be used to conduct virtual office hours. It can, for instance, lighten your advisory load, or at least make it less onerous, if you use it in a focused way. Say, for example, that you tell your students that you will be available for consultations for an hour or two on certain days. If you're in your office, or even your home, you can connect to the Internet and open a chat session, leaving the chat window visible on your screen. As you wait for students to check in, you can do other work, glancing at the screen now and then to see if anyone has arrived.

Once a student has arrived, your conversation (depending on the chat software you're using) can usually be logged; that is, a record of your conversation is automatically saved to a text file. This permits you to edit the text file at some later date, extracting material for your FAQ page.

Some chat software tools now include a whiteboard function. The whiteboard, as you'll recall from Chapter 3, is a communal area where an instructor can draw or type. The students in the chat session can then discuss the instructor's display or present material of their own as part of the online give and take. Newer software tools permit you to display in the whiteboard area any document on your hard disk (such as a PowerPoint presentation or an Excel spreadsheet) or any web page you may have bookmarked; you can do this simultaneously while chatting with your students. More impressive still, the students can do the same thing. Thus you and your students can see the same documents, web pages, or applications at the same time that you are discussing them.

It won't be long before the foregoing capabilities will be augmented by desktop videoconferencing tools. These tools, available now but not widely employed, permit one-to-one or even group video and audio communication. Until recently, desktop videoconferencing was too data intensive for most home modems. Pictures thus conveyed tended to be blurry or sporadic. But as the pipelines carrying the information improve, this form of communication is bound to become more accessible and common. At that point, the instructor will have a broad array of communication tools with which to conduct advisory or small-seminar sessions with a class.

Assigning Group Projects

O ne tool rarely used by instructors but commonly available in most course management software is the ability to divide large classes into small student groups, affording them a private area online in which to collaborate on the production and publication of group projects.

In these private areas the students have access to the full panoply of online tools—message boards, chat rooms, and whiteboards. They can create information, format it into HTML pages, or attach it as downloadable documents to their postings, sharing these items with each other, unseen by the rest of the class. This gives them a virtual workspace, permitting them to work together on a schedule convenient to them—a particular advantage to students with busy schedules or difficult commutes. It also permits you as the instructor to assign group collaborative projects with the assurance that they won't overwhelm the students' time or capabilities.

In a small private school, using a conferencing system to promote group work may seem superfluous. But in a large urban school, where students commute long distances, have jobs, or are raising families, the opportunity to work online overcomes a number of logistical obstacles while at the same time affording a level of intercommunication that wouldn't otherwise be possible. It also helps students learn how to collaborate with one another, a communication skill highly valued in the workplace.

Access to conferencing tools permits you to assign larger research projects than you might have before. By dividing the workload, students can tackle problems of much greater complexity than might have been possible if the assignment were for one student alone. Online conferencing also permits students to bring into their work students or experts from outside their area. Students from different institutions, cities, and even countries can connect via the Internet and work together collaboratively using the same set of tools. Finally, the group projects can be released for viewing to the whole class and form the basis of a vigorous in-class discussion. To explore this subject further, see

Chapters 5 and 6 for discussion of some of the specific options available for group activities.

Using the Web as a Presentation Medium

The Web is a powerful presentation medium, yet it's surprising how rarely it is used to display work created by students as course projects, either individually or in groups. Instructors understandably prefer the more traditional means of expression, such as the research paper or the PowerPoint slide show delivered in front of the class. Frequently, however, there isn't adequate hardware in the classroom—data projectors, for example—to display the information. Perhaps more significant is the inordinate amount of classroom time required to present such projects to the class.

Using the Web to present such reports permits students to use a wider range of media to make their points. Students can create PowerPoint slide shows or compose web pages replete with graphics, sounds, animations, and links. Even without such multimedia embellishments, web-based reports can be read and evaluated by all the students before or after they come to class, leaving class time for discussion, analyses, and critiques.

Assembling such projects as HTML files should no longer be considered a hardship for students. In most cases, it is a skill they can master easily, and one they ought to learn. Using a simple tool such as Netscape Composer (see Chapter 7), or simply saving their word-processed file as an HTML page, as described earlier in this chapter, they should be able to assemble relatively sophisticated web pages with ease.

Web-Based Exercises

The Web is so rich that traditional instructors would be depriving their students of valuable educational resources if they ignored it altogether. No matter what subject you teach, be it molecular biology or cultural anthropology, there is a multitude of sites that can provide you and your students with information, simulations, or resources to consider, critique, analyze, or discuss.

Aside from visiting informational web sites, students can

- participate in global science experiments.
- perform experiments in online labs.
- collaborate and communicate with students from another school, state, or nation.
- analyze and critique articles published online and post reactions to them in a discussion board.
- meet and discuss relevant issues with a "guest host" in a discussion board or chat room.

Here are some pointers for incorporating the Web into your face-to-face class:

- Identify each site you want your students to visit by its URL, both on your web site and in the syllabus. Revisit the site just before you begin teaching the class to make sure it's still alive (sometimes sites are moved to different URLs, or simply no longer work).
- Be very clear when defining what you want your students to see or do when visiting a site. Be respectful of the time they must spend online to accomplish the assigned task. Generally, you'll want to avoid the treasure hunt approach—that is, having your students hunt for information before they can critique it.
- Avoid displaying web sites in class. Connections often fail because of network congestion either at your institution or elsewhere on the Web, making the presentation of web sites in class a risky maneuver.

Team Teaching

Just as students can collaborate easily online, so can teachers. Team teaching a large, lecture-style course requires a great deal of advance planning and preparation. Traditionally, this is done in face-to-face meetings, but using the collaborative tools available on the Web can ameliorate the process, speeding up the production of course materials and easing the task of approving them once they are done.

Once a course is under way, using the Web has its advantages as well. Instructors can spell each other at certain tasks, with one instructor handling lectures in the classroom while the other publishes backup materials on the Web and replies to student inquiries on discussion boards.

In less common cases, instructors may be situated too far apart to commute easily to the physical class. Using the Web is an obvious alternative, permitting the use of "experts" to prepare online lectures, but leaving the discussions to the instructor in the class.

A Final Thought

In this discussion of ways the Internet can be integrated in an on-the-ground class, one key thought underlies our comments.

Important! *Making the use of the Internet optional rather than incorporating it into the curriculum dooms it to failure.*

When you make the Web an integral part of the course work, you automatically make it more relevant and valuable to your students and yourself alike. Treating the web site merely as a repository for chance comments or random postings reduces it to the level of a technological appendage and squanders its considerable potential to enrich what you are doing on the ground.

Resources

Adobe Acrobat. **http://www.adobe.com/store/products/ acrobat.html**

Information about Adobe Acrobat's functions, features, and price.

Hot Potatoes Homepage. **http://web.uvic.ca/hrd/halfbaked/**

Free software for creating web-based quizzes and exercises.

University of Hawaii QuizCenter. **http://www.motted. hawaii.edu/**

Provides quiz-making features, as well as lists and reviews of quiz software available elsewhere on the Web.

IV

New Trends and Opportunities

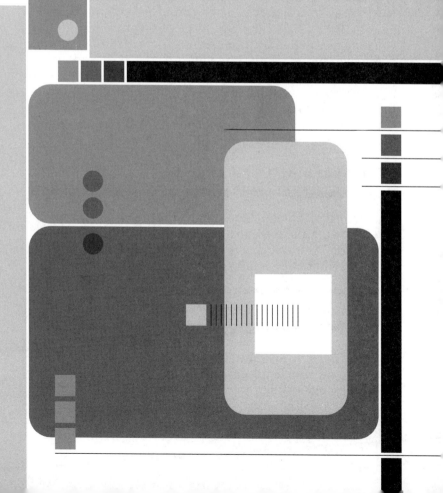

Taking Advantage of New Opportunities

Because online education is a relatively new enterprise, you have an opportunity to make a positive contribution to this growing field. To take full advantage of this new opportunity, you would do well to keep yourself informed of the latest trends and issues and to continually improve your skills and knowledge. Each time you teach online, you have the chance to acquire insights and experience that can be used as the basis for further exploration.

In this chapter, we hope to point out some of the possibilities for your development as an online educator.

What Teaching Online Can Do for You

Although teaching online presents many challenges to the instructor, there are many benefits to be gained from the experience. They have implications for new career directions, as well as for improved performance in the classroom.

Heightened Awareness of Your Teaching

Among instructors who have taught online, the advantage of the process that they most commonly express is that it makes them better teachers.

Few of us in higher education have any training in teaching methods or instructional design. We learn chiefly from osmosis (being in a classroom), from mentoring by more experienced colleagues (if we're lucky), or through time spent as teaching assistants in graduate school.

Teaching online heightens our awareness of what we're actually doing in the classroom. The interactions between our students and ourselves—which often consist of fleeting occasions in the on-campus classroom—are recorded for us online, available for our review and reflection. We also have the opportunity to observe and review how our students respond to our assignments, to track the growth of understanding or incomprehension as they respond to the lessons and activities we set in motion for their learning.

This heightened awareness can be both illuminating and humbling. We find that the instructional design process becomes less implicit and more of a deliberate enterprise. Sometimes this leads us to make changes in the way we do things or to try out new approaches, not only in our online courses but in our on-campus classrooms as well.

Anita Reach, the Kansas City pharmacology instructor cited earlier in this book, remarked on the awareness she gained by online teaching: "What I found out was that I began to rethink everything I did on the ground. Why did I lecture so much? Students are very bright and they have a lot to say, but the way I was teaching wasn't allowing that."

As you reconsider your instructional methods, you may find that the rapid and flexible communication afforded by the Internet fosters some creative new approaches. Tisha Bender, the instructor we quoted in Chapter 10, discovered one such opportunity when teaching a literature class. She related how exciting it was for her to travel to D. H. Lawrence's hometown, spend the day exploring the environment that had shaped Lawrence, and then, that very evening, make a report to her students about her impressions. "There was such immediacy in what I had to tell them!"

When *you* teach online, you, too, may experience that serendipitous moment when the possibilities of the medium and your course objectives suddenly come together. Grasp that moment and shape it to enliven and enrich your students' learning!

New Connections with the Wider World

A great fear among many instructors is that all human interaction online is inevitably superficial and that such a learning environment leads to more alienation between students and instructors, and less meaningful communication among colleagues.

Communication online isn't the same as in person, but it can be both effective and satisfying. It also brings us new opportunities to communicate with, and even to get to know, people we would have no other chance to meet—either because they live at a great distance from us or because their schedules wouldn't otherwise allow them to take our classes.

Tisha Bender mentioned how gratifying it was to be able to teach students who were ballerinas on tour. Another of her students was a convalescent confined to bed. It pleased Bender to know that these students had found a way to continue their education—and that she had a chance to associate with them.

At the risk of sounding heretical, we will venture the proposition that meeting online is sometimes the ideal way to get to know a student or colleague. The by-now-old joke goes, "Nobody knows you're a dog on the Internet," and by the same token, nobody knows whether you're under twenty-one or over sixty-five years old. When one of this book's authors, Susan Ko, met Gerda Lederer online as a colleague at the New School, she formed a picture in her head of a woman of about thirty who had a fresh and open attitude toward life and who was simply bursting with creative ideas and enthusiasm for the new medium. Susan deduced from their extensive online communications that Gerda kept very current in her field of expertise, as well as up to date in her knowledge of culture and education in general. Susan and Gerda got to know each other rather well online, and eventually, when Gerda traveled to Los Angeles, they decided to meet in person. Susan was surprised to discover that Gerda was over seventy years old. Although Susan felt that she was without any bias toward older adults, she had to admit that meeting Gerda's *ideas* before she met her in person had actually been the very best way to get to know her.

Many instructors, including the authors of this book, arrange to meet online students at conferences. Online students will also network among themselves, carry on long correspondences, and sometimes meet in person. In fact, talking extensively with another online, observing that person's interaction with others, and perhaps collaborating on a project can often form the basis of a solid friendship.

New connections with distant colleges also become possible. An instructor residing in Missouri may teach for an institution based in New York, and a professor on leave from a college in California may teach a class from a temporary post in France. Tisha Bender points out that she knows of several instructors who were able to continue their institutional associations with their former colleges after they had moved far away from the home campus site.

New Career Directions

The field of online education has become the preoccupation not only of most institutions of higher education but also of software producers, media conglomerates and publishing houses, and education delivery companies. All of these players are beginning to appreciate the need to employ people with solid academic credentials, experience in the classroom, and, of course, an understanding of how teaching and learning can be effectively handled and enhanced in an online environment.

Because online education ranges from self-paced independent study modules to fully instructor-created and instructor-led courses, career prospects cover a similarly wide range. For instance, you can find new opportunities in areas like these:

- Creation of courseware for your own courses
- Design and creation of courseware to be used by other instructors
- Curriculum development for both nonprofit and profit-making entities
- Course conversion and instructional technology services
- Training and providing support for faculty
- Administrative positions directing online education efforts

Even a cursory look at some of the online job-listing sites demonstrates the range of nonacademia-based jobs for which educators with online expertise might qualify. As technology races ahead of content, those with the intellectual capital to create courseware and shape curriculum will be increasingly in demand.

The example of Anita Reach illustrates some of the possibilities. Anita Reach has moved from her position as an instructor at Kansas City Community College, where she began her online teaching by planning a single course, to her present involvement as instructional technology online project leader, overseeing a program of more than sixty online courses with an anticipated 1,000 students and what is soon to be an associate's degree delivered online.

Of course, there are several features of Anita Reach's background that provided support for this type of move. She was an experienced teacher who had twice received awards for teaching excellence. She had leadership experience as coordinator for the substance abuse program and the addiction counselor program at her college. An advocate of lifelong learning, she has continued to take courses that broaden her awareness and keep her current in her field. In 1997, she was one of the fledgling group who completed the full series of courses in the Online Teaching Program offered by UCLA Extension. Yet Anita's career experience is not unique. As time goes by, more and more instructors will find similar possibilities available to them.

Already, online teaching has revitalized the careers of many longtime instructors, allowing them to experiment with new approaches to teaching and to create courses for an expanded audience of learners. Many have assumed new positions of leadership within their own institutions. For others, online experience has provided an opportunity to start a new career outside of academia, to bring their needed expertise and perspectives to associations and companies engaged in education-related businesses.

Moreover, instructors who are ready to retire may consider extending their teaching lives with online courses. As part of continuing education, online teaching offers new opportunities to retired professionals who have much to offer students in the way of expertise and experience.

What to Do After You've Read This Book

Although this book strives to provide you with a comprehensive guide to online teaching, we hope that it will also inspire you to explore some additional pathways for your continued development as an online educator. Here we'll suggest a few of them.

Further Training

This book was developed as a practical guide for instructors who wish to teach online, but it wasn't meant to replace a formal training program completely. In fact, although a good training program would include at least some of the *information* provided by this book, a training program should also include the *experience* of teaching and learning online.

Important! *Whenever possible, opt for a program that emphasizes online training, not just on-site training.*

Most of us are used to learning in a workshop or lab arrangement, with an instructor hovering over us or directing from the front of the room as we struggle with a software program. Such personalized attention can be very helpful; the face-to-face interchange and the ability to ask questions "on the fly," gaining immediate feedback and support, can be quite valuable.

But trying to learn to use a specific course management system in a workshop environment can have its disadvantages as well. For one thing, some course management software programs, such as WebCT and Blackboard CourseInfo, are simply too complicated to master within a manageable amount of real time (three hours, for instance, which is about as much time as the average instructor has to spare in a single afternoon). This isn't because the software itself is especially difficult to use, but because it contains too many individual parts and functions to cover adequately in the space of a few hours. Learning how to operate the basic functions in software is one thing, but knowing what to do with them is quite another. In a workshop devoted to a course management system, most instructors, especially novices, find the information too plentiful to digest in one sitting. Without repetition over time, much of the experience is lost. Or—and this is probably just as harmful—instructors may leave the workshop thinking they know pretty much all they need to know.

Coupling an on-site workshop with further work online is often the best solution for those eager to learn enough to proceed confidently on their own. Until you've become a student, there's no way you can properly appreciate, or even identify, the problems and pitfalls of learning online. Sitting in a classroom with other instructors is a totally different experience from sitting at home and communicating with your instructor and fellow students online. Using the actual online tools to complete an exercise or post a comment on a bulletin board is entirely different from experimenting with the tools in an onsite workshop.

An added advantage to learning online, rather than in a workshop, is that students can progress at a speed that suits them. Thus the novice can afford to proceed at a slow pace without worrying that he or she may be holding back the rest of the class, while more advanced users can proceed quickly to get to the material they need to learn.

You can learn some fairly complex and technical material online. For example, in a course we taught about how to make effective use of multimedia, instructors learned how to make

On-Site Versus Online Training: One Team's Experience

Jennifer Lieberman, a trainer with the Illinois Online Network, works with a team that offers a complex series of services to some twenty different institutions. The on-site training ranges from inspirational talks to workshops of two to three hours, covering software applications as well as instructional methods and design.

Recently, the team has added an online component for faculty training. The online course was originally designed along the lines of train-the-trainer models, to stimulate activity related to technology as well as online education. However, after seeing the enthusiastic response to the online training, Jennifer's team is considering emphasizing online training rather than on-site visits.

Jennifer offered this comment on her instructors' growing awareness of the value of this modeling of the online experience: "As the weeks unfolded, it became more and more evident that these participants were gaining valuable insight into the dynamics of online learning by experiencing an online course from a student's perspective. Many of them commented that, in addition to learning about online course delivery, this experience was helping them improve their face-to-face teaching as well."

GIF animations, streaming sound files, and even streaming slide shows entirely on their own, submitting their completed work to a web site. Most of these instructors had never used the software before taking the class, yet none of them complained that they could not learn without a live instructor standing by. These instructors were not "techies"; they ranged from English professors to instructors of machine-shop technology in a trade high school. The material they used—narrated slide shows—guided them through the various exercises, and the online discussion board provided a forum in which they could voice their problems and concerns.

Training Outside Your Own Institution   If you have a good training program at your institution, we strongly recommend that you sign up for it. What should you do, however, if your institution isn't offering faculty development training in online teaching?

First of all, you can enroll as a student in an online course of your own choosing. There are many online courses being offered now by institutions all over the world. You might base your choice on any number of criteria:

- A subject you've always wanted to study
- A course that is in your field or similar to your own course
- A course that uses the same software platform your own institution is considering
- A course that simply suits your schedule and budget

Even though such courses won't show you specifically how to teach online, they will give you vital experience as a learner in the online classroom.

In terms of specific training for teaching online, there are now a number of national and vendor-operated programs, including the following types:

- Short online courses and tutorials in particular software platforms, offered by the providers of those platforms, such as Embanet, Blackboard, and Convene
- Short, site-based training courses for particular software platforms, such as the courses offered for WebCT and Blackboard CourseInfo

- Full-scale, comprehensive programs—covering teaching methods, curriculum development, and tools—that aren't specific to any software platform, such as UCLA Extension's Online Teaching Program and Walden University Institute's Online Certified Instructor program

Many of these programs are available completely online, thus eliminating the constraints of geography. Online training is particularly advantageous in that it doesn't involve removing an instructor from the classroom in order to be trained, and it is particularly economical in that it doesn't require the travel and lodging expenses necessary for an off-site workshop.

You may be able to work on an interdepartmental, districtwide, or consortium basis to arrange discounted tuition for yourself and other faculty members. You can also investigate whether any statewide opportunities are available. For example, the Illinois Online Network has developed a pilot program of instruction in online teaching for all of its interested community colleges. The California State University system has periodically run workshops for statewide faculty on online teaching, both on-site and online. Many more opportunities of this sort open up each day.

It is also good to have several instructors from your single institution take an online teacher training course together. You can point out to the administration that training several people at once will provide a seed crop of informed faculty who will go on to share their new insights with other faculty members. Faculty collaboration and sharing will often stimulate others to continue learning. But whether or not your institution is willing to offer financial support for you and your colleagues, taking a course together will provide a mutual support network for all of you.

General Characteristics to Seek in a Training Program   What characteristics should you look for in a training program? First, as we suggested earlier, it is essential that the core of the development program be conducted online.

The ideal training program should also have a flexible schedule, emphasizing asynchronous (not real-time) communication, although there should be a start and stop date to prevent participants from losing focus and motivation. Lessons and activities should be arranged so that students can work on them on a weekly basis, rather than on a specific day. Faculty should participate three to five times a week, for short intervals, in the discussion forums, rather than once a week for longer periods of time. This replicates the ideal online teaching experience.

Ideally, the program should be a minimum of about six weeks in length. This will allow a week for general introduction to concepts and time to get accustomed to the software. Six weeks is really the minimum to ensure that you and your fellow students have adequate time to get up to speed with the software, interact in the online environment, and begin to think about the issues associated with your own courses.

The person leading the training should be someone who has experience in both teaching and learning online, has taught in a live classroom, and has a working knowledge of curriculum design. Perhaps you will find that the training is done by a pair or team in which one of the members is an instructional technologist. That's fine, as long as at least one of the trainers can share the perspective of teaching in a live classroom. Such a person is better able to comprehend the sensitive nature of transferring years of experience in the live classroom to an online setting.

Content to Seek in a Training Program   What content and topics should you look for in a training program? We think there are four important categories of content: software training, facilitative or methods training, personal consultation, and supervised start-up.

1. *Software training.* Naturally, software training is important. In an online teaching program that isn't platform specific, you will learn the software being used for the program and perhaps be introduced to several different platforms. As in the process of learning a foreign language, you will find that learning one platform and analyzing others will improve your facility in learning further platforms. Sometimes these programs will ask you to produce a demo in your own chosen platform. If your program has been specifically designed for your institution, then the software training may include having each participant build a basic shell for a model classroom.

   Training in HTML code or in using a WYSIWYG (what-you-see-is-what-you-get) HTML editor may be included, as well as experience with specific plug-in programs. Your training may also include topics such as academic web page design, the creation of course web pages, and use of online quizzing tools. Good programs combine observation and analysis of how tools are used with opportunities for hands-on experience.

Overall, how much do you need to learn about the software you'll be using? Naturally this will depend on how much help you can expect to receive from support staff. But even if you have technical support, including instructional designers or instructional technologists to assist you and do a good deal of the work for you, we suggest that you learn as much as you can so that you can provide direction and make informed decisions. In the end, because decisions about design and organization affect curriculum, a wise online instructor will seek to be fully involved.

2. *Facilitative or methods training.* The next layer of training is what may be called "facilitative" or "methods, approaches, and techniques." A good training program will give you the chance to explore the differences and similarities between live and online classrooms. For example, it will help you confront the sometimes-troubling issue of the instructor's "voice" and style in the classroom. In large part, a sense of your own online voice will develop as you engage in online communication with others. The trainer as well as other colleagues can help you achieve this vision of yourself through interaction and positive reinforcement. It's difficult to achieve this sense of ease about oneself in a one- or two-week training program; that's one reason why we recommend a course of at least six weeks.

Any comprehensive training program should also include classroom management, course preparation, methods of handling student participation and interaction, the use of web resources, and other areas explored in this book. Moreover, we believe that a substantial portion of the training should involve analysis of case studies in online teaching and learning. You'll want a chance to observe real courses on the Web, both at your own institution and elsewhere. The program should offer guided discussions of the diverse teaching methods and styles present in online courses. Especially in a short-term program, we believe you will find analysis of teaching models as they are actually used in a real course to be more valuable than instructional design theory in the abstract.

3. *Personal consultation.* Either in the final portion of your training or as a follow-up, some personal consultation is desirable. Ideally, training instructors or other staff should be available to work with you on a one-to-one basis to arrive at a course conversion model that will satisfy your particular goals and objectives. Finding a good fit for your own preferred teaching methods and style is paramount here.

4. *Supervised start-up.* Finally, in an ideal training program, the last stage should involve a supervised start-up of your actual course. If this isn't available to you, we recommend that you ask another instructor with experience teaching online to critique your web site.

Learning from Your Own Experience

No matter how good your preparation for teaching online, there's still more to be learned when you actually begin teaching your class. It takes time to feel entirely comfortable teaching online. It's quite common for instructors to feel anxious, lost, confused, or disoriented by the new teaching situation.

The following profile of an online instructor describes some of the stages you may go through as you embark on your first experience in teaching online.

Profile of an Online Instructor

Joanne is a new online instructor assigned to teach a marketing course. Before planning her class, she conscientiously completed the short training and orientation course offered at her institution, and she took advantage of opportunities to consult with support staff. Besides asking for technical assistance, she sought advice about her syllabus and course activities.

After putting together a pack of articles for her course, she submitted it to the program office at her institution, which promised to secure copyright permissions and distribute the material to the online students.

(cont.)

She worked out her syllabus on a weekly basis, making sure she had thought out the activities and readings students would pursue, as well as specific discussion questions she would pose in her discussion board threads. She also thought carefully about the procedures for students to deliver assignments to her and about whether she would schedule virtual office hours via real-time chat. She decided that she would offer real-time chat office hours only by prior appointment (arranged by e-mail), because it was difficult for her to carve out a specific time in her schedule when she would be available each week.

Joanne did have some trouble deciding how to convert one of her favorite assignments to the online setting. She was accustomed to giving students a twenty-minute "quick writing" assignment each week, requiring them to brainstorm rapidly and formulate a basic marketing plan. How would she handle "quick writing" in an asynchronous class? What, she asked herself, was the equivalent of twenty minutes in the asynchronous mode? Or should she use the real-time chat room instead, having each student meet with her there for a twenty-minute period? With twenty-five students, the latter option didn't seem feasible. She finally settled on a two-day window for each "quick writing" topic; that is, from the time she posted a topic in the online classroom, students would have two days to e-mail her their responses. She would then post the best examples online. The entire sequence of procedures would be explained to students beforehand in the syllabus.

Joanne was surprised at the amount of time she ended up devoting to the preparation of her online class. She had created new courses before, and that always took an enormous effort; but because this wasn't an entirely new course, she didn't imagine it would require so much preparation. For example, although she had some lectures already written out in full, most of her lectures existed simply in outline form. Over the years she had been able to speak at length on the basis of the outlines. She hadn't calculated that it would take so many hours to put her previously spoken words into print, and then upload or copy and paste these documents into the course presentation areas.

Joanne also discovered that, despite her extensive preparation, issues that she hadn't anticipated arose during the course. Students required more clarification of assignments than she had supposed they would. The activities and assignments turned out to be too closely scheduled. She suffered problems with her Internet service provider that kept her from logging on for two days during the middle of the course.

(cont.)

It was a very active class, with hundreds of postings from the twenty-five students. As the course progressed, she felt it was successful overall, but she was a bit overwhelmed by the intensity of the experience. She was online nearly every day, and she found herself logging on at odd times, as though she might otherwise be missing something. She was always a little surprised to see how many new postings there were. The little signs indicating new, unread postings began to trigger feelings of anxiety in her. She also found that she was sometimes overlooking a message, or that she had read it quickly and forgotten to respond.

During one particularly difficult and busy week, she discovered that she had made a mistake in announcing the due date for an assignment. She worried that students would lose confidence in her. At this point she e-mailed a colleague, who had been teaching online for a few semesters, to express her feelings of anxiety. The colleague wrote back with what proved to be an important piece of advice: "Anxiety is normal at this stage. Don't be afraid to make a mistake. If you make a mistake, just tell the students as quickly as you can of the corrections needed."

By the fourth week of the eight-week course, she was beginning to feel less anxious. She also started to feel confident that she could take a less interventionist role in her class. She realized that she could pose questions in such a way that students would begin to address each other rather than her. She recognized, too, that she need not answer every single posting. The large number of initial questions on technical issues could be greatly reduced by creating a short FAQ to precede each unit of the course. She implemented these changes for the remainder of the course.

By the sixth week, Joanne was already scrutinizing her class with an eye to improving it next time around. She also contacted a few colleagues with whom she had trained, to find out what had worked or not worked for them in their own online courses. After this review of her course and some useful anecdotal evidence from her colleagues, which seemed to confirm her own conclusions, she decided that she needed a better mix of individual and group activities to reduce the number of individual students' postings on each topic. She also resolved to replace the large number of different assignments with an incremental series of assignments, each building on the preceding one. This change would mean that students could choose a single topic, research it, and structure each successive assignment around it. She felt this approach would save time and provide a more focused, in-depth learning experience.

(cont.)

Joanne enjoyed the remaining portion of the course and felt optimistic about teaching online in the future. She realized that her preparation time had been a wise initial investment and that, despite the revisions she planned for the next go-round, she wouldn't have to totally re-create the course. She resolved to stay in touch with others involved in online teaching at her institution and to spend some time before every term keeping herself informed via the Web about progress in online education.

A few things stand out in Joanne's case history. First, Joanne took good advantage of training opportunities to prepare herself for teaching online. Second, her planning was comprehensive—not only for the overall arrangements, such as distributing reading material and establishing virtual office hours, but also for the week-by-week online classroom activities. Nonetheless, the preparation time involved was more than she had expected. Moreover, despite all her preparation, she went through a period of adjustment in the first weeks of the course, during which she felt great anxiety about her ability to manage the classroom.

She responded to her worries by taking action. Midway through the course, she made certain adjustments that were immediately feasible, and she began to note aspects of the course that could be improved the next time it was offered. By talking with others who were teaching online, she was able to get practical suggestions that confirmed her own best observations.

We imagine that your own experience will be similar to Joanne's. Although you'll do your best to prepare yourself, you'll still have adjustments to make as the course progresses, and you'll find ways to refine it in the future. It's important that you take the time to reflect on and fine-tune your course each time it runs. As we mentioned earlier, the online course, with its recording of student-instructor interaction, permits a higher degree of scrutiny of our teaching methods than a face-to-face classroom.

A good student evaluation designed for the online classroom can provide valuable feedback. If members of your institution's instructional design staff or support staff have observed your course, they may also be able to provide insights about improving it. Of course, this can be a delicate issue, and you may feel uncomfortable with the heightened scrutiny. What we have in mind here is a review for the purpose of improving your online instruction, not for judging or criticizing your performance as an instructor. We want to encourage you to see this process in a positive light. Greater appreciation of what you do will also become possible, and, we hope, greater rewards for excellence in teaching may one day result from this climate of openness.

You may find that you need additional professional development to maximize your potential as an online instructor. You can avail yourself of opportunities for further formal training in online teaching. You may take on the challenge of learning more about your course software so that you can use some of the higher-end tools. Or you may want to explore some entirely different software programs to attain skills in web site design or creation of multimedia. There are many short courses (offered online, naturally), both instructor led and self-paced, that focus on learning a particular set of skills.

Networking with Others Involved in Online Education

At many institutions there are certain faculty members who have succeeded in promoting themselves as chief watchdogs and opponents of online education. They often express the idea that online education has nothing to offer pedagogically and that it will undermine face-to-face interaction between student and instructor. Many of them have no experience in an online classroom, either as student or as teacher. In this sense they resemble the anthropologist of Bali who undertakes all his field research without leaving his apartment in Manhattan.

It's useful, then, to remember that ignorance can be found even in the most erudite academic circles. Don't allow the naysayers to dissuade you from becoming experienced and knowledgeable in the area of online teaching. There are many more of your colleagues in higher education who are excited by the new possibilities afforded by online education and who are anxious to share their enthusiasm and learning. If there are none such on your own campus, they can be found through online discussion forums, at conferences, and through mailing lists. These people can provide a wonderful support network for you.

Becoming a Lifelong Learner

Online education is a continually evolving field. In years to come, it will feel the impact of many technological improvements, from software improvements to online resource availability to the incorporation of high-speed access.

Unfortunately, it is quite common for faculty members to learn one approach and one type of software and convince themselves that these are the answers now and forever. After all, few people relish putting in extra time to learn new programs or retrain themselves. Nonetheless, faculty who want to teach online need to adopt the same attitude they often prescribe for their students—that lifelong learning is for everyone.

Resources

Note: Some of the URLs cited in this section—for specific pages embedded in much larger sites—may change over time. If you find that a URL doesn't work, try starting at the institution's home page.

Networking and Online Educator Sites

ALN Web. **http://www.aln.org/**

The web site for the Sloan Foundation's Asynchronous Learning Networks provides links to discussions, workshops, and magazines of interest to online educators.

DEOS Listserv Archives. **http://www.wested.org/tie/dlrn/ dlsearch.html**

DEOS-L is a popular listserv for distance educators. This archive allows you to search through recent and past archives of messages.

Distance Education Resources. **http://cuda.teleeducation.nb. ca/distanceed/liste.cfm**

A site sponsored by TeleEducation NB of Canada. See the sections on Professional Development, Networking, Online Discussions, and other topics of interest.

League for Innovation in the Community College. **http://www.league.org/welcome.htm**

Offers a searchable database for descriptions of the league's presentations and contact information for presenters.

The Node Learning Technologies Network. **http://thenode.org/**

The Node offers articles on technology in education and provides various types of online forums (some of them open to anyone and some not), as well as archives and summaries of past forums.

Some Training Programs for Online Teaching

California State University, Hayward, Certificate in Online Teaching and Learning. **http://www.online.csuhayward.edu/Certificate/onclass1.htm**

Illinois Online Network, MVCR Online Training Series. **http://illinois.online.uillinois.edu/mvcr.html**

A series of online courses, primarily for Illinois Online Network members, but now open for those outside the state as well. MVCR stands for "Making the Virtual Classroom a Reality."

Nova Southeastern University, Graduate Teacher Education, Online Teaching and Learning Series. **http://www.fcae.nova.edu/gtep/online/OCI500501502.htm**

UCLA Extension, Online Teaching Program. **http://www.onlinelearning.net/CommunitiesofStudy/neighborhoods.cfm?NB=OTP**

Walden Institute, Certified Online Instructor Program. **http://www.waldeninstitute.com/coi/community/COIprog/coiprog.html**

14

Where Do We Go from Here?

This book is based on our knowledge of the technology and software presently available to instructors teaching online. Because it is intended as a practical guide, it has focused on the tools you are most likely to encounter and use, most of which, as you have learned, are asynchronous—conferencing systems, e-mail, web page postings, and the like.

But what would teaching online be like if the tools to deliver it were to change radically? What if, instead of relying on the written word, you could see your students on a monitor and talk to them through a mike, while they in turn did the same with you? What if you could communicate this way from a portable computer no larger than the palm of your hand, rather than from the desktop computer we're familiar with today? What effect would this transformation have on the way classes are conceived and administered? How would it change the way the traditional university or college is organized or built?

And what if the way you created your class materials were different as well? Right now, for example, to create a web page or an animation, you have to use a specific software program, be familiar with its codes, and know where to find the appropriate commands. But what if the software were more "intelligent"? What if, when composing a web page, you could say to your computer, "Reformat that" or "Give me more designs," and the computer would take your content and reshape it, offering you a panoply of best-guess choices based on its understanding of your likes and dislikes? What if the hardware and software for creating and using video were as commonplace as tape or CD recorders are today? How many more instructors would then make the switch from the classroom to the Web?

Finally, consider the dynamism of the open market. Education is now a commodity that is much in demand. Without it, many people can't secure decent jobs or advance in their careers. As of the year 2000, close to 40 percent of the students pursuing a four-year undergraduate degree were older than twenty-five, and the cost of pursuing a degree at a conventional residential institution was skyrocketing out of sight. Online learning doesn't necessarily save money. But if the tools for delivering it become more effective and easier to use, and if the costs for its delivery begin to come down, how many students are going to opt for it rather than for the more expensive traditional courses of study, particularly when online learning allows them to hold a job and support a family while getting a degree?

Online learning as we have described it in this book is still very much in its infancy. In 1997–1998, according to the U.S. Department of Education, the total number of distance learning courses in higher education with discrete catalog listings in the United States was 52,270. The student population thus served amounted to 710,000, or about 5 percent of the total number of students involved in undergraduate higher education in the United States.* In comparison, the International Data Corporation (IDC), an Internet consulting group, predicted in January 2000 that the total number of students taking courses online would rise to 2.23 million—15 percent of the total student population—by the year 2002. Whether this prediction is true is perhaps less important than the fact that some change—and very likely a considerable amount of change—is sure to occur within a short period of time.

It would be nice if we could tell you just what is going to change, and when. But we aren't soothsayers. For us to try to predict what the world of online learning will look like five years—or even one year—into the future would be at best an entertaining

---

* Keep in mind that most of the distance learning courses in the Department of Education survey were taught with very basic tools: a combination of standard correspondence school techniques supplemented by e-mail or listservs. A lesser percentage made use of course management software programs, and only a fraction employed audio or video conferencing techniques.

diversion, and at worst a complete waste of time. At conferences you can find gurus galore delivering keynote speeches with smug aplomb, peering into the future with X-ray eyes. We think it's wiser to remind ourselves that even Bill Gates, in 1993, didn't regard the Internet as a serious pretender to his desktop throne. Now, a mere handful of years later, the Web so dominates our lives that it's hard to remember when it wasn't there.

Like everyone else in the world, instructors are already struggling with the burdens imposed by change. This was made evident in 1999 when the Higher Education Research Institute of UCLA's School of Education released the results of a survey of 33,785 instructors at 378 colleges. Of those surveyed, 67 percent listed "keeping up with new technology" as a major source of stress. For many instructors it isn't just "publish and perish" anymore. It's "keep up with new developments or miss the train."

Finding information about online learning and educational technology is fairly easy. Leading periodicals and newspapers, many of which are available online, cover technology, and distance education in particular, in considerable depth. A teacher seeking to keep up with general trends need look no further than the *Los Angeles Times* or the *Chronicle of Higher Education,* both of which devote extensive space to distance education. Online web sites, such as those of CNN, Yahoo! and CNET, cover technology in detail and report on day-to-day trends. E-mail journals, such as *CIT Infobits,* edited by Carolyn Kotlas of the University of North Carolina, are quite useful. Listservs devoted to online learning, such as AAHESGIT (moderated by Steve Gilbert for the American Association for Higher Education), can provide you with support, resources, and up-to-date information. You can find web addresses for these sources in the Resources section at the end of this chapter.

Making sense of all this information is far more of a challenge than finding it. This is as true for the authors of this book as it is for you. What we can do, however, is share with you our thoughts about some of the areas we regularly keep an eye on. We monitor these areas because we feel they may affect us the most:

- The information pipeline
- Synchronous learning systems

- Software and hardware for the average person
- The educational marketplace and student expectations

The Information Pipeline

Throughout this book we've emphasized the importance of paying close attention to the issue of accessibility to the Internet when planning an online class. The "pipeline" between the university and the student determines what you can put online, how much and how complex your course material can be, and how easy or difficult it will be for your students to learn the material online. The pipeline we're talking about is the Internet itself—most particularly, the final segment of it, the part that brings information directly into the home or office. At the moment, for most students who work at home, this segment takes the form of a regular telephone line, which is connected in turn to a modem in or near the student's computer.

The modem gets its name from the function it serves: it *mod*ulates and *dem*odulates digital information. Information received via telephone lines is in analog format. The modem converts this into digital information that a computer can read. Conversely, the information a computer produces is converted by the modem into analog format so that it can be conveyed to another computer via the telephone line. The speed by which the modem can perform this function determines in large part how much information can get in or out of the computer.

Several years ago, most students had either 14.4 kbps or 28.8 kbps modems. At present, most students and instructors have modems that work at 56.6 kbps. Even at this speed, however, information such as web pages and digital video arrives at the average home computer in sporadic chunks; that is, either it takes a long time to download or, when it arrives, it's missing bits and pieces of the original file.

The speed limitation imposed by modem communication has required that online education make extensive use of text-based tools: text-based asynchronous conference boards, text-based chat, and text-based HTML pages enlivened by a graphic or two. This is the case because text travels more efficiently than multimedia. It's less data intensive, less complex. But if the speed limitation were removed, an instructor might soon be able to have a genuine, real-time, two-way conversation with a student or a class of students via the Internet, using all the visual and vocal cues that are the basis for human interaction. Such a change in technology would no doubt alter the way both instructors and students perceive online education.

Expanding the Pipeline

How swiftly the pipeline expands depends almost entirely on developments beyond the home and the university—in the outside world where cable companies are merging with telephone service providers, who in turn are being snapped up by software conglomerates or computer hardware manufacturers. In the wake of these dynastic wars and financial couplings will come solutions that allow us to receive information via one or more high-speed connections:

1. Cable TV hookups (cable modems)
2. Telephone lines equipped with special data modems (such as DSLs, or digital subscriber lines)
3. Separate lines that connect the home computer to the main data backbone (for instance, ISDNs, or integrated services digital network lines)
4. Satellite or wireless modems that send signals through the air

Each of these technologies has its pros and cons. For example, cable modems, in theory, can receive and transmit far more information than DSL lines, but most cable connections are capable of only one-way communication from the cable company to your computer or TV set. A relatively small number of homes can send a signal back to the cable company. For that reason, many new cable lines must be installed and activated before cable modem connections become widespread. DSL service, in contrast, can be installed in homes using the same telephone lines already in use. Using a special modem, a DSL line can split voice and data so that the user can remain connected to the Internet while talking on the phone (especially useful if you're talking to tech support about a malfunction on your computer!). ISDNs require a separate, dedicated-line connection, and thus its availability and cost vary considerably from place to place. Wireless modems don't use landlines, but they require a considerable amount of hardware to receive the signals.

What this situation leads to is a series of *if*'s. *If* one (or more) of these methods prevails, and *if* the costs of adopting it are reasonable, and *if* a significant number of students decide to make use of it, *then* the consequences for online learning may be quite significant. There really is no way to predict which system will win out or how long such a change may take. But it is reasonable to assume that, with the amount of e-commerce presently taking place on the Web, the financial incentive to increase the flow of information to and from the home will speed the process considerably.

Implications of a Larger Pipeline

From the educator's point of view, a bigger pipeline to and from the home means that the way instruction is structured and delivered may change as well. Whereas most Internet instruction to date has been asynchronous, with bulletin boards, newsgroups, and listservs serving as the primary vehicles of communication, the larger pipeline may focus more attention on synchronous forms of learning. In that case, these changes seem likely:

- Instead of logging onto chat rooms and typing in their comments, users will speak directly to each other—the flow of the discussion moderated by software that permits only one student to speak at a time.

- Instructors and students alike will make more frequent use of video and audio for presentations and assignments, using less expensive digital cameras to collect material and more user-friendly software to display it.

- Virtual office hours will become more commonplace, with software that lets instructor and student easily view and control each other's computer screens, run software applications, display documents in a common whiteboard area, troubleshoot problems, and explore new ideas.

High-speed connections will affect the asynchronous world as well. Whereas in the past information was conveyed primarily with text and graphics, the future, with its better tools and high-speed connections, will make multimedia elements such as digital video and 3D animations far more feasible. Until now, most multimedia elements have been created by highly paid programmers and designers working for well-funded institutions or private companies intent on controlling the production and distribution of courseware. Instructors have been relegated to the role of *content provider,* the accepted industry term for the scholar with valuable information stuffed in her head. But in a high-bandwidth world, where instructor and student can communicate with greater facility, instructors will have the option of becoming both the creators and the providers of information. The ability to do so depends on the availability of lower-cost hardware and more accessible software, an eventuality we discuss later in this chapter. If these developments occur, however, they will significantly affect the quality of online learning and the ability of instructors to retain a measure of control over the courses they teach.

Bits and pieces of this new educational landscape exist today. There are software programs that connect a single student or class of students synchronously to an instructor. Some employ two-way audio and video; others use web-based "workspaces" (whiteboards where common documents can be marked up) augmented by telephone hookups; and still others use customized browsers specifically designed for teaching online. In the next section we'll explore some examples.

Synchronous Learning Systems

The course management systems we've been examining in this book, such as WebCT and Blackboard CourseInfo, have all been asynchronous systems. Although most of them include the ability to chat online (a synchronous tool), all assume that, for the most part, students will log on at a time of their choosing, view posted material, and perform most of their work offline.

But imagine that the developments we described in the preceding section have already taken place. High-speed connections are the norm, and synchronous online learning is more and more common. Now you find that you have to *go* to school online—that is, attend a class online at a specific time, when you join the instructor and the other students in using tools that allow a constant two-way flow of information. In this case, how will student activities be structured? What will the role of the instructor be?

This is one of those phenomena that are hard to imagine until you've experienced it—much as online learning itself is a mystery to many until they've taken a class themselves. Yet we recently had the opportunity to take part in such a synchronous class.

We used a system devised by Rotor Learning Systems, one of several firms experimenting in this area.* The class originated at California State University at Dominguez Hills. To participate, we had to download a browser especially designed by Rotor Learning. This browser divided up the screen into several areas, including (1) a window where the instructor could be seen as he or she lectured and (2) tabs enabling the student to select several discrete functions (Figure 14.1).

The instructor broadcasts a lecture live, using a camera and software provided by Rotor Learning. The student can use the tabs to ask the instructor a question (Figure 14.2), take a quiz, or join in a general discussion. Students can watch a video while simultaneously discussing it (Figure 14.3). Throughout these various activities, the instructor can control the options that are available. For example, the instructor can suspend the use of the discussion or polling areas while lecturing or while using the main window to display graphics, a PowerPoint slide show, or a

---

* For a comprehensive list of such products, along with brief reviews and links to the manufacturers' home pages, see Robert H. Jackson's incisive Web Based Learning Resources Library at **http://www.outreach.utk.edu/weblearning/**.

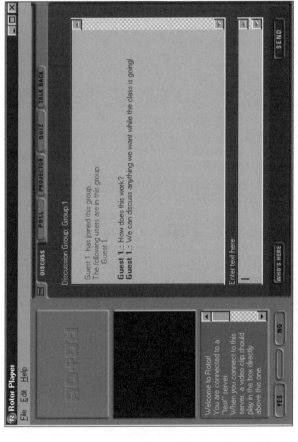

Figure 14.1 The Rotor Learning Browser. Note the tabs denoting particular functions along the top. In this view, the browser is in Discuss mode. The Projector tab would be used for displaying a video or slide show created by the instructor. The Quiz tab is used to take tests. The Yes and No buttons on the lower left permit the instructor to quickly poll students about their understanding of the content.

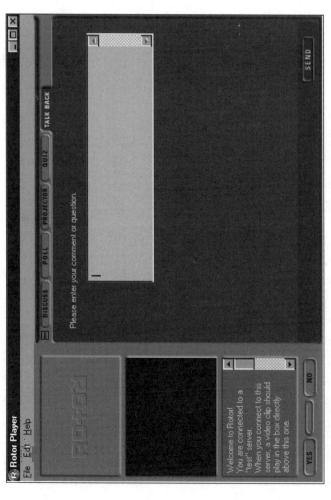

Figure 14.2 Sending a Question. In this view of the Rotor Learning browser, the student has selected the Talk Back tab in order to send a question to the instructor. If the instructor decides to answer it, she can display it to the rest of the class in the text box at the lower left.

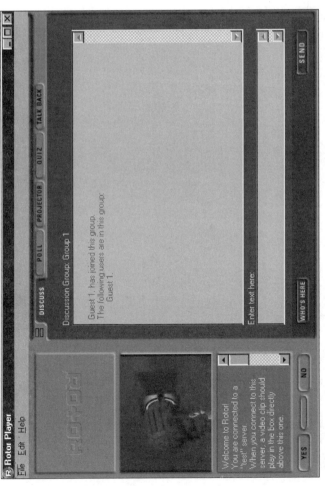

Figure 14.3 Streaming Video on Rotor Learning. On the left a video is streaming to the Rotor Learning browser, while on the right students can discuss its content. The area in which the video appears could also be used to display the instructor as he or she gives a lecture.

live, streamed video. At the conclusion of the presentation, the instructor can then unblock these functions, permitting the students to discuss the content of the presentation, ask specific questions, or take a quiz. After a quiz, the results can be displayed immediately online, enabling further discussion.

The effect of attending a class like this is quite unique. You feel as if you've really gone to school, interacting directly with your instructor and fellow students in the same controlled environment that exists in most classrooms or seminars. Nevertheless, sophisticated as the system may be, it is still limited in scope. Audio and video communication is one way only, from instructor to student. Were this coupled with an asynchronous system, permitting students to view or review classes at a convenient time, and were students able to communicate using audio and video as well, it would perhaps offer an experience that competed favorably with traditional courses on the ground.

Rotor Learning is just one of many synchronous learning systems in development. Others—often referred to as "real-time collaboration systems"—offer a host of functions within one virtual environment. Some feature document sharing in a common space, coupled with the ability to use pooled telephone connections to facilitate a group chat. Others permit an instructor to run an application, such as a spreadsheet program, on her computer and then pass control of the screen to a student, who then can run an application of his own.

A few of these systems are experimenting with the use of two-way video. White Pine Software, for example, has a sophisticated web-based video system called ClassPoint, which permits a group, or several groups, of students to communicate with each other across the Web. In Figure 14.4, for example, an instructor is talking to several groups in different geographical locations. In Figure 14.5, the students are viewing a slide show the instructor made. This sort of web-based conferencing software is very effective in a high-bandwidth environment such as a university or a corporate network, although it doesn't function successfully when streamed to modems at home. No doubt when the pipeline is larger, access more widespread, and hardware and software less expensive, this sort of two-way video communication will become more commonplace.

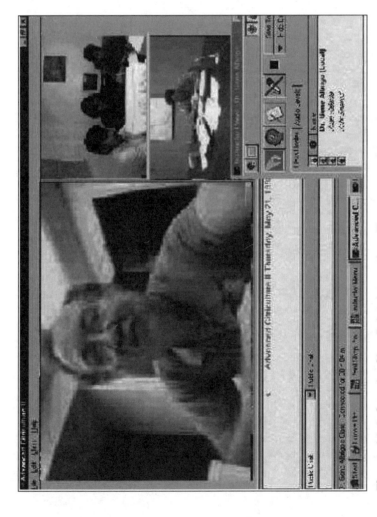

Figure 14.4 Sample ClassPoint Interaction. The screen shows the Instructor Panel with incoming video from student sites.

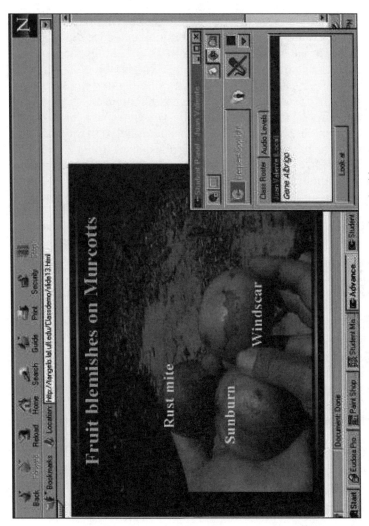

Figure 14.5 Another Example of ClassPoint Interaction. In this case, the Student Panel is receiving class materials.

Software and Hardware for the Average Person

One of the major obstacles blocking the development of online teaching is the lack of inexpensive and easy-to-use tools. Many types of hardware (digital cameras, computer systems, scanners) and software (image editors, web page editors, video editors) are too expensive and complicated for the average instructor. A video camera that costs "only" $100 may sound cheap to the manufacturer, but to the consumer struggling to raise a family, it's just one more high-ticket item that can't be purchased without sacrifice. Nor is it soothing to open an image-editing program and learn that, if need be, you can view a "histogram of the luminosity of a graphic" you just scanned. Can the average instructor be blamed if perhaps he or she doesn't understand?

However, the dot.com culture in which we now live, coupled with the imperatives of e-commerce, is driving companies to produce less expensive hardware and software that the general public can use. RealNetworks, for example, has produced a number of free software products available to anyone who visits the company web site. With RealNetworks software, which we described in some detail in Chapter 7, one can produce some very sophisticated applications (streaming audio files or narrated slide shows) without pursuing a degree in computer science. RealNetworks, of course, offers free software in the hope that the end user will purchase some of the company's more high-end products; yet the ubiquity of such free products on the Web has forced other companies to follow suit.

Hardware manufacturers are following a similar trend. Equipment that used to be available only to labs or corporations is now being produced at prices more people can afford. New products are constantly being developed and improved: for instance, hand-held computers costing a few hundred dollars but capable of sending or receiving e-mail and surfing the Web; hand-held e-books in which a student can store the material of one or several textbooks, as well as graphics, video, and sound; and game decks aimed at the family living room that do double duty as computers for surfing the Web.

The breakneck pace with which products are created, polished, and brought to market is changing every sector of society, forcing us all to rethink the way we produce, sell, and deliver almost everything, from pizzas to encyclopedias. As more and more options and technologies become available, institutions of higher education are being forced to rethink the concept of the university itself, from the way campuses are built to the way that teaching and learning take place. The prospects are exciting, scary, and exquisitely unpredictable.

The Educational Marketplace and Student Expectations

Academics live in a world in which, for the most part, they control their own fate. Academic senates convene and vote to make changes; administrators sit on committees and devise policies; and trustees meet to set tuition schedules. The pace is unhurried, especially when academics must wait for legislatures to allocate tax monies to fund expansive plans. Yet the leisurely pace with which academic change takes place may no longer meet the needs of those living outside academia. As the workplace evolves and becomes more dynamic, as adults find they must upgrade their skills and knowledge every three to five years, as older citizens hunger to return to school, as corporations search for employees with cutting-edge skills, as young students desperate for a decent education find they can no longer afford the cost of residential colleges, people may increasingly turn to online learning, with its improved tools and easier access, as not just a viable alternative but a more desirable one.

Already there are signals that this process is under way. Such vaunted institutions as Harvard, Brown, NYU, and Columbia have created online entities to market courses and even degree programs to the public at large. As these shock waves rumble through the academic world, smaller colleges, such as the New School and the Maricopa Community Colleges, have established a presence online far out of proportion to the size of their physical plants. What leads students to choose one over the other may be the cost and quality of the education provided, or it may be the cachet of a famous name. But competition in this arena is bound to add more pressure for such institutions to make swifter changes.

We're used to thinking that change in the academic world takes place from within, as though a vote by the academic senate, a decree from a "visionary" chancellor, or a policy set down by a governor can control the shape and rate of social change. But it may well be that in the case of online learning the marketplace itself will dictate the pace of change.

We hope that this book has provided some valuable techniques to help you take advantage of new opportunities in the changing educational marketplace. Who knows? In five years, in order to polish up our skills, we may find ourselves in an online course taught by you.

Resources

Synchronous Learning Systems

Web Based Learning Resources Library. **http://www.outreach. utk.edu/weblearning/**.

Compiled by Robert Jackson, this site offers an incisive review of the full range of synchronous learning systems, including video and audio chat sites. The list is complete with comments and links.

Keeping up with New Technology

The Chronicle of Higher Education. **http://www.chronicle.com/**

A weekly journal replete with articles and job listings for instructors. Distance learning resources are accessible to non-subscribers.

CIT Infobits. **http://www.unc.edu/cit/infobits/infobits.html**

A monthly e-mailed newsletter dealing with news and developments in technology and education; edited by Carolyn Kotlas at the University of North Carolina.

CNET. **http://www.cnet.com/**

An excellent site for news of technology developments, reviews, and downloads of popular software.

CNN. **http://www.cnn.com/**

A good source for daily articles dealing with business and technology.

Los Angeles Times. **http://www.latimes.com/**

Offers regular features dealing with distance learning and instructional technology, with past issues available to nonsubscribers.

The TLT Group. **http://www.tltgroup.org/**

Affiliated with the American Association for Higher Education, this site offers resources, news, and the AAHESGIT listserv, used by instructors worldwide.

Yahoo! **http://www.yahoo.com/**

This popular portal and directory offers quick links to a multitude of news and media sources pertaining to computers and the Internet.

Glossary

asynchronous   Occurring at different times; for example, electronic bulletin boards are said to be an asynchronous form of communication because messages are typically posted at one time and read at another.

bookmark   A feature of a web browser that allows you to record URLs of web sites so that you can easily return to those sites at a later time.
browser   See *web browser.*
bulletin board   See *electronic bulletin board.*

cc   An e-mail function that allows you to send copies of a message to one or more people other than the main recipient; the term was originally an abbreviation for *carbon copy.*
chat   Online communication that occurs synchronously; that is, in real time. Usually, chat conversations are conducted with typed text, but some employ audio or video.
chat room   The online area where a chat is held. Typically, it consists of a window where messages are displayed, as well as a message box where each individual can type in a response.
conference area   See *electronic bulletin board.*
course management system   A software program that contains a number of integrated instructional functions; also known as *integrated application software, online delivery system, educational delivery application,* or *online tool suite.*

dial-up access   Access to a network or to the Internet by modem through a regular telephone line.
discussion board   See *electronic bulletin board.*
distance education   Any form of learning that does not involve the traditional classroom setting in which student and instructor are in the same location at the same time. Examples range from correspondence courses to videoconferencing to online classes.
download   To retrieve a file from a remote computer and save it on your own computer.

educational delivery application   See *course management system.*

electronic bulletin board   A software program that permits you to "post" messages online (much as you would post a message on a corkboard with a tack) and allows others to reply to your posting with one of their own; also known as a *discussion board, forum, conference area,* or *threaded discussion area.*

Ethernet   The most common technology for local area networks, usually relying on coaxial cables or special "twisted-pair" wires.

fair use   The allowable use or reproduction of material without specific permission from the owner. Although copyright law itself outlines the extent of fair use, various rules and guidelines have extended the definition for educators.

FAQ   Acronym for "frequently asked questions"; typically an online list of common questions and their answers.

forum   See *electronic bulletin board.*

freeware   Software available free of charge.

GIF   Graphics Interchange Format, a compression format useful for graphics files with a limited number of colors.

home page   The principal or initial screen display of a particular web site; the main entry point for that site.

HTML   Short for Hypertext Markup Language, a coded language that defines the format of onscreen text or graphics through a series of descriptive tags.

hyperlink   An element on a web page (typically an image, icon, or highlighted word or phrase) that makes something happen when you "click" on it with the mouse. Typically, it takes you to another web page, but it can also cause a digital movie or audio file to play. Also known simply as a *link.*

integrated application software   See *course management system.*

ISP   Internet service provider; that is, an organization that provides the user with access to the Internet.

JavaScript   A program that works with HTML to make web pages interactive.

JPEG   A compression format useful for photographs; the acronym stands for Joint Photographic Experts Group.

link   See *hyperlink.*

listserv   See *mailing list.*

local area network (LAN)   A network made up of interconnected computers in a relatively small geographic area, ranging from a single office or lab to a campus.

mailing list (listserv)   An online discussion group, administered by a software program, in which each message is sent to a common e-mail address, which then forwards the message to all members of the list.

modem   A device that converts information sent over a telephone line into a form that a computer can understand and, conversely, converts computer data into a form that can be sent to another computer via a telephone line.

multimedia   A combination of two or more different communication media, such as text, graphics, audio, animation, and video.

online delivery partner   A private business set up to assist institutions or businesses in delivering courses online.

online delivery system   See *course management system.*

online tool suite   See *course management system.*

operating system   The software that controls a computer and allows it to perform its most basic functions.

PDF   Acronym for Portable Document Format, an electronic file format designed to be readable by different operating systems. A PDF document can be created with Adobe Acrobat software and viewed with the free Adobe Acrobat Reader.

pixel   Short for *picture element,* the individual dots that make up images on an electronic screen. A screen's resolution is defined by the number of pixels in a given area, usually expressed as dots per inch (dpi).

plug-in   An application that supplements a web browser, automatically activating itself when it is needed.

post   To contribute a message to an electronic bulletin board; more generally, to place any message or document on a web site.

scanning   Using a device that will convert hard-copy materials (text, graphics, or slides) into a format a computer can read.

server   See *web server.*

shareware   Software available for a free trial period, with the stipulation that a fee (usually small) be paid if use continues beyond that period.

streaming media   Audio or video files that are sent in a continuous stream from a source computer (usually via a web site) to a receiving computer. Using a "player" software program, the recipient can hear or view the content in real time.

synchronous Occurring simultaneously. For instance, a synchronous online discussion is one in which users can communicate immediately; examples include online chats and Internet telephone calls.

thread An ordered row of online comments on a particular topic; a number of threads in a single bulletin board area constitute a *threaded discussion*. See also *electronic bulletin board*.
threaded discussion area See *electronic bulletin board*.

upload To transfer a file from your computer to a remote computer; the reverse of *download*.
URL Short for Uniform Resource Locator, the address for a site on the Internet. An address such as **http://www.ucla.edu/** is a URL.

virtual classroom Any online area in which instructors and students "meet," via their computer connections, for course activities.

Web See *World Wide Web*.
web browser A software program that permits you to view and interact with material on the World Wide Web. The two most popular browsers are Netscape Communicator and Internet Explorer.
webmaster Person who administers and maintains a web server; usually a programmer.
web server Software that "serves" out, or disseminates, web pages across the Internet; also may refer to the computer on which this software has been installed.
web site The "place" on the World Wide Web where online teaching and learning generally take place. A site typically includes a series of pages (a "page" is equal to a screenful of information) containing text, images, and hyperlinks to other web pages.
whiteboard The online equivalent of a chalkboard, on which one or more users can write or draw.
World Wide Web A vast network of Internet locations that share common protocols, allowing displays of text and multimedia as well as hyperlinks between one site and another.
WYSIWYG An acronym for "what you see is what you get," referring to screen displays that match the appearance of the eventual product; for instance, Netscape Composer is a WYSIWYG web page editor that allows you to create an HTML page without using the actual HTML coded tags.

Zip disk A portable hard disk that allows you to store and retrieve files.

Guide to Resources

In this section we have gathered together the various resources mentioned throughout the text, organized them into a few simple categories, and added a number of other references. Our intent is not to be exhaustive, but rather to concentrate on sources that are useful and practical. Most of the sites and texts listed here include their own hyperlinks or references to other resources. For updates and additional ideas, see our web site: go to **http://college.hmco.com** and select "Education."

FUNDAMENTALS OF THE WEB AND DISTANCE LEARNING

Distance Education Clearinghouse. **http://www.uwex.edu/ disted/definition.html**

Offers definitions of distance learning and links to other distance education resources.

Learn the Net.com. **http://www.learnthenet.com/**

A good site for learning the basics of web navigation, how to download files, and much more.

Webmonkey. **http://hotwired.lycos.com/webmonkey/**

Offers a "How-to Library" with sections on authoring of web material, design, multimedia, and more, as well as feature articles and reference guides.

ONLINE TEACHING: THEORY AND PRACTICE

Beaudin, Bart. "Keeping Online Asynchronous Discussions on Topic." *Journal of Asynchronous Learning Networks* 3, no. 2 (November 1999). **http://www.aln.org/alnweb/journal/ Vol3_issue2/beaudin.htm**

This article presents results of research into techniques used by instructors in managing asynchronous online discussion.

Boettcher, Judith. "Cyber Course Size: Pedagogy and Politics." *Syllabus Magazine* 12, no. 8 (April 1999). **http://www.syllabus.com/syllabusmagazine/apr99_magfea2.html**

> Boettcher, of the Corporation for Research and Educational Networking (CREN), discusses the question of class size in online courses.

Cotton, Eileen Giuffre. *The Online Classroom: Teaching with the Internet,* 4th ed. Bloomington, IN: Grayson Bernard Publishers, 1998.

> An excellent book for K–12 educators.

French, Deanie, et al. *Internet Based Learning: An Introduction and Framework for Higher Education and Business.* Sterling, VA: Stylus Publishing, 1999.

> Aimed at both educators and trainers.

Grabe, Mark, and Cindy Grabe. *Integrating the Internet for Meaningful Learning.* Boston: Houghton Mifflin, 2000.

> A fine introduction to strategies and resources, aimed at K–12 educators.

Greatest Hits Discussions. **http://online.usu.edu/openhouse/greatest/greatesthits.html**

> Sample asynchronous discussions from a Utah State University instructional technology course, "Online Chats and Discussions in Education," demonstrate a moderator's use of different approaches and strategies.

A Guide to Online Teaching and Learning Activities. **http://cleo.murdoch.edu.au/eddesign/resources/onlinelearning/guide/index.html**

> Romana Pospisal of Murdoch University in Australia offers this useful guide.

Institute for Higher Education Policy. *Quality on the Line: Benchmarks for Success in Internet-Based Distance Education.* Washington, DC, April 2000. **http://www.ihep.com/quality.pdf**

> A study on what makes a successful online education program.

Khan, Badrul, ed. *Web-Based Instruction*. Englewood Cliffs, NJ: Educational Technology Publications, 1997.

A collection of writings on various aspects of web-based instruction.

Learner's Corner and *Instructor's Corner.* **http://olt-bta. hrdc-drhc.gc.ca/learning/index.html** and **http://olt-bta. hrdc-drhc.gc.ca/pract/index.html**

These resource pages from the Canadian Office of Learning Technologies offer glossaries, directories, and various guides to support technology in education.

O'Bannon, Deborah, Jill Scott, Margaret S. Gunderson, and James Noble. "Integrating Laboratories into Online Distance Education Courses." *The Technology Source: Case Studies,* January/February 2000. **http://horizon.unc.edu/TS/cases/ 2000-01a.asp**

A short article about the challenges of providing hands-on lab activities in online courses.

Palloff, Rena, and Keith Pratt. *Building Learning Communities in Cyberspace: Effective Strategies for the Online Classroom*. San Francisco: Jossey-Bass, 1999.

Emphasis on strategies for creating a sense of community among online learners.

Scaling Up Class Size in Web Courses. **http://pegasus.cc.ucf. edu/~jmorris/resources/ScalingUp2.html**

Joan Morris from the University of Central Florida offers strategies for handling workload in online courses.

Virtual Resource Site for Teaching with Technology. **http://www.umuc.edu/virtualteaching/**

A resource site, sponsored by the University of Maryland and Bell Atlantic, offering case studies and examples of the use of web-based media (including web pages, audio, video, and animation) in different teaching approaches and learning activities.

Winiecki, Donald J. "Keeping the Thread: Adapting Conversational Practice to Help Distance Students and Instructors Manage Discussions in an Asynchronous Learning

Network." *DEOSNEWS* 9, no. 2 (1999). **http://www.ed.psu.
edu/acsde/deos/deosnews/deosnews9_2.asp**

> Winiecki compares the patterns of face-to-face and online
> asynchronous conversations and suggests some strategies
> for more effective communication.

Creating a Syllabus

Faculty Orientation Online Syllabus Checklist. **http://online.
valencia.cc.fl.us/Faculty/VOfacultysyllabuscheck.htm**

> Valencia Community College's guidelines for online course
> syllabi.

The Online Course Syllabus. **http://ollie.dcccd.edu/Faculty/
InfoForFaculty/DistrictResources/secure/olsyll2.htm**

> A syllabus template offered by Dallas TeleCollege of the
> Dallas County Community College District for the district's
> distance learning "telecourses."

Syllabus. **http://oit.idbsu.edu/fp/syllabus.htm**

> Skip Knox at Boise State University Computing Services offers
> guidelines on the basic elements of an online syllabus and tips
> on how to use an online syllabus for a face-to-face class.

Instructional Design and Learning Styles

Address Diverse Learning Styles. **http://depts.washington.
edu/catalyst/method/learning_styles.html**

> One of the Method Guides from the University of
> Washington's Catalyst resource site, this page offers a num-
> ber of useful suggestions.

*Addressing Diverse Learning Styles Through the Use of
Multimedia.* **http://www.vpaa.uillinois.edu/tid/resources/
montgomery.html**

> A paper by Susan Montgomery, University of Michigan,
> based on the use of multimedia in an engineering class.

An Anonymous Asynchronous Web-Based Role Play. **http://
www.bus.uts.edu.au/fin&econ/staff/markf/roleplay/rp_
outline.html**

Description of an innovative role-playing activity at the University of Technology in Sydney, Australia, plus a link to a paper by Mark Freeman and John Capper about this experience.

DVC Learning Style Survey for College. **http://silcon.com/~scmiller/lsweb/dvclearn.htm**

Prepared by Suzanne Miller of Diablo Valley College in California, this site explains various learning styles and offers a survey to determine your preferred learning style.

Instructional Design Models. **http://www.cudenver.edu/~mryder/itc/idmodels.html**

Martin Ryder at the School of Education of the University of Colorado at Denver offers this collection of links organized according to different models or theories of instructional design.

Instructional Design for Online Course Development. **http://illinois.online.uillinois.edu/IONresources/instructdesign.html**

From the Illinois Online Network, this page explores topics related to instructional design and development of online courses. The information is presented in clear and easy-to-read fashion for nonspecialists.

Instructional Innovation Network. **http://bestpractice.net/**

At this site sponsored by Arizona State and Cal Poly Pomona, follow the links to the Cooperative Learning Homepage and the Case Study Homepage, which contain explanations of each method, along with teaching materials and resources. Linked articles explain the difference between group projects and true cooperative learning.

Learning Styles and the Online Environment. **http://illinois.online.uillinois.edu/IONresources/learningstyles.html**

This Illinois Online site offers a short explanation of learning styles and a collection of links to other resources on the subject.

Teaching and Learning Styles That Facilitate Online Learning.
http://www.tafe.sa.edu.au/lsrsc/one/natproj/tal/index.htm

The Australian National Training Authority sponsors this site on designing online courses with diverse learning approaches in mind.

COURSE MANAGEMENT SYSTEMS AND CONFERENCING TOOLS

Anlon: Products and Services. **http://www.anlon.com/products/**
Links to descriptions of Anlon's IntraKal course management tool.

Blackboard CourseInfo. **http://company.blackboard.com/courseinfo/** or **http://product.blackboard.net/courseinfo/**
Details on Blackboard CourseInfo software.

Centrinity Products. **http://www.softarc.com/products/**
The entry page for information about FirstClass software.

ClassPoint Product Information. **http://www.wpine.com/products/ClassPoint/**
White Pine Software's web-based video system.

Conferencing Software for the Web. **http://thinkofit.com/webconf/**
David Woolley's annotated lists of conferencing software, including both free and commercial varieties.

Convene.com. **http://www.convene.com/**
Convene's online distance education program.

eCollege.com. **http://www.ecollege.com/**
The home page for eCollege's varied products and services.

Embanet Corporation. **http://www.embanet.com/**
The home page for Embanet's tools for online learning.

HyperNews.org. **http://www.hypernews.org/**
Offers a free system for discussion forums.

IntraLearn. **http://www.intralearn.com/**
Information about IntraLearn's software platform for online learning.

LearningSpace Website Homepage. **http://www.lotus.com/ products/learnspace.nsf/wdocs/homepage/**
Introduction to LearningSpace's "distributed learning environment."

MadDuck Technologies. **http://www.wcbinfo.com/** or **http://www.madduck.com/**
MadDuck, manufacturer of the popular Web Course in a Box software, announced its acquisition by Blackboard in March 2000; these sites offer information about developments in the product line.

NetMeeting Home. **http://www.microsoft.com/windows/ netmeeting/**
Information about Microsoft Windows NetMeeting conferencing software.

Nicenet's Internet Classroom Assistant. **http://www.nicenet.org/**
A free course management tool.

Online Educational Delivery Applications: A Web Tool for Comparative Analysis. **http://www.ctt.bc.ca/landonline/**
Bruce Landon's site designed "to help educators evaluate and select online delivery software"; offers reviews, comparisons, and links to the major providers of course management software.

Rotor Learning Systems. **http://www.rotorcom.com/**
Rotor Learning is one of the firms experimenting with synchronous courseware.

Virtual-U. **http://virtual-u.cs.sfu.ca/vuweb/**
The entry point for descriptions of the Virtual-U software and research project.

WBT. **http://www.wbtsystems.com/**
Information about TopClass software.

Web Based Learning Resources Library. **http://www. outreach.utk.edu/weblearning/**
Maintained by Robert Jackson, University of Tennessee, Knoxville, this site contains information on many types of

web educational resources. See especially the sections on "Asynchronous Web Based Software Suites" and "Synchronous (Real-Time) Web Based Training Solutions."

WebBoard. **http://webboard.oreilly.com/**

Overview and demonstration of the WebBoard software.

WebCT.com. **http://www.webct.com/**

Home page for information about WebCT's course management software.

OTHER SOFTWARE APPLICATIONS: PRODUCTS, INFORMATION, AND SAMPLE USES

Adobe. **http://www.adobe.com/**

Links to information about Adobe's many well-known products, including Acrobat, Acrobat Reader (a free download), Photoshop, and PageMill.

Animation Projects. **http://www.ac.wwu.edu/~stephan/ Animation/animation.html**

This page by Ed Stephan, offering a sampling of his animations, is an inspiring demonstration of what can be done with animation software.

Email Discussion Groups/Lists and Resources. **http://www. webcom.com/impulse/list.html**

A useful page designed to be a one-stop information resource about mailing lists (listservs).

A Guide to the Educational Use of Multimedia. **http://www. csu.edu.au/division/oli/celt/edtech/multimedia/mmintro. htm**

Charles Sturt University in Australia offers this guide to interactive, computer-based multimedia, including principles of design and evaluation.

Interface Design. **http://www.csu.edu.au/division/oli/celt/ edtech/interface/interfac.htm#top**

Tom Lawson of Charles Sturt University, Australia, provides an introduction to interface design comprised of three parts:

"Interface Design and Human-Computer Interaction," "Web-Site Design," and "Web-Page Design."

LView Pro Home Page. **http://www.lview.com/**

A useful and relatively inexpensive image-editing program.

Macromedia. **http://www.macromedia.com/**

Home page for the manufacturer of Fireworks, Dreamweaver, Flash, Shockwave, Director, and other popular software products.

Paint Shop Pro. **http://www.jasc.com/psp.html**

The image-editing product from Jasc Software.

Ulead Systems. **http://www.ulead.com/**

Home page for the company that makes Ulead SmartSaver, a useful image-compression tool.

Web Page Composers

FrontPage. **http://www.microsoft.com/frontpage/**

Microsoft's web page composing tool.

Netscape Composer. **http://www.netscape.com/**

Composer is a useful composing tool included in the Communicator web browser; a free download is available.

Sound

Labtec. **http://www.labtec.com/**

A manufacturer of computer microphones and other peripheral equipment.

RealProducer. **http://www.real.com/** or **http://www. realnetworks.com/products/**

Access to information about the RealProducer software for streaming audio.

Narrated Slide Shows

PhotoPoint. **http://www.photopoint.com/**

A web hosting service for slide shows and graphics.

PowerPoint. **http://www.microsoft.com/office/powerpoint/**
Microsoft software that can be used for narrated slide shows.

QuickTime. **http://www.apple.com/quicktime/**
Apple's well-known software for narrated slide shows, video, music, and other types of multimedia presentations.

RealSlideshow and *RealPresenter.* **http://www.real.com/** or
http://www.realnetworks.com/products/
These sites will lead you to information about RealNetworks' software for slide shows.

Quiz-making

Hot Potatoes Homepage. **http://web.uvic.ca/hrd/halfbaked/**
A useful, free suite of software for creating web-based quizzes and exercises.

University of Hawaii QuizCenter. **http://www.motted.
hawaii.edu/**
Provides quiz-making features as well as lists and reviews of quiz software.

EDUCATIONAL RESOURCES ON THE WEB

AudioOnDemand. **http://www.wrn.org/ondemand/**
The World Radio Network provides "on demand" audio programs from radio stations all over the world.

EcEdWeb: Economic Education Web. **http://ecedweb.
unomaha.edu/home.htm**
Links to resources and lesson plans for incorporating web resources on economics and related topics.

Educational Object Economy. **http://www.eoe.org/**
Follow the links to the EOE Learning Community and then to Learning Objects and the educational Java applet library.

E-Learning Communities. **http://www.webct.com/global/
home/**
WebCT's education portal has faculty-led resource sites in different subject areas. Good source for evaluated, high-quality web resources as well as book reviews.

The ImageBase, Fine Arts Museums of San Francisco.   **http:// www.thinker.org/fam/thinker.html**

A searchable collection of art.

Internet Scout Project.   **http://scout.cs.wisc.edu/index.html**

An annotated and continually updated site reporting on selected educational web resources.

National Archives Online Exhibit Hall.   **http://www.nara. gov/exhall/exhibits.html**

The National Geographic Map Machine.   **http://www. nationalgeographic.com/resources/ngo/maps/**

ZoneZero.   **http://www.zonezero.com/**

A bilingual (Spanish and English) site dedicated to contemporary photography.

News and Magazine Sources

The Economist.   **http://www.economist.com/**

The Internet Public Library: Online Newspapers.   **http:// www.ipl.org/reading/news/**

A searchable resource that offers links to news sources worldwide, by country and language.

Maclean's Online.   **http://www.macleans.ca/index.stm**

The New York Times.   **http://www.nytimes.com/**

Salon.   **http://www.salon.com/**

Sources for Information on Technology

The Chronicle of Higher Education.   **http://www.chronicle.com/**

A weekly journal replete with articles and job listings for instructors. Distance learning resources are accessible to nonsubscribers.

CIT Infobits.   **http://www.unc.edu/cit/infobits/infobits. html**

A monthly e-mailed newsletter dealing with news and developments in technology and education; edited by Carolyn Kotlas at the University of North Carolina.

CNET. **http://www.cnet.com/**

An excellent site for news of technology developments, reviews, and downloads of popular software.

CNN. **http://www.cnn.com/**

A good source for daily articles dealing with business and technology.

Los Angeles Times. **http://www.latimes.com/**

Offers regular features dealing with distance learning and instructional technology, with past issues available to non-subscribers.

The TLT Group. **http://www.tltgroup.org/**

Affiliated with the American Association for Higher Education, this site offers resources, news, and the AAHESGIT listserv, used by instructors worldwide.

Yahoo! **http://www.yahoo.com/**

This popular portal and directory offers quick links to a multitude of news and media sources pertaining to computers and the Internet.

Guides to Web Search and Evaluation

Advanced Web Searching. **http://www.atl.ualberta.ca/ articles/web/advance.cfm**

Kenton Good of the University of Alberta explains how to get the most out of using a web search engine.

Evaluating Web Resources. **http://www2.widener.edu/ Wolfgram-Memorial-Library/webeval.htm**

Jan Alexander and Marsha Ann Tate at Widener University's Wolfgram Library offer checklists for evaluating sites and teaching modules on related subjects.

Search Engines. **http://illinois.online.uillinois.edu/ ionpointers/ionpointers.html**

From Illinois Online Network's "Pointers and Clickers" technology tips (October 1999), a succinct explanation of the differences among different types of search engines.

Thinking Critically About World Wide Web Resources. **http:// www.library.ucla.edu/libraries/college/instruct/web/critical. htm**

Esther Grassian of UCLA College Library provides a checklist of questions to ask in evaluating a web site.

Webhound. **http://www.mcli.dist.maricopa.edu/webhound/ index.html**

This Maricopa Community Colleges site offers tutorials on web searching skills, as well as links to other guides and tutorials. See especially the link to "What a Site!" (**http://www. mcli.dist.maricopa.edu/show/what/index.html**), which focuses on how instructors can find and integrate web resources into student activities.

Computer-Based Simulations

Coglab, Purdue University. **http://coglab.psych.purdue. edu/coglab/**

Cognitive psychology demonstrations, designed mostly for specific classes. To see demonstrations, use *guest* as the user ID and password. (Note that, with guest access, you cannot save data on the server.)

The Java Gas Turbine Simulator. **http://memslab.eng. utoledo.edu/~jreed/jgts/JavaGasTurbineSimulator.html**

The University of Toledo College of Engineering offers a gas turbine simulator that students can manipulate.

Solar System Simulator. **http://space.jpl.nasa.gov/**

Sponsored by the Jet Propulsion Laboratory of the National Aeronautics and Space Administration (NASA), this simulator allows one to view parts of the solar system.

Virtual Chemistry. **http://neon.chem.ox.ac.uk/vrchemistry/ default.html**

Research students in the department of chemistry at the University of Oxford maintain this site, which features online interactive experiments. Access is free.

COPYRIGHT AND INTELLECTUAL PROPERTY ISSUES

About.com. **http://www.about.com/**
At this popular portal, a search for "password protection" will lead you to resources on the subject.

Copyright Clearance Center. **http://www.copyright.com/**
One of several online services that will help you find a copyright owner and secure permission to use material.

Copyright Considerations. **http://twist.lib.uiowa.edu/ resources/fairuse/index.html**
Sponsored by the University of Iowa, this is a well-thought-out selection of links dealing with various issues of copyright, fair use, and intellectual property.

Distance Learning: Intellectual Property. **http://distance learn.about.com/education/distancelearn/msubip.htm**
Kristin Hirst's unique compilation of links to sites dealing with various issues of intellectual property.

The UT System Crash Course in Copyright. **http://www. utsystem.edu/ogc/intellectualproperty/cprtindx.htm**
Provided by the University of Texas, this is another well-designed and comprehensible site dealing with copyright and intellectual property. The "crash course" is extremely useful.

Webmonkey. **http://hotwired.lycos.com/webmonkey/**
Search for "password protection" to find useful information about the subject.

PROFESSIONAL DEVELOPMENT

ALN Web. **http://www.aln.org/**
The web site for the Sloan Foundation's Asynchronous Learning Networks provides links to discussions, workshops, and magazines of interest to online educators.

DEOS Listserv Archives. **http://www.wested.org/tie/ dlrn/dlsearch.html**

DEOS-L is a popular listserv for distance educators. This archive allows you to search through recent and past archives of messages.

Discussion Logs for EDTECH. **http://h-net.msu.edu/ cgi-bin/logbrowse.pl?trx=lm&list=EDTECH**

EDTECH is one of the lists of the H-Net mailing list discussion network. This site contains a log of its discussions.

Distance Education Resources. **http://cuda.teleeducation.nb. ca/distanceed/liste.cfm**

A site sponsored by TeleEducation NB of Canada. See the sections on "Professional Development," "Networking," "Online Discussions," and other topics of interest.

League for Innovation in the Community College. **http:// www.league.org/welcome.htm**

Offers a searchable database for descriptions of the League's presentations and contact information for presenters.

The Node Learning Technologies Network. **http://thenode.org/**

The Node offers articles on technology in education and provides various types of online forums (some of them open to anyone and some not), as well as archives and summaries of past forums.

Office of Learning Technologies. **http://olt-bta.hrdc-drhc. gc.ca/**

The entry point for a useful site sponsored by the Canadian government, offering a wealth of information for instructors and learners as well as a listserv database.

Tapped In. **http://www.tappedin.org/**

A mostly synchronous (real-time) forum for K–12 educators, especially those with an interest in technology and education.

Selected Training Programs for Online Teaching

California State University, Hayward, Certificate in Online Teaching and Learning. **http://www.online.csuhayward. edu/Certificate/onclass1.htm**

Illinois Online Network, MVCR Online Training Series. **http://illinois.online.uillinois.edu/mvcr.html**

> A series of online courses, primarily for Illinois Online Network members, but now open for those outside the state as well. MVCR stands for "Making the Virtual Classroom a Reality."

Nova Southeastern University, Graduate Teacher Education, Online Teaching and Learning Series. **http://www.fcae.nova.edu/gtep/online/OCI500501502.htm**

UCLA Extension, Online Teaching Program. **http://www.onlinelearning.net/CommunitiesofStudy/neighborhoods.cfm?NB=OTP**

Walden Institute, Certified Online Instructor Program. **http://www.waldeninstitute.com/coi/community/COIprog/coiprog.html**

Sample Orientation Programs and Guides

DIAL program, New School University. **http://www.dialnsa.edu/stdsrv5a.htm**

George Mason University's WebCT Resource Page. **http://www.irc.gmu.edu/WebCT/default.asp**

Illinois Online's WebBoard Tutorial. **http://illinois.online.uillinois.edu/online/webboardtutorial/starthere.htm**

IntraKal. **http://www.anlon.com/techsupport/**

> An instruction manual can be downloaded.

OnlineLearning.net. **http://www.onlinelearning.net/**

> Choose the tab for "How Online Learning Works."

SUNY Learning Network. **http://sln1.esc.edu/admin/sln/original.nsf**

> Follow the link for "Getting Started."

University of Central Florida. **http://reach.ucf.edu/~coursdev/learning/orient/**

Web Course in a Box.   **http://www.madduck.com/**

As of this writing, the Web Course in a Box orientation documents were available from this site; however, changes may occur in the wake of the company's announced merger with Blackboard.

WebCT Student Guide.   **http://www.webct.com/v2/guide/**

Credits

Figure 1.1: Reprinted with permission of WebCT™. Copyright WebCT 2000.

Figure 1.2: Courtesy of Dr. Greg Bothun, Department of Physics, University of Oregon.

Figures 4.1, 5.1, 5.3–5.5, 12.3–12.6: Printed with permission of Blackboard, Inc. All rights reserved. Blackboard released Blackboard 5 in July 2000 with additional functionality not covered in the version depicted here.

Figures 7.2–7.8, 9.1–9.3: Netscape Communications Corporation has not authorized, sponsored, endorsed, or approved this publication and is not responsible for its content. Netscape and the Netscape Communications Corporate Logos are trademarks and trade names of Netscape Communications Corporation. All other product names and/or logos are trademarks of their respective owners.

Figures 7.9–7.10: Courtesy of UCLA Faculty New Media Center.

Figure 7.11: Digital photo by Steve Rossen.

Figures 7.12: UMAX, the UMAX logo, MagicScan, VistaScan, and MagicMatch are the property of UMAX Data Systems, Inc. All rights reserved.

Figure 7.13, 7.15–7.16: From Paintshop Pro, Courtesy of Jasc Software. Copyright © 1995–1999, Jasc Software, Inc. All Rights Reserved.

Figures 7.17–7.24: Copyright © 1995–2000 RealNetworks, Inc. All rights reserved. RealNetworks, RealAudio, RealVideo, RealSystem, RealPlayer, RealJukebox, RealProducer, RealSlideshow, and other names or logos are trademarks or registered trademarks of RealNetworks, Inc.

Figure 7.25: Courtesy of Dr. Ed Stephans, professor emeritus, Western Washington State University.

Figure 7.26: From Ocrat web site: http://www.ocrat.com.

Figure 7.27: Courtesy of Mandeville Special Collections Library, University of California, San Diego.

Chapter 8, letter, page 184: Courtesy of CETUS, The Consortium of Educational Technology in University Systems.

Figures 8.1–8.2: Adobe and Acrobat are either registered trademarks or trademarks of Adobe Systems Incorporated in the United States and/or other countries. Reprinted with permission.

Figures 14.1–14.3: Courtesy of Rotor Learning Systems, Inc.

Figures 14.4–14.5: Courtesy of CuseeME Networks, Inc.

Index ||||||||